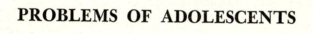

PROBLEMS OF ADOLESCENTS

Publication Number 956

AMERICAN LECTURE SERIES®

A Publication in

The BANNERSTONE DIVISION *of*
AMERICAN LECTURES IN SOCIAL AND REHABILITATION PSYCHOLOGY

Editors of the Series

JOHN G. CULL, Ph.D.
Director, Regional Counselor Training Program
Department of Rehabilitation Counseling
Virginia Commonwealth University
Fishersville, Virginia

and

RICHARD E. HARDY, Ed.D.
Diplomate in Counseling Psychology (ABPP)
Chairman, Department of Rehabilitation Counseling
Virginia Commonwealth University
Richmond, Virginia

The American Lecture Series in Social and Rehabilitation Psychology offers books which are concerned with man's role in his milieu. Emphasis is placed on how this role can be made more effective in a time of social conflict and a deteriorating physical environment. The books are oriented toward descriptions of what future roles should be and are not concerned exclusively with the delineation and definition of contemporary behavior. Contributors are concerned to a considerable extent with prediction through the use of a functional view of man as opposed to a descriptive, anatomical point of view.

Books in this series are written mainly for the professional practitioner; however, academicians will find them of considerable value in both undergraduate and graduate courses in the helping services.

PROBLEMS OF ADOLESCENTS

SOCIAL AND PSYCHOLOGICAL APPROACHES

RICHARD E. HARDY

JOHN G. CULL

CHARLES C THOMAS · PUBLISHER
Springfield · Illinois · U.S.A.

Published and Distributed Throughout the World by
CHARLES C THOMAS • PUBLISHER
BANNERSTONE HOUSE
301-327 East Lawrence Avenue, Springfield, Illinois, U.S.A.

© *1974, by* CHARLES C THOMAS • PUBLISHER
ISBN 0-398-03163-0
Library of Congress Catalog Card Number: 74-3232

With **THOMAS BOOKS** *careful attention is given to all details of
manufacturing and design. It is the publisher's desire to present
books that are satisfactory as to their physical qualities and artistic
possibilities and appropriate for their particular use.* **THOMAS
BOOKS** *will be true to those laws of quality that assure a good name
and good will.*

Printed in the United States of America
N-1

Library of Congress Cataloging in Publication Data

Hardy, Richard E.
    Problems of adolescents.

    (American lecture series, no. 956. A monograph in
the Bannerstone division of American lectures in social
and rehabilitation psychology)
    1. Juvenile delinquency. 2. Drugs and youth.
3. Social work with youth. I. Cull, John G., joint
author. II. Title. [DNLM: 1. Adolescent psychology.
2. Drug abuse—In adolescence. 3. Juvenile delinquency. WS462 P962 1974]
HV9069.H3168   364.36   74-3232
ISBN 0-398-03163-0

CONTRIBUTORS

STEPHEN CHINLUND: Was graduated *Cum Laude* from Harvard University and received an additional degree from Union Theological Seminary. He is Director of the Manhatten Community Rehabilitation Center. Formerly, he was the Asssitant Director of Exodus House, a Rehabilitation Center in East Harlem; founder, administrator, trainer, and therapist in the Addict Rehabilitation Program at Greenhaven State Prison; he was involved in similar work at the Great Meadow Correctional Institution and was co-founder and administrator of Reality House in Central Harlem. Prior to becoming Director of the Manhatten Rehabilitation Center of the New York State Narcotic Addiction Control Commission, Mr. Chinlund was involved in in-service training for group counseling at facilities operated by the Commission. He also is involved in training at the Bedford Hills Correctional Facility. Mr. Chinlund is very active in community and professional affairs in New York and is a consultant and board member of numerous programs and projects.

MELVIN COHEN, Ph.D.: Research Associate and Principal Investigator, Drug Abuse Studies, Hillside Hospital, Glen Oaks, New York; Adjunct Associate Professor, Psychology Department, School of General Studies, Queens College, Flushing, New York. Formerly, Instructor and Research Associate in Social Psychology, Downstate Medical Center, Brooklyn, New York; Research Assistant, Department of Psychology, New York University and Research Assistant, Walter Reed Army Medical Center, Washington, D. C.

CRAIG R. COLVIN, M.Ed.: Currently a Doctoral Candidate for Ed.D. at the University of Virginia's Department of Counselor Education. Formerly, Assistant Professor, Regional Counselor Training Program, Department of Rehabilitation Counseling, School of Community Services, Virginia Commonwealth University; Associate Editor of *Job Placement Division Digest*. He has also held positions with the North Carolina Division of Vocational Rehabilitation as a counselor for the mentally retarded as well as holding a general caseload. Mr. Colvin was the State Coordinator acting as a liaison representative between Vocational Rehabilitation and the Department of Correction in North Carolina; he is co-author of *Contemporary Field Work Practice in Rehabilitation*. He has made several contributions to the professional literature.

ROBERT G. CULBERTSON, Ph.D.: Assistant Professor, Department of Criminology, Indiana State University, Terre Haute, Indiana. Doctor Culbertson is a member of the Indiana Criminal Justice Planning Agency's Task Force; Vice-President of the Board of Directors of Big Brother—Sister Youth Service Bureau; member of the Social Service Planning Council for the Vigo County Coordinating Council. Formerly, Doctor Culbertson was a probation

counselor and probation department supervisor in Dayton, Ohio at the
Montgomery County Juvenile Court; Secretary of the Board of Directors for
Halfway House, Inc.; Team member Suicide Prevention Center; Instructor,
Evening College, University of Dayton; Taft Fellow, University of Cincin-
nati. Doctor Culbertson is the senior author of *Jails and Lockups In Indiana*
and has contributed several articles to the criminalogical literature.

JOHN G. CULL, Ph.D.: Professor and Director, Regional Counselor Train-
ing Program, Department of Rehabilitation Counseling, Virginia Common-
wealth University, Fishersville, Virginia; Adjunct Professor of Psychology and
Education, School of General Studies, University of Virginia, Charlottesville,
Virginia; Technical Consultant, Rehabilitation Services Administration,
United States Department of Health, Education and Welfare, Washington,
D.C.; Editor, American Lecture Series in Social and Rehabilitation Psychol-
ogy, Charles C Thomas, Publisher; Lecturer Medical Department, Woodrow
Wilson Rehabilitation Center; Formerly, Rehabilitation Counselor, Texas
State Commission For The Blind; Rehabilitation Counselor, Texas Rehabil-
itation Commission; Director, Division of Research and Program Development, Virginia State Department of Vocational Rehabilitation. The following
are some of the books which Doctor Cull has co-authored and co-edited: *Drug
Dependence and Rehabilitation Approaches, Fundamentals of Criminal Behavior and Correctional Systems, Rehabilitation of the Drug Abuser With
Delinquent Behavior,* and *Therapeutic Needs of the Family.* Doctor Cull has
contributed more than sixty publications to the professional literature in psychology and rehabilitation.

RICHARD E. HARDY, Ed.D.: Diplomate in Counseling Psychology (ABPP)
Professor and Chairman, Department of Rehabilitation Counseling, Virginia
Commonwealth University, Richmond, Virginia; Technical Consultant,
United States Department of Health, Education and Welfare, Rehabilitation
Services Administration, Washington, D.C.; Editor, American Lecture Series
in Social and Rehabilitation Psychology, Charles C Thomas, Publisher; and
Associate Editor, *Journal of Voluntary Action Research,* formerly Rehabilita-
tion Counselor in Virginia, Rehabilitation Advisor, Rehabilitation Services Ad-
ministration, United States Department of Health, Education and Welfare,
Washington, D.C., former Chief Psychologist and Supervisor of Professional
Training, South Carolina Department of Rehabilitation and member of the
South Carolina State Board of Examiners in Psychology. The following are
some of the Books which Doctor Hardy has coauthored and co-edited: *Drug
Dependence and Rehabilitation Approaches, Fundamentals of Criminal Behavior and Correctional Systems, Rehabilitation of the Drug Abuser with Delinquent Behavior, and Therapeutic Needs of the Family.* Doctor Hardy has
contributed more than sixty publications to the professional literature in
psychology and rehabilitation.

GILBERT L. INGRAM, Ph.D.: Coordinator, Mental Health Programs and
Chief Psychologist, Federal Correctional Institution, Tallahassee, Florida; Ad-

junct Lecturer, Department of Psychology, Florida State University; Consultant, Georgia State Department of Family and Children Services, Waycross Regional Youth Development Center; Book Reviewer, *Correctional Psychologist*. Formerly, Chief Psychologist, Robert F. Kennedy Youth Center, Adjunct Assistant Professor, West Virginia University; Instructor, Alderson-Broaddus College, Chief Psychologist, National Training School for Boys and Research Project Director, Federal Bureau of Prisons. Doctor Ingram has contributed numerous articles to the professional literature in correctional psychology, crime and delinquency.

NORMAN MANASA, Jr.: Director, Project SUMMON, University of Miami, Miami, Florida; Machinist Class II; Past member of Teamsters Union; Educational Consultant to the United States Office of Education; Member, National Study Commission on Higher Education and the Education of Teachers, University of Nebraska; Recommended for the nomination of Youth Representative on the Advisory Council on Education Professions Development.

CARSON MARKLEY: Associate Warden, Federal Reformatory for Women, Alderson, West Virginia. Formerly, Supervisor of Education, Federal Correctional Institution, Danbury, Connecticut; Assistant Supervisor of Education, United States Penitentiary, Marion, Illinois; Teacher and Recreational Specialist, Federal Reformatory, Petersburg, Virginia; Guard, Teacher, Captain of the Guard, and Recreation Specialist at the West Virginia Medium Security Prison, Huttonsville, West Virginia. Mr. Markley reecived his BS at Davis and Elkins College, Elkins, West Virginia and his MS Degree from Southern Illinois University, Carbondale, Illinois. He was a Fellow at Harvard Law School, Cambridge, Massachusetts (1971-72), University of Minnesota, St. Paul, Minnesota (1968) and University of Indiana, Bloomington, Indiana (1965). Article published in March, 1973 *Federal Probation* regarding Furloughs and Conjugal Visiting in Adult Correctional Institutions.

RICHARD L. RACHIN, M.P.A.: Chief, Bureau of Group Treatment, Florida Division of Youth Services, Tallahassee, Florida. He is Editor, *Journal of Drug Issues*. Formerly, Chairman, (Florida) Governor's Task Force on Narcotics, Dangerous Drugs and Alcohol Abuse; Resident Director, New York State Division for Youth, J. Stanley Sheppard Youth Rehabilitation Center; Mr. Rachin has contributed numerous articles to the literature on corrections and social problems.

HENRY RAYMAKER, Jr., Ph.D.: Chief, Psychology Service, Veterans Administration Center, Dublin, Georgia; Consultant, College Street Hospital, Macon, Georgia; Consultant, Officer of Rehabilitation Services, Atlanta, Georgia; Consultant, Regional Youth Development Center, Sandersville, Georgia; Consultant, Department of Family and Children's Services, Atlanta, Georgia; Private practice, Dublin, Georgia. Doctor Raymaker has been a licensed clinical psychologist in the State of Georgia since 1957. He received his doctorate in Clinical Psychology from Vanderbilt University.

PAUL L. ROSENBERG, M.D.: Resident in psychiatry, Camarillo State Hospital, Camarillo, California; School Consultant, Santa Monica, California; Consultant to the Santa Monica Child Care Centers; Cofounder of the Los Angeles Free Clinic, Los Angeles, California. Doctor Rosenberg is interested in parapsychology and bio-energetics. He has had extensive experience in the drug abuse field. He resides in Topanga Canyon outside Los Angeles.

JEFFREY L. SCHRINK, Ed.D.: Assistant Professor, Criminology Department, Indiana State University. Formerly: Indiana public school teacher; State Director of Classification and Treatment, Indiana Department of Correction; and Executive Director of Research, Planning and Statistics, Indiana Department of Correction. Professional membership includes: American Psychological Association, American Correctional Association, American Correctional Psychologist Association, and Indiana Correctional Association. He has had articles published in *Federal Probation* and *Library Occurrent*.

Paul Caron
Ron and Jackie Hall
James McClary
Warm Friends and Concerned Citizens

Selected texts appearing in the Social and Rehabilitation Psychology Series include:

UNDERSTANDING DISABILITY FOR SOCIAL AND REHABILITATION SERVICES
  John G. Cull and Richard E. Hardy

REHABILITATION OF THE URBAN DISADVANTAGED
  John G. Cull and Richard E. Hardy

VOCATIONAL EVALUATION FOR REHABILITATION SERVICES
  Richard E. Hardy and John G. Cull

REHABILITATION OF DRUG ABUSER WITH DELINQUENT BEHAVIOR
  Richard E. Hardy and John G. Cull

SPECIAL PROBLEMS IN REHABILITATION
  A. Beatrix Cobb

AVOCATIONAL ACTIVITIES FOR THE HANDICAPPED
  Robert P. Overs, Elizabeth O'Connor, and Barbara Demarco

FUNDAMENTALS OF CRIMINAL BEHAVIOR AND CORRECTIONAL SYSTEMS
  John G. Cull and Richard E. Hardy

INTRODUCTION TO CORRECTIONAL REHABILITATION
  Richard E. Hardy and John G. Cull

MEDICAL AND PSYCHOLOGICAL ASPECTS OF DISABILITY
  A. Beatrice Cobb

LAW ENFORCEMENT AND CORRECTIONAL REHABILITATION
  John G. Cull and Richard E. Hardy

PREFACE

THIS BOOK IS AN OUTGROWTH of our interest and that of our colleagues in attempting to offer practical information to students and professional personnel serving youth. The scope of this book is broad of necessity in that the problems associated with adolescents are multifaceted and most complex.

We have meticulously selected those individuals who could most ably contribute practical materials. These persons are those who are involved on the "firing line" in attempting to help adolescents in their adjustment to a changing social and physical environment. As could be expected, these persons are practitioners of high order. We have gained much from our work with them and are pleased to offer the results of combined efforts.

It is hopeful that this book will be of real value to all professional personnel concerned with problems of adolescents. This will include medical doctors specializing in adolescent treatment, psychologists, rehabilitation counselors, social workers, psychiatrists, sociologists, and others. The book offers a good deal of useful material on special problems of the disadvantaged boy, the girl, special problems of the family, the runaway and his behavior, drug related concerns including types of drugs and the relationship of drug abuse to juvenile delinquency and other behavior. It also offers therapeutic material in chapters on positive peer pressure, young people as volunteers, vocational rehabilitation and its role, and development of meaningful employment opportunities for young persons in difficulty.

RICHARD E. HARDY
JOHN G. CULL

CONTENTS

PROBLEMS OF ADOLESCENTS

CHAPTER 1

THE MALE JUVENILE DELINQUENT
AND HIS BEHAVIOR

RICHARD L. RACHIN

〰〰〰〰〰〰〰〰〰〰〰〰〰〰〰〰〰〰〰〰〰〰〰〰〰〰〰〰〰〰〰〰〰〰〰〰

- ☐ WHO ARE THE DELINQUENTS
- ☐ BELIEFS AFFECT BEHAVIOR
- ☐ THE IMPORTANCE OF SELF-ESTEEM
- ☐ UNDERSTANDING SHOULD RESULT IN CHANGE

〰〰〰〰〰〰〰〰〰〰〰〰〰〰〰〰〰〰〰〰〰〰〰〰〰〰〰〰〰〰〰〰〰〰〰〰

J UVENILE DELINQUENCY is not a term with any precise meaning. As it is commonly used, it would describe a range of generally disapproved behaviors engaged in by young people. The term is heavily laden with the values of our dominant white, middle-class culture and is most frequently directed at activities which appear to fly in the face of prevalent customs and beliefs. The fact that since time immemorial youth and particularly young males have had a penchant for developing or expressing oppositional life styles and behavior with no untoward societal consequences seems lost on each succeeding generation. Briefly put, the definition offered above is frequently used informally to describe behavior such as dress styles and grooming habits, keeping the "wrong" friends, staying out late, getting poor grades, and so on. Even attitudes in conflict with the prevalent ethic towards school or work, for example, could result in the label unofficially being affixed.

3

Of course there is a more "serious" host of activities which may result in some formal type of "official action" legitimizing the use of an official label. Some of the behavior described above could result in this if engaged in repeatedly and usually after several unheeded warnings. In addition, running away from home, truancy from school, "willful disobedience" towards a parent, "ungovernability," drinking alcoholic beverages, and so forth, would describe examples of so-called juvenile status offenses; that is to say, offenses for which only juveniles can be charged, adjudicated and committed.

Finally, and most seriously, juvenile delinquency describes violations of the criminal law, running the gamut from trespassing to sometimes murder when committed by youth generally under the age of eighteen.

Contrary to what may be believed, behavior which most frequently gets young people into trouble with the police and courts is the so-called juvenile status offenses. Thanks to the pressure of court decisions many states have revamped their juvenile court laws establishing Child-In-Need-Of-Supervision categories for status offenders. Prior to this, youth could be processed only as delinquents regardless of the offense. CINS cases, however still frequently become recipients of the same sanctions as delinquents. A boy could be committed to a reform school regardless of whether he simply played hooky or had committed a violation of the criminal law. And in many cases status offenders have stayed longer than boys who have committed criminal acts. Consequences of such actions are evident in the dismal record of accomplishment achieved by the juvenile justice system.

The likelihood that a large percentage of male youths will come to the official attention of the police and courts for non-criminal matters is great enough to raise serious questions about the intent and accomplishments not only of the juvenile law and practices, but its philosophical and historical roots as well.[1] De-

[1]*The Challenge of Crime in a Free Society: A Report by the President's Commission on Law Enforcement and Administration of Justice.* (Washington D.C.: U.S. Government Printing Office, 1967), p. 55. It is reported that ". . . one in every six male youths will be referred to juvenile court in connection with a delinquent act (excluding traffic offenses) before his 18th birthday."

signed to legitimate the values of moral reformers, the court proposed to accomplish this in an essentially nonjudicial, nonpunitive setting.[2] While intended to provide protection and help for children ostensibly in need of its care and control through informal and nonadversary proceedings, the juvenile court much too frequently, and certainly unintentionally, has ended up harming children rather than helping them.[3] Most children referred to the Juvenile Court need not be; and most children processed by the court, should not be.

WHO ARE THE DELINQUENTS

It would be best to make clear that the expression "boys will be boys," may have much more significance than many may be aware. Not many boys grow up without doing something illegal. It is also unlikely that any one population group is more likely, prone, or disposed to delinquency than any other, statistics and the conventional wisdom notwithstanding.[4]

The popularly held image of the male delinquent may be as distorted as the many theoretical explanations of young offender behavior. This does not mean young people identified as delinquent fail to fit the typical delinquent statistical profile. Emphasis must be placed on the word *identified*. That is to say, there is no assurance that youth who are caught are representative of the overwhelmingly greater number of boys who escape detection and apprehension. Interestingly, there is good reason to believe that just the opposite may be true.[5] It may be helpful to

---

[2]Edwin Lemert, *Instead of Court: Diversion in Juvenile Justice* (Chevy Chase, Md., National Institute of Mental Health, Center for Studies of Crime and Delinquency, 1971), p. 6.

[3]*The Challenge of Crime in a Free Society*, p. 80. "Official action may actually help to fix and perpetuate delinquency in the child through a process in which the individual begins to think of himself as delinquent and organizes his behavior accordingly. . . . While statutes, judges, and commentators still talk the language of compassion and treatment, it has become clear that in fact the same purposes that characterize the use of the criminal law for adult offenders—retribution, condemnation, deterrence, incapacitation—are involved in the disposition of juvenile offenders too."

[4]Bill Haney and Martin Gold, "The Juvenile Delinquent Nobody Knows," *Psychology Today*, September, 1973, pp. 49-55.

[5]*Ibid.*

examine what is known about juvenile crime about which everyone seems to know so much and yet so little at the same time.

Statistics about youth crime unfortunately provide an extremely unreliable index of the extent, frequency and often the meaning of juvenile delinquency. In the first place there is an enormous disparity between the number of offenses reported and the actual incidence of youth crime. Self-report studies disclose that as many as ninety percent of all youth have engaged in behavior which could have resulted in their referral to the juvenile court.[6] Second, the collection of juvenile crime statistics is subject to varying problems of accuracy, definition and administrative emphasis. Not only is it likely that different police departments report their statistics in unique and varying ways, but any examination of trends is limited by the changes many police agencies have made over the years in their own reporting systems.[7] The Uniform Crime Reports which the U.S. Department of Justice compiles and analyzes from reports submitted by approximately 10,000 law enforcement agencies have been described as almost worthless.[8] It is these same reports which are customarily used for making the usual pronouncements concerning crime and delinquency. U.S. crime statistics have been described as the worst among all major nations in the Western World.[9] An additional caveat must be stressed in cautioning against the ready tendency to compare delinquency rates over different time periods. That is the need to consider the development of various technological aids and sharpened and more sophisticated investigative skills during the past several years.

Keeping all this in mind, as well as other criticisms of the means by which crime statistics are compiled and interpreted, juvenile delinquency is reported to have increased significantly in recent years.[10] While arrests of girls under eighteen years of age

---

[6]*The Challenge of Crime in a Free Society*, p. 55.

[7]Criminal Statistics (Rockville, Md., National Institute of Mental Health, Center for Studies of Crime and Delinquency, 1972), p. 3.

[8]"Crime Statistics Often Numbers Game," *New York Times*, (February 4, 1968), p. 58.

[9]H. D. Graham and T. R. Gurr (eds.), *Violence in American Education*, (Washington, D.C., U. S. Government Printing Office, 1969), p. 372.

[10]*The Challenge of Crime in a Free Society*, p. 56.

were reported to have increased sixty-two percent during the five year period 1967 to 1972, compared to twenty-one percent rise in arrests of boys under eighteen, nevertheless total male arrests reportedly surpassed female arrests by six to one.[11] During 1965, five times more boys than girls under eighteen were arrested and four times as many boys were referred to juvenile court.[12] Considering only Crime Index offenses (murder, forcible rape, aggravated assault, burglary, larceny and auto theft) solved by the police in 1972, young people under eighteen years of age accounted for twenty-seven percent of the total, although youth between ten and seventeen comprise only about sixteen percent of the population.[13] It is likely that the great majority of these offenses were committed by young males.[14] While such statistics may seem to indicate a greater propensity for youth to commit serious crimes than adults, it should be understood that youth are much more likely to be arrested than are adults. In addition, youth are more likely to commit crimes accompanied by peers, not only increasing the probability of their apprehension, but making it likely that more youth than adults will be arrested for the same offense. The greater sophistication, skills, and resourcefulness of adults are additional factors which may influence the apparent disproportionate representation of young males in arrest statistics.

Looking at the number of arrests reported for all offenses during 1972 it is interesting that almost 200,000 (more than ten percent) of approximately 1,800,000 youth under eighteen years of age arrested were charged as runaways. Only one other offense category (larceny-theft) accounted for any greater number of arrests (337,000).[15]

Although male arrests increased twenty-one percent from 1967 to 1972 for all offenses (not counting traffic related arrests) arrests of young people under eighteen rose during this same period by twenty-eight percent.[16] Considering Crime Index Offenses only,

[11]*Crime in the United States: Uniform Crime Reports,* 1972, (Washington D.C., U. S. Government Printing Office, 1973), p. 34.
[12]*The Challenge of Crime in a Free Society,* p. 56.
[13]*Crime in the United States,* p. 34.
[14]*The Challenge of Crime in a Free Society,* p. 56.
[15]*Crime in the United States,* p. 34.
[16]Ibid.

the F.B.I. reported an overall increase in arrests of thirty-six percent during this five year period. Youth under eighteen registered twenty-five percent of this increase compared to a forty-seven percent rise in arrests for people over eighteen. Between 1960 and 1965, a fifty-two percent increase in Crime Index Offenses was reported for people under eighteen.[17] Not only then does there appear to be a significant reduction in the rate of increase for Index Offenses among youth during these two time periods (1960 to 1965 and 1967 to 1972) but the relatively greater increase among youth for all offenses during 1967 to 1972 may be explained in part by the precipitous rise in drug related offenses during this period.

Separating the four violent crime categories (murder and non-negligent manslaughter, forcible rape, robbery and aggravated assault) from Index property crime arrests (burglary and larceny), youth under eighteen registered a sixty percent increase in arrests for violent crimes and a twenty-two percent increase for property crime arrests.[18] Adult arrests for both crimes of violence and property increased by forty-seven percent for each category during this same five year time span.

In Table 1-I all reported arrests (1,793,984) during 1972 for youth under eighteen are presented in the frequency with which the offense occurred. Although the five year trend (1967 to 1972) indicates a significant rise in the volume of violent crimes committed by youth under eighteen, it is important to note that of the total number of arrests reported, more than ninety-five percent were property crimes or other nonviolent offenses. Males continue to dominate the violent crime categories. Only ten percent of these arrests during 1972 were of females.[19]

A sharp rise in "narcotic drug law violations" of 291 percent from 1967 to 1972 also marked a significant change in the increased vulnerability of youth under eighteen to arrest during this time period.[20] During 1972 alone, arrests of total drug related

---

[17]*The Challenge of Crime in a Free Society,* p. 56.
[18]*Crime in the United States,* p. 34.
[19]Ibid.
[20]Ibid.

TABLE 1-I.
ARRESTS OF PERSONS UNDER 18 IN THE UNITED STATES**
1972

Non-Index Offenses		Index Offenses
	336,983	Larceny-Theft
Runaways	 199,185	
	160,376	Burglary-Breaking or entering
Disorderly Conduct	 127,756	
Curfew & Loitering	 116,126	
Narcotic Drug Laws	 98,308	
Vandalism	 91,586	
Liquor Laws	 76,894	
	65,255	Auto Theft
Other Assaults	 60,322	
Drunkenness	 40,625	
	34,823	Robbery*
	27,256	Aggravated Assault*
Stolen Property	 21,988	
Weapons, carrying possessing, etc.	 18,656	
Suspicion	 12,421	
Sex offenses except forcible rape & prostitiution	 10,977	
Driving Under the Influence	 7,568	
Arson	 6,203	
Vagrancy	 5,547	
Forgery & Counterfeiting	 4,311	
	3,842	Forcible Rape*
Fraud	 3,705	
Gambling	 1,728	
	1,634	Murder & Non-Negligent Manslaughter*
Prostitution & Commercialized Vice	 1,399	
Offenses against Family & Children	 1,034	
Embezzlement	 379	
Manslaughter by Negligence	 282	
TOTAL		*TOTAL*
1,163,815		562,614 Property Crimes
		67,555 Violent Crimes*
		────────
	GRAND TOTAL	630,169
	1,793,984	

**Revised under Table 33—"Total Arrest of Persons Under 15, Under 18, Under 21, and Under 25 Years of Age, 1972" *Uniform Crime Reports*—1972, p. 128.

offenses by themselves ("narcotic drug laws," liquor laws, drunkenness and "driving under the influence") totalled 223, 395 youth under eighteen, or more than eighteen percent of all non-Index arrests made during 1972 for this age group.[21]

To make sense of the apparent increase in juvenile crime consider the following:

1. There is no assurance that higher juvenile arrests are actually related to a comparable increase in juvenile crime. There is reason to believe that improved investigative techniques, greater concern about youth crime, varying reporting procedures in different places and at different times, and a greater emphasis on the official handling of juvenile crime may account for part of this rise.

2. Although the public, and others who should know better, are prone to interpret crime statistics as proof that youth are more delinquent, violent and rebellious than ever; there are no grounds to validate such beliefs.

3. There is no way of determining the extent to which the reported increase in juvenile crime is attributable to a greater prevalence of delinquent behavior among youth or greater numbers of group arrests (for auto thefts, drugs or gang related activities, for example) for single offenses. In addition, aggregate arrest figures provide no clues of the extent to which rate increases are related to repeat arrests of the same juveniles. While juvenile arrest figures are disproportionately high for their percentage of the population, it is important to consider that this may mean little other than this age group has a higher percentage of repeat offenders. The fact that the group arrested most frequently are those under twenty—of all offenders under twenty years of age arrested during 1970 to 1972 forty-three percent were repeaters—would seem to lend credence to this assumption.[22] In addition, as the population base has increased over the time frames discussed, it is likely that the same

[21]Ibid., p. 128.
[22]Ibid., p. 36.

percentage of repeat offenders account for significantly greater numbers of arrests.

Reasons have been suggested for proceeding cautiously in interpreting delinquency statistics as barometers of youth crime conditions. Statistics by themselves provide no clues to understand changes in behavior, or for that matter, behavior itself. It makes as little sense to take measures to remediate this problem as it would any other about which so little is known. Tilting at windmills may satisfy a need to do something, but it is highly unlikely any real benefits will result. And it may be no exaggeration to suggest that continued assaults on the symptoms rather than the more substantive issues will continue to produce, if not exacerbate, the very problems antidelinquency measures are intended to correct.

BELIEFS AFFECT BEHAVIOR

Popularly held beliefs about delinquents, who they are, where they come from, the kinds of behavior they engage in, owe their existence to the dictates of "common sense" notions mixed in with personal experiences and a myopic misconception of the prevalence, incidence and nature of delinquency. Much of this stems from inferences made about the very small percentage of youth who commit offenses and are apprehended. Not only is it unlikely that the police arrest a representative sample of all delinquents, but it is at best speculative that the juvenile courts adjudicate and commit the most serious offenders.[23] And anyone familiar with institutions to which delinquents are committed is well aware of the large percentage of boys who are sent there for truancy, running away, disobedience, ungovernability and petty violations of the criminal law. Not too well known is the large number of youth sent to reform schools not because it is believed desirable, but as one well-intentioned juvenile judge put it, because there were no other alternatives. The best of intentions aside, that is like sending a coronary patient to a veterinarian because no physician is available. The sterotype of the male delinquent as typically black or other minority group member from a lower

---

[23]Haney and Gold, *op. cit.*

socioeconomic class and a broken family, characterizes little other than boys apprehended, identified and officially labelled as delinquents.[24] Ignored or overlooked is the fact that certain factors predispose particular *classes* of young males to a greater likelihood of arrest and adjudication than is true for other classes. The popular image of the potential delinquent as likely to be true to this long prevalent caricature contributes to the greater arrest vulnerability of this group. Not only that, but it also increases their likelihood of adjudication, commitment and rearrest. Considering all this, it should not be surprising to learn that minority group members, and especially those from broken and economically disadvantaged homes, are disproportionately represented in offender statistics.

It would be naive to assume all this has not had an effect on the behavior of youth. No one is born more likely to become delinquent than anyone else. Theories once advanced which explained offender behavior as biologically determined have little credibility today. Interestingly, however, attempts to explain criminal behavior by linking its occurrence to certain atavistic characteristics, e.g., sloping forehead, flattened nose, scanty beard, are strikingly similar in making the same preposterous assumptions as some present day theorizing which hypothesizes a casual connection between race, poverty, broken families and delinquency. Delinquency is no more traceable to a boy's being black or white, poor or rich, or his living in an intact or broken family; than is more acceptable, socially approved behavior. It is the greater vulnerability of certain genetically sired and socioeconomic *groups* to societal fallout, and membership in these groups, which accounts for the individual's increased risk of becoming delinquent. The vulnerability quotient increases in direct proportion to the expectations which teachers, police, social workers, and others have for these groups. Boys from such groups who "make it" then obviously do so with much slimmer odds than is true for members of more culturally advantaged groups. Accordingly, it should not be difficult to understand that while it is commonly assumed that youth are equally vulnerable to arrest, adjudication and commitment, membership in culturally disad-

___
[24]Ibid.

vantaged groups in our society significantly increases the risk. It may not be, as is commonly assumed, that the incidence of delinquent behavior is so much greater among disadvantaged group members, but rather that only the likelihood of being arrested is significantly greater. Delinquency then cannot adequately be explained as an individual phenomenon or even as a function of the individual's membership in certain groups; it can only be understood as the individual and his group memberships are considered in relationship to a social system in which they are involved and a part.[25] It is a generally prevalent and shared set of cultural beliefs which unwittingly sometimes, and intentionally at other times, fosters the more likely occurrence of delinquent behavior among some groups than others.

Keeping this in mind it should not be difficult to understand how invidious comparisons of intelligence, aptitude, motivation, social skills, and so forth, often give short shrift to children from less culturally advantaged groups. If we have come to look with a jaundiced cultural eye at the relative abilities of various groups of people as opposed to others, it may not be unreasonable to attribute the occurrence of a higher incidence of socially disapproved behavior in part, to such class and cultural expectations. Few children under the age of six engage in what could be called criminal activities. Prior to the time they enter school, it would be extremely difficult to find discernible substantive differences in behavior. It remains for the school to seize upon what may be relatively unimportant variations in skills—it would probably be more accurate to say *perceived* variations—and begin the "I am good" (because I possess these attributes) and "I am bad" (because I do not) treadmill towards failure. While there is no simple explanation to account for the reasons certain *groups* of children are statistically more likely to become delinquent than others, it is not far-fetched to reason that school begins the process.

Accepting this line of reasoning one should argue strongly against such pedagogical techniques as compartmentalizing chil-

---

[25]Richard A. Cloward and Lloyd E. Ohlin, *Delinquency and Opportunity: A Theory of Delinquent Gangs* (Glencoe, IL., The Free Press, 1960), p. 211.

dren on the basis of their relative abilities. That is, their relative abilities as measured against predominant cultural norms. Invariably, the "problem classes" in which children are placed, are made up of a disproportionate number of youth owning membership in poor, minority group families whose observed and tested level of performance may be more a measure of societal barriers and expectations, than it is actual ability.

If what we have come to identify as delinquent symptoms are observable anywhere at an early age, the school room is the place to look. It is in the classroom where children from less advantaged families, usually the poor and minority groups, first react to culturally imposed restrictions on their emotional and socially productive development. The conflict between prevalent cultural values and norms and their cultural and subcultural counterparts erupts first for most children in school. This conflict becomes sharpened and more pronounced as the child grows older. We see this vividly in dress codes which include not only the types and colors of clothing permitted, but in hair styles, jewelry, beards, mustaches and so forth. Recall the well publicized incident last summer where a school in the Southwest denied a youngster the opportunity to attend her graduation because her hand sewn dress was not up to snuff. Numerous other incidents occur with regularity because of boys wearing earrings, hair styles being "unacceptable," clothing being too "provocative." T shirts unfittingly emblazoned with "unacceptable" slogans, etc., etc.

The more isolated and restricted a group perceives itself to be from attaining culturally valued goals in a socially approved manner, the more likely it is the group will seek alternative means of expression. Psychologically it also appears that groups who perceive the dominant culture as hostile, repressive or restrictive will also find ways to fend off and attempt to combat the anxieties and assaults on feelings of self-worth which such perceptions bring about. Unwittingly again, it appears that instead of making efforts to combat such perceptions schools frequently respond by reinforcing these beliefs. Usually the more alien the behavior of groups, the more threatening it becomes to teachers and school administrators who, after all, tend to be carriers and enforcers of the dominant culture. The more distant group values, norms and expectations are from those of the adult white, middle-class culture, the more frequently and severe its members' behavior appears sanctioned by authorities representing the dominant system.

Labelling and other ritualistic school practices follow, none of which appear to have the effect intended. One of the more futile and counter-productive measures is the segregating of children into various classes based upon conduct and perceived abilities. Lumped together and reminded daily in many subtle and some not too subtle ways that they are "bad students" and "bad students" are never really expected to "measure up," children too often respond accordingly. For many, this becomes a self-fulfilling prophecy regardless of their true ability. The opposite behavior, of course, might easily be observed were these same children expected, encouraged and given opportunities to behave in a manner which is believed normative for children owning membership in more advantaged groups.

This does not mean that white, middle and upper class children as individuals are any less likely to respond poorly to school. But not owning membership in groups which our prevalent culture views invidiously, such children when they do behave "improperly" or poor grades do occur, more often than not find their behavior described as prankish and more likely to be ignored or forgiven. At most times these children are described as simply not performing at the level they are believed capable. Only rarely are these more advantaged groups of children assigned to the "problem" classes, even when there is little to distinguish their behavior from others placed in these classes. It is also unlikely that more advantaged group members are as vulnerable to having permanent records record their misbehavior as it is for other children. Couple all this with the attitude and mistaken beliefs of many teachers and school administrators that parents of culturally disadvantaged students are not likely to have the same interest or concern about their children as other mothers and fathers and unwittingly again, the child is given an additional nudge towards becoming delinquent.

THE IMPORTANCE OF SELF-ESTEEM

We have postulated that not all youth are equally disposed to encounter some of the factors which appear related to school children becoming identified delinquents. Nor are they all likely to become ensnared in what may very well be web-like educational traps which, in fact, if not intentionally, may contribute to the very type of behavior they are designed to head off. Once the child becomes known as a slow learner or problem student—and regardless whether this has any basis in fact—a whole host of other labels seems ready to attach, much like tacks to a magnet. Given the current predelection to attribute learning problems to underlying emotional difficulties, the child becomes vulnerable to a number of stigmata which further greases the skids as he begins to accelerate towards fulfilling the expectations many already have for him. Further steps to monitor his behavior and additional labels, e.g., disruptive, problem-prone, unmotivated, seem to follow. Failing or finding it difficult to achieve recognition for socially acceptable endeavors, it should not be surprising that in company with others who have found themselves similarly processed, the boy begins to seek recognition and status in an antisocial manner. Often the choice is between passively accepting membership in a group which on the face of it does little for one's sense of self-esteem, or rebelling in a fashion which may be as necessary as it often is self-defeating. Denied opportunities to achieve recognition and status in legitimate ways, youth may seek this through esteem and status which being "slick," "cool," or "mean" confers from peers also finding it difficult "making it" in the conventionally approved and socially responsible manner. Since school is often responsible, albeit unintentionally, for the youth's first negative appraisal of his own skills and abilities, his negative behavior towards school, formal learning and teachers who are powerful early authority figures, seems quite understandable. School and all it represents seems a natural target for his hostility. Problems which so many children have during adolescence with authority figures is certainly not unrelated to these frustrating and embarrassing only learning experiences.

It is human nature to avoid stressful situations. Being embarrassed, feeling inadequate and failing to "measure up" are psychologically untenable, especially when we consider that school may offer little respite from this for practically half a waking day and for what must appear to be an eternity lying ahead. Most young people finding themselves in such predicaments obviously are not about to accept it casually.

As we have mentioned, if delinquency is born and nurtured anywhere it would be a reasonably good assumption to look to school as the place. And it does not necessarily follow that the student puts into motion the process by which he may end up coming to the official attention of the police and courts. Long before he may actually have committed any violation of the law, in the eyes of many who witness some of the understandable antics of boys shunted to the "problem" classes, he is already labelled and expected to behave "delinquent." The concept of delinquency is considerably broader than its legal application.[26]

School administrators and teachers must become sensitive and do something about the important part school plays in a child's becoming delinquent. Not until this happens and teachers, administrators and students become involved and care about one another, rather than acting as if each were from another world and could care less, will the situation improve.[27]

UNDERSTANDING SHOULD RESULT IN CHANGE

We have attempted to discuss some factors which appear involved in the development of juvenile delinquency. Contrary to what may popularly be believed, delinquency cannot be understood by reference to the individual alone. No one is born "bad" or more likely than anyone else to steal cars, play hooky, or smoke pot. Nor is it likely that much juvenile behavior occurs without reference to the influence which young people have on one another. The behavior which results in the arrest and referral of

---

[26]R. K. Merton, "The Social-Cultural Environment and Anomie," in Helen L. Witmer and Ruth Kotinsky, *New Perspectives for Research on Juvenile Delinquency* (Washington, D.C., U. S. Department of Health, Education, and Welfare, Children's Bureau, 1956), pp. 24-50. Vilhelm Aubert, "White-Collare Crime and Social Structure," *American Journal of Sociology*, (1952), p. 270.

[27]William Glasser, *Schools Without Failure* (New York: Harper and Row, 1969.)

some youth to the juvenile court, for far many more is as common-place as it is unidentified.

Adolescent behavior, regardless whether in dress styles, types of music or dance, sexual conduct, fighting, stealing, or what have you, for most youth is a function of peer group affiliation and pressure. Adolescence is a period of rapid physical and emotional change, uncertainty, testing and an overwhelming need to belong and conform. It is an age of experimentation, establishing a fairly permanent self-identity and a time perhaps when the need to prove oneself to others is greater than during any other period in life. It is also a time when many laws are broken and where risks are freely taken and seemingly sought after despite the consequences. As one youth put it:

> It was the idea of being defiant, of going on the tracks, with the trains going by and the third rail down there and cops. I've run away from the cops and it was a thrill. But isn't that what adolescence is supposed to be, defying authority?[28]

From the perspective of the predominant culture, adolescence is viewed as a mystifying, trouble-filled, tumultuous time. It is a period in which authority is challenged, physical and intellectual equality must reluctantly be recognized, and most sacred and important beliefs are questioned and the frailties and inadequacies of adults confronted and sometimes exposed.

The adolescent years are frequently marked by behavior which not only appears unfathomable to adults, but seems cast in direct and challenging opposition to the values and norms of the dominant culture. While, of course, there often is a wide disparity between what adults espouse and what they do, nevertheless there is an obvious double standard when it comes to judging and reacting to the behavior of youth. Youth have recognized and oftentimes used this to rationalize and sometimes justify their own behavior. And in some contexts this obviously has been a potent argument to defeat. That is not to excuse conduct which on the fact of it appears destructive and injurious, but simply to sharpen our focus on the dynamics and complexity of human behavior and our

---

[28]"An Underground Graffitist Pleads from Hospital: Stop the Spraying," *New York Times*, October 18, 1973, p. 43.

understanding of what makes kids "tick."

As we have observed, juveniles brought to the attention of the police and courts are disproportionately poor and minority group youth. Surely this does not mean youth from more culturally advantaged circumstances are innately more law abiding, socialized or likely to grow up better citizens. Nor does it mean that kids who break the law are either sinful or sick (whatever these terms may mean), as seems popularly to be believed. It would be highly unusual if not troubling to find many boys growing up in communities recognized and identified as delinquency areas who were not involved in delinquency. If studies of unreported delinquency have validity, it would probably be mistaken to identify any one community as opposed to any other as a delinquency area. As George Vold observed, ". . . in a delinquency area, delinquency is the normal response of the normal individual . . . the nondelinquent is really the 'problem case,' the nonconformist whose behavior needs to be accounted for."[29]

It is important to recognize that delinquency (perhaps of a different kind or degree, and that is a big perhaps) is probably as prevalent in more "advantaged" communities populated predominately by middle and upper-middle class majority group members as it is in the more "likely" areas where it is customary to look and do research. While delinquency may be more covert or, for other reasons, less apparent, it is mistaken to assume that its occurrence is any less frequent or prevalent. The shock, for example, which white middle-class mothers frequently express when confronted with a son's delinquent activities belies only our cultural inability to accept the reality or seriousness of behavior for kids, "who had anything they ever could have wanted."

We are geared to expect delinquency from certain groups and lacking in understanding how normal delinquency is for most youth, regardless what their origins or socioeconomic circumstances. It is society's reaction to the anticipation of such behavior and the actual behavior itself, when it is identified, which seems

[29]F. Lovel Bixby and Lloyd W. McCorkle, "Discussion of Guided Group Interaction and Correctional Work," *American Sociological Review*, (August, 1951), p. 460.

crucial to understanding and attacking the problem. It is not likely much is going to change until we alter our understanding of juvenile delinquency as "deviant" and more characteristic of one group as opposed to any other. In addition, it is unlikely that many changes will take place until class, cultural and racial barriers between educators, clinicians, justice system workers and youth whose behavior becomes officially identified are removed. Steps must also be taken to revamp and curtail the overreach of the law and the juvenile court. It is about time we learned that problems are not really solved by passing laws which prohibit and penalize conduct we do not like.[30] The Juvenile Justice system, for example might profitably barred from jurisdiction over the whole range of noncriminal matters which currently fall within its purview and authority. Even in the more "progressive" states it is not unusual to find as many as one-third of all commitments sent to juvenile institutions to be truants, runaways, dependents and other noncriminal cases for whom the justice system, no matter how treatment oriented or benign, does little good. As Martin Silver observed, "The detection of a proclivity to bad behavior is facilitated by the court's treatment process."[31] It may be just as fruitless and irrational to continue treating delinquency in the traditional fashion as it would be to attack poverty as evidence of deviance.

If one change more than any other would seem important it would be the elimination of our egregious labelling systems which compartmentalize, stigmatize and too frequently harm young people. Despite what we have become conditioned to believe, most delinquent behavior is anything but evidence of underlying pathology.[32] As Dick Gregory once remarked, "Being black

---

[30]John W. Oliver, "Assessment of Current Legal Practices from the Viewpoint of the Court," in J. R. Wittenborn, *et al,* (eds.), *Drugs and Youth,* (Springfield, Charles C Thomas, 1969), p. 229.

[31]Martin T. Silver, "The New York City Family Court: A Law Guardian's Overview." *Crime and Delinquency,* (January, 1972), p. 95.

[32]William Glasser, *Reality Therapy: A New Approach to Psychiatry* (New York: Harper and Row, 1965), David L. Bazelon, *Equal Justice for the Unequal,* Issac Ray Lectureship Award Series of the American Psychiatric Association, University of Chicago, 1961.

is not needing a psychiatrist to tell you what's bugging you."[33] One of these days we may understand what this means and act accordingly.[34] A lot of good may come as a result of it.

[33]Silver, Supra, p. 95.

[34]William Glasser, *The Identity Society*, (New York, Harper and Row, 1973); Charles Mangel, "How to Make a Criminal out of a Child," *Look* (June 29, 1971), pp. 48-53; Thomas S. Szasz, *The Myth of Mental Illness*, (New York, Dell, 1961). Richard L. Rachin, "Reality Therapy: Helping People Help Themselves," *Crime and Delinquency*, (January, 1974); Karl Menninger, *The Crime of Punishment* (New York, Viking Compass, 1966); O. Hobart Mowrer, *The New Group Therapy* (Princeton, N.J., Van Nostrand Rheinhold Co., 1964).

CHAPTER 2

THE FEMALE JUVENILE DELINQUENT AND HER BEHAVIOR

Carson Markley

☐ THE MEANING OF DELINQUENCY
☐ NATURE AND CAUSES OF JUVENILE DELINQUENCY
☐ SIGNIFICANCE AND BEHAVIOR

THIS CHAPTER CONCERNS ITSELF with the female juvenile delinquent and her behavior. In surveying literature pertinent to this subject, I found there is very little information available concerning the female juvenile delinquent. I discovered that articles regarding juvenile delinquency indicated that female delinquency is not a significant factor in crime and delinquent behavior.

I feel in order to present a more current or up to date view of female juvenile delinquency, it is necessary to attempt to define juvenile delinquency; discuss the nature and causes of juvenile delinquency; and discuss the behavior and apparent significant increase in female juvenile delinquency.

THE MEANING OF DELINQUENCY

The most difficult problem in writing about juvenile delinquency, whether male or female, is defining the term itself. It is generally agreed that juvenile delinquency refers to the antisocial acts of young people. According to Carr, delinquency actually has many meanings. There are legal delinquents (those committing antisocial acts as defined by law), detected delinquents (those exhibiting antisocial behavior), agency delinquents (those detected who reach an agency), alleged delinquents (those apprehended, brought to court), and adjudged delinquents (those found guilty).[1]

Gisela Konopka states that those acts performed by juveniles which are considered delinquent fall into three basic categories:

a. Those which are considered delinquent regardless of whether committed by a juvenile or an adult, because they violate criminal laws. Examples are stealing or assault on human life.
b. Those which violate societal morals as agreed upon generally in our particular society, regardless of whether the person is a juvenile or an adult. An example is certain forms of sex behavior.
c. Those which are violations only because the person is a minor. This is exemplified in truancy from school or teenage drinking. These violations are governed by different laws in states, and therefore will make a youngster a delinquent in one state and not in another.

Ms. Konopha adds that delinquent acts of girls fall into all three categories, though most delinquent girls have some problems in relation to sex. This assortment of offenses alone shows it is impossible to talk about one kind of delinquent personality. One can only say that those designated as "delinquent" are so by virtue of having been adjudicated as such, which means having been judged by the court.[2]

Clyde Vedder also indicates that juvenile delinquency is not a disease or a clinical entity. It is a descriptive term referring to a huge agea of asocial and antisocial behavior.[3]

When discussing the misconduct of young people, the terms juvenile and youth are not specific or precise definitions of people. This becomes a problem because the age which the term juvenile

---

[1]Lowell J. Carr, *Delinquency Control* (New York, Harper and Brothers, 1950), pp. 89-92.
[2]Gisela Konopka, *The Adolescent Girl in Conflict* (Englewood Cliffs, New Jersey, Prentice-Hall, Inc., 1966), pp. 18-19.
[3]Clyde B. Vedder, *Juvenile Offenders* (Springfield, Illinois, Charles C Thomas, 1963), p. 4.

covers ranges from six years to twenty-one years of age. In some states, people are legally juveniles until they pass their eighteenth birthday, but in other states they stop being juveniles after they pass their sixteenth birthday. In other states they remain juveniles until they are twenty-one.

Almost all youths commit acts for which they can be arrested and taken to court. But it is a much smaller group that ends up being defined officially as delinquent.

A second problem in writing about female juvenile delinquency is that most research concerning delinquency and crime is focused on the male delinquent. It has been suggested that the male delinquent is a more serious threat to the public, and the female juvenile delinquent represents a minor threat to the public. Other writers contend that females commit only self-destructive acts such as sexual promiscuity and running away from home.

This shortage of material on the female juvenile delinquent is significant in that the delinquent girl has often been rejected, brutalized, abused, poorly understood, and almost forgotten in the correction of delinquent behavior. Virginia W. McLaughlin, Warden at the Federal Reformatory for Women, Alderson, West Virginia, states that, "If you are female, black, or poor in our society, the dice have been loaded against you."

The female delinquent can play a significant role in the delinquency of boys. Girls can exert a great deal of influence on gang activity by preventing boys from stealing, getting drunk, etc.; or they can cause these acts of antisocial behavior. But, we usually find that gangs are typically male dominated and the female role is primarily supportive.

NATURE AND CAUSES OF JUVENILE DELINQUENCY

Many studies have been conducted in an effort to acquire information revealing the causes of juvenile delinquency. Vedder indicates that among these are the legalistic approach (the juvenile treated as an adult offender, based on the assumption that age is a correlative of increasing responsibility), the individual approach (a case study method), the group approach (a study of gangs and other youth groups, with implications for the delinquent or studies of delinquency in relation to social situations), the cultural approach (the effects of culture conflicts are culture contacts on the delinquent), and the ecological approach (the study of spatial and temporal factors as they are related to the physical setting) .[4]

These approaches over the years have been on a hit and miss basis; and law enforcement agencies, the courts, and correctional institutions have attempted to implement various educational and recreational programs in an attempt to reduce the seriousness of juvenile delinquency. However, young people still come before the courts. Literally thousands of young people appear to be involved in delinquent acts. Many students indicate that perhaps 90 percent of all young people have committed at least one act for which they could have been brought before juvenile court. Many of these offenses are relatively trivial-fighting, truancy, running away from home, etc.

The appearance of a girl in juvenile court may be taken more seriously since it frequently indicates that she has failed to conform after previous measures have been taken, or that the offense is serious enough to warrant adjudication as a delinquent; personal and situational characteristics justify the severe action the court may take. Such factors perhaps are considered much more seriously in the case of girls since they may be less compatible with the sterotype image of the female role in our society.[5]

Vedder states that there seem to be nearly as many causes of juvenile delinquency as there are individuals who have studied the problem. Delinquency has been attributed to bad companions, adolescent instability, mental conflicts, extreme social suggestibility, early sex experience, love of adventure, motion pictures, school problems, poor recreation, excessive street life, vocational dissatisfaction, sudden impulses, bad habits, obsessive ideation, poor physical structure, ill health, or premature puberty. Yet, most children have experienced one or more of these causes and have never become officially delinquent.[6]

Juvenile delinquents are concentrated disproportionately in the cities, and particularly in the larger cities. Arrest rates are next

---

[4]*Ibid.*, p. 8.

[5]Peter G. Garabedian and Don C. Gibbons, *Becoming Delinquent* (Chicago, Aldine Publishing Co., 1970), p. 87.

[6]Vedder, op. cit., p. 9.

highest in the suburbs, and lowest in rural areas.

Delinquents generally do badly in school. Their grades are usually below average. Many have dropped one or more classes behind their classmates or have dropped out of school entirely. The delinquent girl usually becomes a problem in school. This can be caused because of the economic conditions of the home or the emphasis placed on the importance of school. School is probably the most important community agency in the effort to prevent delinquency since it reaches almost all children at an early period of their growth. Unfortunately, school has little relationship to life at home for many delinquent girls and cannot overcome the behavioral difficulties of the child.

Delinquents tend to come from backgrounds of social and economic deprivation. Their families tend to have lower than average incomes and social status. But perhaps more important than the individual family's situation is the area in which a youth lives. One study has shown that a lower class youth has little chance of being classified as delinquent if she lives in an upper class neighborhood. Numerous studies have revealed the relationship between certain deprived areas; particularly the slums of large cities and delinquency.

Many times social class largely determines whether female misbehavior is labeled delinquency or emotional disorder. Doctor Halleck discovered while directing a student health psychiatric clinic at a large university, and at the same time serving as a consultant at a nearby training school, that girls at both institutions behaved similarly but were treated differently. The rate of promiscuity among the students was about equal to that of the delinquent group. It was unheard of however, for a college girl to be defined as a delinquent because of sexual misbehaving. He also found that shoplifting and other petty theft occurred with considerable frequency in both groups, but in the college girl it was almost always considered to be a sign of emotional disorder. In lower class girls, identical behavior led to a label of delinquency. Many kinds of pranks and attitudes of contemptuousness toward authority occurred in both groups, but again they received differential treatment. The college girls sometimes flaunted rules and regulations as though they were made to be broken. This was defined as either "healthy" rebelliousness or as a sign of personality disturbance. No such luxury was allowed to lower-class girls, who were more likely to be defined as antisocial or incorrigible.[7]

Doctor Halleck further added that he could recall participating in a conference at the training school in which discussion centered about community reaction to a girl who had made several long distance phone calls and had illegally charged them to local businessmen. Everyone was convinced that community reaction against this girl was so negative that she could never be paroled to that area. Doctor Halleck stated that he also found himself sharing this sentiment until he recalled that he had recently sat in on a much more benign and optimistic conference designed to deal with an epidemic of this same behavior at the university.[8]

Middle-class girls, of course, are more careful to test limits of inappropriate behavior. They know when it pays to be respectful and obedient since they have more often been rewarded for such behavior. It is also true that stealing among upper or middle-class girls has a more apparently unreasonable quality since it is less likely to be governed by economic need. Yet, the peculiarities of our society's reaction to female misbehavior are such that in seven years of consulting to a state school for girls, Doctor Halleck stated that he never heard of the commitment of an upper-middle or upper-class girl. During this time, a number of serious crimes, including murder, were committed by girls of these classes which received much publicity throughout the state. In every instance, the girls were either put on probation or sent to a mental hospital.[9]

Doctor Halleck concludes that punishment is mainly imposed upon those girls who do not have "respectable" homes or access to sufficient resources to protect against institutionalization. Many of the girls who end up in a training school are sent there simply because their families are unwilling or unable to care for them and there is nowhere else to send them. After a period of time, of course, the lower-class girl who is labeled delinquent does become hardened, angry and antisocial. Subcultures form which are dedi-

---

[7]Seymour L. Halleck, *Psychiatry and the Dilemmas of Crime* (Harper and Row, New York, 1967), pp. 138-139.

[8]*Ibid.*, p. 139.

[9]*Ibid.*, p. 139.

cated to an attack on middle-class institutions and morality. It is hard to see how these attitudes could fail to develop. The average female delinquent knows she is more of a victim than a miscreant and quickly perceives adult hypocrisy when she is told to "be good" or to reform.[10]

According to Gisela Konopka, many delinquent girls come from economically deprived families where the parents themselves live with frustration, where poverty not only means not having money, but also means ignorance, fear, and degradation. Children are a nuisance, especially when they get older and assert themselves.[11]

Delinquency rates are high among children from broken homes, and a number of studies have shown that abnormal or defective family relationships are much more prevalent among families of delinquent children than among families of comparable children who do not become delinquent.[12]

Most delinquents grow up in homes where no father is present, and where the mother has to be everything. These girls have no experience with a father person. Men hardly exist, or they exist as an occasional intruder in the family. The road to a healthy development toward womanhood through affection for the male and identification with mother simply does not exist.[13]

Parental deprivation and abuse seem to occur more frequently among female delinquents. The child receives inadequate attention from the mother and attempts to seek these gratifications from the father. With the onset of adolescence, this close relationship with the father (if there is a father in the home) cannot be maintained because of the sexuality of the relationship, and she seeks affection elsewhere. The price for this affection is usually sexual intercourse. You see the same pattern develop in normal development, but usually these girls have received sufficient gratification from the mother so that their need for the father does not take on a desperate "oral" quality.[14]

---

[10]*Ibid.*, p. 139.

[11]Konopka, op. cit., p. 49.

[12]David Dressler, *Readngs in Criminology and Penology* (New York, Columbia University Press), 1964, p. 268.

[13]Konopka, op. cit., p. 50.

[14]Halleck, op. cit., p. 141.

Halleck further indicates that a surprisingly large percentage of delinquent girls claim that their first initiation to sexual experience occurred during latency and that they were seduced by an older man.[15]

All adolescents are uneasy about their self-image. Many have a very low self-esteem and a dissatisfaction with their own worth. Unlike girls from middle-class families, delinquent girls have not been praised during childhood for small accomplishments. They have never felt important and have never known success. They remember their childhood as a painful experience, and only recall the scoldings and beatings for something they have done wrong. It had been conveyed early to them that they were less than important, that they were a nuisance.

The adolescent female is usually eager to discuss her self-image and self-attitudes. Self-attitudes are unique in that the person holding the attitude and the object toward whom the attitude is held are the same.[16]

Our attitudes toward ourselves are very importantly influenced by the responses of others toward us. Membership in a minority group in one's neighborhood—especially among children—may produce exclusion and rejection, and, through the medium of reflected appraisals, feelings of inadequacy. Children in different social groups are likely to be exposed to characteristic reactions from others which may be decisive in the formation of self-esteem. Every society or group has its standards of excellence, and it is within the framework of these particular standards that self-evaluation occurs.[17]

According to Rosenberg, research regarding social class and self-esteem, the highest-class girls are only slightly more likely than the lowest-class girls to have high self-esteem.[18]

Anxiety represents an important element of neurosis which is widely acknowledged. The lower the subject's self-esteem level, the more likely was she or he to report experiencing various physiologi-

---

[15]*Ibid.*, p. 141.

[16]Morris Rosenberg, *Society and the Adolescent Self-Image* (Princeton, N.J., Princeton Univ Press, 1965), p. 10.

[17]*Ibid.*, p. 13.

[18]*Ibid.*, p. 41.

cal indicators of anxiety—hand trembling, nervousness, insomnia, heart pounding, pressures or pains in the head, fingernail biting, shortness of breath when not exercising or working hard, palmar perspiration, sick headaches, and nightmares. People with low self-esteem were also more likely to report that they had suffered from nervousness, loss of appetite, insomnia, and headache during the past five years.

In addition to these psychophysiological indicators, Fromm-Reichmann has suggested that anxiety is manifested by (1) "interference with thinking process and concentration," (2) "a frequently object-less feeling of uncertainty and helplessness," (3) "intellectual and emotional preoccupation," and (4) "blocking of communication."[19]

Horney contends that the child, through a variety of adverse circumstances in the family, develops a fundamental fear, a basic anxiety. In order to cope with this anxiety, the child retreats into the world of imagination where she creates an idealized image which gives her a sense of strength and confidence. This image is so admirable and flattering that when the individual compares it with her actual self, this latter self is so pale and inferior by comparison that she feels a hatred and contempt for it.[20]

Rosenberg further contends that low self-esteem contributes to four conditions: (1) instability of self-image, (2) the presenting self, (3) vulnerability, and (4) feelings of isolation. These conditions in turn tend to generate anxiety; and if we control these factors, the relationship of self-esteem to anxiety will decrease.

People with low self-esteem often present a false front to the world. Their aim is to overcome the feeling of worthlessness by convincing others they are worthy.

People with low self-esteem are (1) much more likely to be sensitive to criticism, to be deeply disturbed when they are laughed at, scolded, blamed, criticized, etc.; (2) are much more likely to be bothered if others have a poor opinion of them; (3) are much more likely to be deeply disturbed if they do poorly at some task they

---

[19]Frieda Fromm-Reichmann, "Psychiatric Aspects of Anxiety," in M. R. Stein, A. J. Vidich, and D. M. White, eds., *Identity and Anxiety* (Glencoe, The Free Press, 1960), p. 129-130.

[20]Karen Horney, *Neurosis and Human Growth* (New York, Norton, 1950).

have undertaken; (4) are much more likely to be disturbed when they become aware of some fault or inadequacy in themselves.[21]

The adolescent afflicted with pangs of self-contempt may develop at least two solutions to the problem of feelings of worthlessness: (1) she or he may retreat into the world of imagination where she can dream of herself as worthy, and (2) she may put up a false front to others to convince them that she is worthy. But as is so often the case with neurotic solutions, they may generate consequences more devastating than those they were designed to alleviate. One of these consequences would appear to be the development of feelings of isolation.[22]

The private world of daydreaming and the public pose-tend to separate the person with low self-esteem from others, make it impossible for her to share herself with others fully, freely, and spontaneously. For these reasons we would expect such people to experience a fundamental feeling of loneliness.[23]

The feeling of loneliness is not just a matter of being physically alone. A person is lonely who cannot make contact with others, communicate with them, get through to them, share feelings, ideas, and enthusiasm with them; and these are things the person with low self-esteem has difficulty in doing because of her involvement in her private world of imagination and her public pose.[24]

M. Hodgkiss' study of Chicago girls disclosed that sixty-seven percent of the delinquent girls and forty-five percent of the controls came from broken homes. Various other studies have shown that the children with intact families have a clear and persistent advantage over those from broken homes. This is especially true for the females. In addition, the home of the delinquent child appears to be much more "defective," "immoral," or "inadequate" than are homes in general. In broken homes one seems to find a conjunction of deprivations and positive influences toward criminal behavior.[25]

T. Hirschi also found that middle adolescence is the period of

---

[21]Rosenberg, op. cit., p. 158.
[22]*Ibid.*, p. 161.
[23]*Ibid.*, p. 162.
[24]*Ibid.*, p. 162.
[25]Dressler, op. cit., p. 270.

maximum delinquent activity. The relation between mother's employment and delinquency is not particularly strong, but the linearity of the relation from full-time employment to part-time to housewife, suggests that some aspect of direct supervision and not some characteristic of the mother or of the child accounts for the relation. It is not that the child is less likely to be supervised; it is not that she is more likely to feel estranged from the mother; it is not that the child is more likely to engage in delinquency-producing activities with her friends. Children from large families are more likely than children from small families to commit delinquent acts. It has been discovered that relation between size of family and delinquency is untouched by controls for affectional ties to and interaction with parents; it persists when the effects of these variables and parental supervision are removed. The middle child is most likely to commit delinquent acts. There are apparently many good reasons why only eldest, and youngest children should be less likely than middle children to commit delinquent acts.[26]

The preceding comments have been an effort to discuss the nature and causes of juvenile delinquency. There is substantial evidence to state unequivocally that children from broken homes, those living in slums, those who do not complete school, those having a low self-image, those running away from home, etc. are the children coming before the courts and other law enforcement agencies. However, not all children having these problems get involved with the courts or commit delinquent acts.

SIGNIFICANCE AND BEHAVIOR

The President's Commission on Law Enforcement and Administration of Justice states in its report *The Challenge of Crime in a Free Society:* "Official delinquents are predominantly male. In 1965 boys under eighteen were arrested five times as often as girls. Four times as many boys as girls were referred to juvenile court."

The report continues: "Boys and girls commit quite different kinds of offenses. Children's Bureau statistics based on large city court reports reveal that more than half of the girls referred to

---

[26]Travis Hirschi, *Causes of Delinquency* (Berkeley, California, Univ. of Calif. Press, 1969), p. 309.

juvenile court in 1965 were referred for conduct that would not be criminal if committed by adults; only one-fifth of the boys were referred for such conduct. Boys were referred to court primarily for larceny, burglary, and motor theft, in order of frequency; girls for running away, ungovernable behavior, larceny and sex offenses."[27]

Doctor Halleck stated that if one were to make a case for the maladaptive nature of criminality or the similarity of mental illness behavior and criminal behavior, he could find no better population to study than adolescent female offenders. It is doubtful if most female offenders ever cause harm to anyone but themselves. The two commonest forms of female delinquency, sexual promiscuity and running away from home, frequently offend our sense of propriety, but they are in no sense dangerous to our persons or to our possessions.[28]

Nationwide juvenile court statistics regularly report one girl delinquent to four, five or six boys. Furthermore, the majority of offenses by boys year after year involves some kind of theft or destruction of property, whereas most girls are charged with delinquency because of sexual misbehavior, whether so identified or listed as truancy, running away, or being ungovernable or incorrigible. However, as Ms. Konopka found in her study in the poverty areas in Minneapolis that girl delinquents numbered not one to five boys, but one girl to two boys.

The Federal Bureau of Investigation's *1972 Uniform Crime Reports* certainly indicates a tremendous increase in female delinquency and the trend is toward more violent crimes. According to the *1972 Uniform Crime Reports* "male arrests outnumbered female arrests by almost six to one in 1972. Male arrests rose by one-half of one percent, while female arrests were up two percent. Eighteen percent of arrests for Crime Index offenses were of female persons. Ten percent of the arrests for violent crimes in 1972 involved females and arrests of females for these types of crimes increased nine percent over 1971. Again, as in prior years, their involvement was primarily for larceny which accounted for nineteen

[27]The President's Commission on Law Enforcement and Administration of Justice, *The Challenge of Crime in A Free Society* (U. S. Government Printing Office, Washington, D.C., 1967).

[28]Halleck, op. cit., p. 138.

percent of all female arrests. In fact, twenty percent of all property crime arrests in 1972 were of females. Females accounted for twenty-five percent of the forgery, thirty percent of the fraud, twenty-six percent of the embezzlement, and fifteen percent of the narcotics arrests. Over one-half of the run-away—police custody cases—were girls under eighteen years of age."

"The five-year arrest trends, 1967 to 1972, revealed that arrests for young females under eighteen years of age increased sixty-two percent, while arrests for young males under eighteen years of age rose twenty-one percent. When the serious crimes as a group are considered, arrests of males 1967 to 1972, were up eighteen percent and female arrests increased seventy-two percent."

The total arrest trends by sex 1960 to 1972, show violent crimes for females under eighteen years of age increased by 388.3 percent, while the increase for males under eighteen years of age rose 203.2 percent. The increase for the female committing property crimes rose by 300.6 percent, while the increase for the males was 71.0 percent.

The total arrest trends, 1971 to 1972, show violent crimes for females under eighteen years of age increased by 12.1 percent, while the increase for males under eighteen was 8.3 percent.[29]

Many persons studying crime and delinquency and other persons working in the criminal justice field, not directly involved with female delinquents, register no alarm at this apparent increase in female juvenile delinquency. They appear to believe that the percentage is rising, but misleading since the total number is not as great as the total number of male delinquents.

One must be aware that in our culture female offenders are not considered as much of a threat to the public as male offenders and the various agencies of the criminal justice system, (e.g. police, courts, probation, etc.) are more lenient in dealing with females.

Walter C. Reckless found that citizens are willing to report the behavior of males much more readily than of females. Judicial process in America are supposed to be very much more lenient with women than men. Consequently, female offenders have a much bet-

---

[29]Federal Bureau of Investigation, *1972 Uniform Crime Reports* (U. S. Government Printing Office, Washington, D.C., 1972).

ter chance than male offenders of not being reported, of not being arrested, and of dropping out of the judicial process, that is, of remaining uncommitted.[30]

Jean Scozzari indicates that many delinquent girls coming into contact with juvenile authorities for truancy, ungovernable behavior, running away from home, sexual promiscuity, etc. end their involvement with the courts at this stage. A large percentage of these girls appear to be defying their parents or acting out because of a lack of supervision. Many are placed in foster homes or other community social agencies and their delinquency ends at this time. Still others, who are pregnant, are placed on the Aid to Dependent Children Program rolls; and others who have serious behavior problems and resist all efforts at community correction are placed in training schools.[31]

The most significant change taking place in this century is the emancipation of women, and as women become more involved in the world of work the trend for criminal involvement will increase. Professor Radzinowicz states that women have traditionally made up only one-eighth of the criminal population, however, if the present trend continues they will soon be closing the gap. He continues that the trend will continue as long as women continue to liberate themselves from their traditional place in the home. During the World Wars, when women were forced to do tasks performed by men, their crime rate went up. When the men came back after the wars, the criminality receded to its normal ratio. Professor Radzinowicz further adds that any member of society who starts to take an increasing role in the economic and social life of that society will be more exposed to crime and will have more opportunities and therefore will become more vulnerable and more prone to criminal risk.[32]

Correctional administrators are beginning to see a significant change in females being admitted to their institutions. It is becoming more common to find that the new admission is charged with

---

[30]Walter Reckless, *The Crime Problem*, 3rd ed., (New York: Appleton-Century-Crofts, 1961), p. 37.

[31]Interview with Ms. Jean Scozzari, Chief Classification and Parole, FRW, Alderson, W. Va., Sept., 1973.

[32]Sir Leon Radzinowicz, *Time*, Vol. 102, No. 11, (September 10, 1973), p. 48.

the more violent crimes, (e.g. murder, armed robbery, assaults, etc.). This new delinquent is oftentimes the leader and aggressor in the criminal act and not the follower as was the case in the past. She has participated in criminal activities since early childhood and has become wise to the ways of the street.

Seymour Halleck's observations that a sizeable number of female juvenile delinquents who regularly participate in antisocial behavior demonstrates a collection of character traits which define what psychiatrists refer to as the hysterical personality. The hysterical personality is typically a girl who is seductive and flirtatious, and often promiscuous. She tends to be histronic and is adept at dramatizing her own plight. She is prone to periods of deep depression and anxiety, which follow one another with rapidity. Such a person is both superficial and flexible. Acutely aware of the needs of others, she learns to play upon them and accommodate herself to a variety of roles. Her sense of self is poorly developed. She is illnessprone and will develop a bewildering variety of physical and emotional complaints whenever the sick role is available and serves her needs. She is loath to acknowledge responsibility for many of her behaviors and can conveniently repress affects which are troubling. Above all, she is dependent. Her dependency has a demanding, "sticky" quality, and she sometimes reacts aggressively when dependency needs are frustrated.

It should be apparent that the hysterical personality describes a person who is prone to impulsive actions, a person who can easily become involved in sexual misconduct and delinquency. The oppresed girl, limited in physical strength, in mobility and in access to socially acceptable aggression, fights back by using her best weapons, exaggerated femininity and controlling passivity. She becomes particularly adept at employing the message, "I can't help myself," to manipulate others and control her environment. Such behaviors describe many female delinquents.[33]

Virginia W. McLaughlin contends that much of the anger and hostility delinquents display are really a cover-up for their deep hurt, and they find it easier to act out than to cry.[34]

---

[33]Halleck, op. cit., p. 140.

[34]Interview with Virginia W. McLaughlin, Warden at the Federal Reformatory for Women, Alderson, W. Va., Sept., 1973.

Whatever the causes or reasons, female delinquency is increasing at an alarming rate, and the delinquent girl is displaying a more violent behavior.

Most delinquent girls appear to have lost much of their respect for themselves and anyone in authority. Homosexuality appears to play an important part in their relationships, and the emotional involvement often results in violence to one of the parties. It appears that these girls are looking for emotional support in their relationships. Many of these relationships continue to exist throughout adolescence and into adulthood.

I interviewed probation officers, police officers, marshals, jailers, and correctional administrators in writing this chapter. Many of these persons did not see the female delinquent as a significant problem in the criminal justice system, however, all of these persons expressed surprise and alarm after they had been exposed to the female delinquent and her behavior patterns. Suddenly, they feel that others in the criminal justice system need to be made aware of this phenomenon, and measures need to be taken to upgrade planning and implementing effective programs of prevention and correction.

In conclusion, I feel there is a need for more research in the area of female juvenile delinquency. In order for the public and the various agencies of law enforcement to make any significant advances in curtailing female delinquency, it will be necessary for them to become more aware of the problems facing young women in our society.

〰〰〰〰〰〰〰〰〰〰〰〰〰〰〰〰〰〰〰〰〰〰〰〰〰〰〰〰〰

CHAPTER 3

FAMILIES IN CRISIS

Gilbert L. Ingram[1]

〰〰〰〰〰〰〰〰〰〰〰〰〰〰〰〰〰〰〰〰〰〰〰〰〰〰〰〰〰

☐ HISTORICAL PERSPECTIVE ON THE FAMILY
☐ THE FAMILY AND DELINQUENCY
☐ DISRUPTED HOMES AND DELINQUENCY
☐ PARENTAL REJECTION AND DELINQUENCY
☐ PARENTAL CONTROL TECHNIQUES AND
   DELINQUENCY
☐ WORKING WITH THE FAMILY IN CRISIS
☐ THE HOSTILE FAMILY
☐ THE INADEQUATE FAMILY
☐ THE FAMILY OF THE INCARCERATED
   DELINQUENT
☐ THE FUTURE

〰〰〰〰〰〰〰〰〰〰〰〰〰〰〰〰〰〰〰〰〰〰〰〰〰〰〰〰〰

THE FAMILY as a viable social unit is under attack from many different sources in modern American society. The assaults have increased in both intensity and number, ranging from criticism concerning the family's lack of effectiveness in producing adaptable members of society, to demands for elimination of the family as it is

---

[1]This chapter represents opinions of the writer and does not represent official policy or attitudes of the Federal Bureau of Prisons or the United States Public Health Service.

presently constituted (Cooper, 1970). An immediate result of these assaults is exemplified in the present chapter; many researchers and practitioners are being compelled to look closely at what is happening.

The spectacle is depressing and indeed presents a sad commentary on the family's efficacy as a social unit. Because fifty percent of delinquents come from broken homes, the fact that families are increasingly being broken by desertion and divorce is of immediate concern. Of those units that manage to remain intact, the adult family members manifest their social and emotional problems in various ways, such as alcoholism, drug addiction, crime, and suicide. These problems naturally extend to children of the unhappy families.

Past dissatisfactions of observers toward the family generally were aimed at the lower class of society and thus were more easily dismissed as problems peculiar to that segment of the population. Today, the delinquent products of inadequate, unstable family units are visible in every social class and cannot be so easily ignored.

Theorists and practitioners of diverse persuasions seem to agree that the family is of fundamental importance in the occurrence of delinquency. Every involved discipline, despite differences in emphasis, joins in the general castigation of the family. Typical of these views are the following: It is a truism that for every juvenile delinquent, there is a delinquent home environment. Children are not born delinquent; they are made that way by their families, usually by their parents (Communications Research Machines Books, CRM's, *Developmental Psychology Today* 1971, p. 291). The more thorough a study of juvenile delinquency is, the greater the emphasis laid on the family as a social unit (Pettit, 1970, p. 191).

The family is frequently cited as the villian of many social evils but with regard to delinquency there is almost unanimous agreement. Even in those cases in which other economic, cultural and psychological factors play a major role, the family still remains significant by its failure to counteract these other forces.

Research results notwithstanding, it is possible that this consensus is nothing more than an empty generalization, devoid of any real meaning and worthless for purposes of prevention or treatment. In fact, such a broad indictment of the family may seduce some into thinking that they now understand the problem, when obviously, this is not the case.

Another fallacy in this area is the tendency to use preliminary research results to place a label on a family that seems to breed delinquency. Once this label is available, the assumption is made that a grasp on the cause of delinquency is at hand. Hypostatization is a comforting but nonproductive enterprise. The causes of delinquency are undoubtedly complex and varied; not unitary.

It is not the intention to present a comprehensive review of all literature pertaining to the effect of the family on delinquent behavior. This task, although necessary, has been accomplished by others, including an excellent review by Peterson and Becker (1965). Rather, the goal is an overview of the area emphasizing general conclusions that appear to have some merit and more importantly, that may have some applicability. Problems in working with the families of delinquents are discussed and specific examples of tactics are presented that may facilitate successful intervention.

HISTORICAL PERSPECTIVE ON THE FAMILY

The modern concept of childhood was unknown in the Middle Ages. At that time, childhood was viewed exclusively as a transition stage before adulthood. As the rate of infant mortality and the demand for productive work decreased, the family began to focus on the child as an individual in his own right. Children were able to go to school and refrain from work. Especially during the Seventeenth and Eighteenth Centuries with the increased opportunity for education, childhood assumed the status of a separate stage of development. Adolescence as a separate stage was even later in evolving, not appearing in its present state until the late Nineteenth and early Twentieth Centuries.

During most of the Nineteenth Century, the agrarian-based culture predominated with its independent family unity and a cohesive community life. As the industrial culture grew, family structure loosened with the concentration of populations in the large, heterogeneous communities. The shift was not only rural to urban, but also included an increased immigration from Europe to the big cities of this country. It should be noted that separate courts for juveniles were first established in the late Nineteenth Century after the large metropolitan courts were swamped with an increasing number of juvenile offenders.

Long cited as a puzzling and difficult stage, adolescence gained society's concentrated attention after the late Nineteenth Century. Because of the rapid technological advances and the influence of mass media, the present situation provides even more stress for the teenager and the family. As Mead aptly stated, "Parents have been rearing unknown children for an unknown world since about 1946 (Mead, 1972, p. 586)."

Added to the ordinary pains and adaptations that occur in growing up during any historical period, today's teenager is placed in various conflicting situations. While being bombarded with provocative stimuli and the sight of hedonistic behaviors of adults, the adolescent is taught to remain economically unproductive and to postpone immediate satisfaction for long range goals. Yet, after a prolonged period of protection and abstinence from 'adult' activities, he is supposed to emerge somehow from this dependent status into adulthood fully capable of behaving in a responsible manner. Added to these contradictory messages, which confuse and frustrate most adolescents, are the other social changes that have altered family life.

The size of the typical family has decreased so that each member is interacting with fewer other members, making individual contributions all the more important. At the same time, shared family activity or 'togetherness' has diminished, and this restricts the number of intrafamilial interactions. This trend sometimes prevents the family's carrying out its prescribed social function. The once biological contribution of the family was that of providing economic and physical safety for the members. Today, society expects the family to serve primarily as a socialization mechanism for the child and to provide satisfaction of psychological needs for all family members.

Leadership of the family has shifted in many ways from a patriarchal type to a more democratic or shared method of decision making. The former role of the father, that of providing explicit authority and fulfilling visible economic duties, allowed the children to model after him. He was quickly accepted as the authority figure. The mother's role was also definite and visible. Changing roles plus the extensive impact of mass media have created a situation in which children are less likely to accept the parents as models of behavior. Riesman (1969) has written of the increasing separatism of teenage culture and the massing in schools of large numbers of young people. The atmosphere engendered by this phenomenon is one of questioning the legitimacy of adult authority. In fact, Riesman believes the young become 'captives' of each other.

The shift in parental roles also has direct effects on the child when problems occur between the parents. One immediate result is seen in the handling of child custody cases. Until recently, fathers were considered to own all family property, including the children. The mother for all practical purposes had no legal rights to them. Today, an almost automatic preference obtains for the mother over the father in such court decisions.

Another characteristic of modern families is their increased mobility. Many writers describe the family as completely inefficient social units, citing the nomadic nature of their existence and resultant lack of stability. All of these modern trends in the life style of family units have dramatic effects on the children. The smaller size of the family plus the frequent changes in residence creates a lack of personal ties with others. Most modern families work and recreate as separate individuals outside of their home neighborhood. It is no great surprise that children of such families feel alienated, disenchanted, and at odds with the world around them.

Granted that modern families have unique problems and do not seem to be satisfying society's expectations; why though do seemingly privileged teenagers become delinquent, especially in terms of violent acting-out behavior? The attribution of such behavior to lower-class versus middle-class persons had been accepted as a general belief in both lay and professional circles. More recently, Stark and McEvoy (1972), among others, have challenged this assumption. Using data compiled by the National Commission on the Causes and Prevention of Violence, they cited statistics supporting the idea that, in fact, the middle class is more prone toward physical assault than the poor. Stark and McEvoy suggested that violence among the poor is more likely to become a police matter because of lack of privacy and little recourse to professional counselors or influential friends.

Keniston (1968) has cited one reason for some of the problems of modern families that offers a different perspective on violence. The adolescent's constant exposure to social upheavals occurring during the past decades has afforded an excellent opportunity for disagreeing with parental values and for perceiving the discrepancy between what parents say and what they do. Keniston acknowledges there has always been a failure to live up to professed ideals, but heretofore the adolescent has learned when parents can be reasonably expected to practice what they preach. Today, this "institutionalization of hypocrisy" does not occur so easily because rapid social change does not allow for the easy definition of exceptions to the rule and it is much easier for youth to detect such discrepancies. Ironically, the young hold to those values (love of fellow man, equality for all) which their parents espouse but do not practice. Having been raised in an affluent environment, the adolescent feels outrage over the lack of opportunities for those less fortunate. Added to this general feeling of anger and disappointment with his parents is the ever-present fear caused by the threat of the bomb and possible technological death. The awareness of violence is continually reinforced by frequently publicized mob behaviors.

Whether the cause is frustration over living conditions, personal inadequacies, or as Keniston has suggested, an obsession concerning violence in general, there is little doubt that the tendency to act out antisocially is increasing among youth in all social classes.

Today, if the family were considered to be a small business enterprise, it might have to declare bankruptcy. The task of turning out a useful social product is not being accomplished. In a recent large-scale study, the authors concluded that most teenagers do not achieve emotional autonomy, detachment from the family, or a personal ethical code of behavior (Douvan & Adelson, 1966). Although these manifestations of inadequate families are possibly as significant as delinquency, none produce such immediate and tangible damage against society. While the financial cost of delinquency is astronomical by all estimates, the psychological and sociological effects are undoubtedly a greater liability for everyone.

THE FAMILY AND DELINQUENCY

Numerous studies have been conducted in the investigation of family characteristics and delinquent behavior. Too many of these studies suffer from severe methodological weaknesses. The typical strategy used in these studies that seem to satisfy research requirements has been a comparison of families of delinquents with families of nondelinquents. This shotgun approach has been necessary because no systematic theory is available to guide inquiry and to organize existing data. The growing emphasis on differential classification programs and the concomitant development of differential treatment approaches acknowledge what every practitioner knows: i.e. delinquents do not present themselves as a homogeneous group for research or treatment purposes. Similarly, families of delinquents have their own particular 'personality' and do not as a single group share similar characteristics.

Rubenfeld (1967) identified the lack of a framework for family classification as a serious drawback in any attempt to determine the effect of family life on delinquent behavior. However, his suggestion for categorizing families by use of child-rearing patterns, such as those determined by the Fels Institute, may also be a waste of time. For example, after reviewing the enormous amount of data on the effect of different child-rearing practices, McCandless (1967) presented his advice which seems most appropriate: . . . mothers [parents] who are well-meaning and who try relaxedly to do what they sincerely believe is best for their children—particularly when this is in harmony with the cultural ways of the community with which they are most closely associatied—obtain the best results with their children (McCandless, 1967, pgs. 127-128). We have little reliable data on the subject considering the widely scattered attention directed toward it.

Despite the lack of information concerning the family, research findings have indicated possible characteristics that may bear on the problem. Three general types of families have consistently been identified with delinquent behavior: an unhappy, disrupted home with poor structure; a home in which parental attitudes of rejection prevail; and, homes demonstrating a lack of consistent and adequate discipline. Whenever possible, representative studies from both the earlier and the more current literature are presented.

DISRUPTED HOMES AND DELINQUENCY

Families may be disrupted by the physical loss of a member through death, divorce, or separation, or by the lack of structure caused by disturbed or criminalistic parents. Many studies in this area have been devoted to the effect of father absence on delinquent males, but the investigation of that variable has been a recent phenomenon.

A widely held assumption had been that the mother produced the major effect on the children and the father was relatively unimportant. Freud's writings were largely responsible for this focus on the mother's role, and even his critics seemed to agree with him on this one issue. The effect of maternal deprivation dominated the literature for many years. However, as more interest developed concerning the father's role, studies began to demonstrate the influence of the father, particularly concerning delinquency. Glueck, and Glueck (1962) cited repeated instances of alcoholism, nonsupport, brutality, and frequent absence from home in the fathers of delinquent boys. Extreme difficulties with male authority figures were frequently noted (see Medinnus, 1965) but disturbed relations with mothers were present only for a few delinquents (Brigham, Rickets, & Johnson, 1967).

As attention was directed more toward the father, new problems were encountered which interfered with research. If the family is intact, fathers usually work during the day and have to be contacted on evenings or weekends. Because this involvement entails the loss of leisure time, fathers are less likely to cooperate. Fathers also view themselves as having little to do with their children's problems because they share the same cultural bias that others have. If the father is unavailable, researchers have frequently adopted another approach which has severe limitations; namely, interviews are held with the mother to obtain information about the father. Distorted perceptions are typically obtained, either positively biased when the home is intact or negatively biased when the home is broken. Both kinds of distortions interfere with comparisons of fatherless homes and intact homes.

Available data from those studies that have been conducted on the effect of fatherless homes indicate that the way in which the father leaves the family is an important variable. For example, loss of either parent through death does not seem to be as harmful an experience as a separation because of parental discord.

When the father is absent from the home, the effect apparently centers on disturbed social behaviors for boys. Father absence produced poor sex typing (Bach, 1946) and poor social relations (Stolz, 1954). Because these factors have been associated with delinquency, the effect of father absence on delinquent behavior seems quite important. The question of the relation of the child's age when father absence occurs to subsequent delinquent behavior is another issue far from being settled. Lynn and Sawrey (1959) and Siegman (1966) found that father absence before age five often produced compensatory masculine behavior in adolescence. More recently, Biller (1971) reviewed the literature and concluded that absence during the elementary school years was most important for the development of delinquency.

The importance of father absence for delinquency is not limited to lower class children. Siegman (1966) asked a group of medical students anonymously to reveal their early histories. Minor behavior problems such as cheating in school were equally likely to occur in both father-absent and father-present groups, but serious acts such as theft of property occurred more frequently in the father-absent group.

Recognizing the importance of a variable and isolating its particular effect are two entirely different problems. Although many studies do support the notion that fatherless homes frequently result in delinquency, approaching the problem simply in terms of father-absence versus intact homes has yielded no definitive answers. Hertzog and Studia (1968) reviewed fifty-nine studies dealing with the effects of fatherlessness on children in general and thirteen studies dealing directly with delinquency. They found general support for a relationship between delinquency and fatherless homes, but also noted qualifying factors. Their suggestions for future research included a shift from single variable analysis to a study of interacting clusters of factors. The fact that approximately six million children in the United States are being raised in fatherless homes indicates the urgency of proceeding with definitive studies.

Contrary to earlier writings, absence of the mother is not frequently cited as a major factor in the area of delinquency. Most researchers apparently agree with Becker, Peterson, Hellmer, Shoemaker, & Quay (1959) who reported the role of the father as being apparently more important than that of the mother in the development of delinquent behavior. More recently, as the role of the mother has shifted in our society, some attention has been directed toward the possible influence of working mothers on children. However, most studies indicate that type of temporary absence is not a significant factor.

Emotional disturbance on the part of either parent, which also produces a lack of structure in the home, seems to be instrumental in producing disturbed delinquents. Delinquents who are regarded as emotionally disturbed often have disturbed parents (Becker, et. al., 1959; Liverant, 1959; Peterson, Becker, Hellmer, Shoemaker, & Quay, 1959; Richardson & Roebuck, 1965). Many practitioners have discovered that delinquents have character-disordered parents when they attempted unsuccessfully to work with them (Reiner & Kaufman, 1959). The presence of disturbed or criminalistic parents does not distinguish delinquents from other groups, but it does indicate that homes disrupted by disturbed as well as absent parental figures may indeed contribute to antisocial behavior.

Homes may also be disrupted by the lack of physical space and by the chaotic life style that accompanies such an environment. These characteristics typically describe the lower-class family, but as already stated, lack of structure is not confined to the physical aspects of the home. In this sense, middle-class children also are often exposed to a living style that precludes a stable pattern of existence. One immediate result of such disrupted homelife for children from all social classes is to make them more vulnerable to the influence of antisocial peer groups (Peterson & Becker, 1965).

The specific ways in which broken and disrupted homes contribute substantially to the delinquency problem are just beginning to be identified. For example, Wood, Wilson, Jessor, & Bogan (1966) found that the overwhelming feelings of powerlessness that delinquents have in dealing with society can be attributed partly to the lack of meaningful structure in their family life. As yet, few research findings in this area have been substantiated and none have been shown to offer meaningful ideas for application in the real world.

PARENTAL REJECTION AND DELINQUENCY

Rejection of the child by either or both parents has long been cited as one important factor in aggressive behavior by numerous researchers. For instance, Updegraff (1939), in reviewing the literature concerning the influence of parental attitudes upon the child's behavior, found a positive relation between maternal rejection and overt aggression in the child. Similarly, Baldwin, Kalhorn, and Breese (1945), using data from the Fels project, found that rejected children showed a marked tendency toward quarreling, increased resistance toward adults, and sibling hostility. Bandura and Walters (1959) and Andry (1960) found rejection by the father to be a significant pattern for their delinquent samples. McCord, McCord, and Howard (1961) conducted an extensive study involving direct observations of behavior for more than five years. One of their relevant findings was that parents who generally rejected their sons were most likely to produce aggressive boys.

More recently, McCord, McCord, and Howard (1963) suggested that antisocial aggression depends more on the degree of rejection and other parental behaviors than simply the absence or presence of parental rejection.

A great deal more has been written about the effect of parental rejection on a particular type of delinquent or criminal, namely the psychopath. This cruel, defiant person who personifies the laymen's stereotype for all delinquents deserves some special attention because he exhibits extreme variations of behavior found in many delinquents.

Lipman (1951) presented a view which may be taken as a general orientation. He said the psychopathic child is one who has been rejected from the beginning. Subsequent aggression is almost a compulsive act and no feeling for other people is present. Bender (1961) stated that psychopathic behavior occurs when the child is exposed to early and severe emotional and social deprivation attributable either to impersonal institutional care or to critical blocks in the mother-child relationship. Fox (1961) proposed that the psychopath's lack of internalization of cultural values could result from his unfortunate first contact with society, i.e. extreme rejection by the parents.

This has an interesting analogy in research conducted on animals. Harlow (1962) found that monkeys raised in isolation had severe social abnormalities that could be compared to psychopathic behavior. Among other types of behavior, they showed exaggerated aggression and an absence of affectional ineraction. This seems to indicate the influence of early social relationships on aggressive behavior may hold despite species differences.

Psychopathic behavior has been proposed to stem from parent-child relationships other than extreme rejection. Greenacre (1945) reported the fathers of psychopaths to be usually men who spend little time at home and who act in a cold manner toward the child. The mother was not a steady parent in her interactions with the child or with others. Jenkins (1960) proposed, in addition to the possibility of organic involvement, the child may have been exposed to a confusing situation for social training. All of these proposals are generally in agreement with the research cited above. Despite the post facto nature of the writings, they point to a rejecting environment early in life as a causal factor in aggressive behavior and possibly in the etiology of psychopathy.

PARENTAL CONTROL TECHNIQUES AND DELINQUENCY

There are three general ways in which parental reactions seem to contribute to delinquency: (1) Parental attempts at discipline are inadequate to control antisocial behavior; (2) Parental re-actions provide a punitive model for the child to imitate; and (3) The parents deliberately encourage the child's inappropriate be-havior.

The inadequacy of parental discipline in controlling the de-linquent's behavior has been noted by many researchers. Healy and Bronner (1926) and Burt (1929) noted that defective pa-rental discipline was an important social determinant of delin-quent behavior. Merrill (1947) determined most of her delin-quents came from homes with lax, erratic, or overly strict disci-pline. Glueck and Glueck (1950) found the delinquent's parents, particularly the father, had the same difficulty with discipline. Bandura and Walters (1959), Bennett (1960), and McCord, *et al.,* (1961) cited the inconsistent handling of problem behavior by parents as a factor in delinquency.

The effect of inadequate discipline is hypothesized by Hoffman and Saltzstein (1967) to be the weak development of conscience frequently found in delinquents. Apparently the type of discipline exerted by the parents does not facilitate the increased resistance to temptation which is necessary to prevent antisocial acts.

The second way in which parental control techniques may lead to delinquency is by providing an aggressive model for the child. Bandura, Ross, and Ross (1961, 1963) found that children, espe-cially boys, are influenced by viewing aggressive behavior, and more importantly, become more aggressive themselves in other situations. The significance of these studies is magnified by the fact that parents of delinquents resort more often to aggressive behavior for punishment than do other parents (Glueck & Glueck, 1950; McCord, *et al.,* 1961).

Physical punishment may effectively suppress behavior for a

short period but it frequently causes a great deal of frustration and provides another opportunity for the delinquent to learn to be aggressive. As Sears, Maccoby, and Levin (1957) found in their classic study, the pattern of child-rearing producing the most aggressive children is when the parents disapprove of aggression but punish its occurrence with their own physical aggression or threats of aggression.

The third, and perhaps most insidious manner by which parents may influence the expression of delinquency, is the deliberate encouragement of antisocial acts. A great deal of data has been collected which supports the hypothesis that delinquent behavior is reinforced by the family. Shaw and McKay (1942) and Glueck and Glueck (1950) both found that their delinquents came from homes in which other criminals were living. McCord and McCord (1958) discovered that a criminal father plus the absence of maternal warmth was the one combination most likely to lead to delinquent behavior. Similarly, dropping out of school, which typically accompanies delinquency, is related to the parents exhibiting the same behavior (Williams, 1963).

The above examples of general reinforcement of delinquency are overshadowed by the occurrences of direct antisocial instruction by the parents. Bandura and Walters (1959) noted that parents of aggressive boys tended to encourage aggression. Bandura (1960) found that mothers of aggressive boys were punitive when aggression was expressed toward them but became more tolerant when the aggression was expressed toward peers or siblings. Becker, Peterson, Luria, Shoemaker, and Hellmer (1962) reported that mothers who frequently used physical punishment also frequently told their children to fight other children whenever necessary.

WORKING WITH THE FAMILY IN CRISIS

Although increasing evidence indicates families are doing a poor job of rearing children, one conclusion remains inevitable under our present system of justice; the family can not be ignored in either the prevention or treatment of delinquents.

In reviewing the history of the development of juvenile courts in this country, Mennel (1972) concluded: Today, as then, we can no longer disqualify parents from caring for their children simply because they are poor or unfamiliar with the principles of child psychology. Parents may indeed abuse or fail to exercise their disciplinary authority. There is, however, little historical evidence to indicate that public authorities in the United States have provided viable and humane alternatives (Mennel, 1972, p. 78).

Until realistic alternatives are available or society changes its viewpoints regarding the sacrosanctity of the family, involvement of the family is necessary. Even after the delinquent's behavior has become completely unmanageable, the situation in which he does not have to return to his basic family unit would be the rare exception. Unfortunately, even in this case or after incarceration has been effected, the courts have no legal authority to insist upon the parent's involvement in the treatment of the child.

Experience to date indicates successful involvement of the family in the prevention or treatment of delinquency often is dependent upon the individual expertise and initiative of the change agent in overcoming bureaucratic inertia. Few specific suggestions are available from the research literature. However, a full understanding of many of the problems facing the family in crisis better prepares the worker to facilitate this involvement. Several parental reactions to delinquency occur frequently enough to warrant some attention. These reactions include a denial of blame with subsequent anger directed toward society, guilt after-the-fact and a feeling of helplessness, and finally, passivity and a relinquishing of responsibility because it is now out of their hands.

THE HOSTILE FAMILY

Many families confronted with the fact of their child's delinquency react very negatively. Typically, these are multi-problem families for whom delinquency poses an additional crisis. Already overwhelmed with financial and social misfortunes, the family is ill-prepared to deal realistically with the child's situation. Most hostile families fall into society's lower social classes.

Previous interactions between family members and society's

representatives usually have been in relation to problems in the educational system and frequently have been negative experiences. Against this background, the appearance of another 'helper' in the life of the family may be greeted with anger and sometimes overt hostility. Communication often breaks down because of real differences which exist between the values and language of the worker and the family.

Not only do the disadvantaged have their own particular vocabulary and style of speech but their concerns in life may differ significantly from the middle-class culture (Miller, 1958). Typical middle-class workers, regardless of discipline, probably share common beliefs about human nature (Dole & Nottingham, 1969). Frequently, the workers' beliefs conflict with the family's own values and communication channels break down. For example, the middle-class emphases on frugality and responsibility probably are not shared by disadvantaged families. Similarly, the family may seem unconcerned with long-term plans because their energies are focused on present problems. Confronted with an unwelcome stranger who talks differently and places a high value on the 'wrong' things, family members may directly indicate their disagreement and displeasure. Any helper, finding his well-intentioned overtures to be greeted thusly, can fall into the trap of assuming an authoritative posture and a condescending manner. The interaction undoubtedly will proceed downhill from this point.

What can be done to work with such a family? The answer depends upon the ability of the helper to understand and accept the members for what they are. This means he must entertain the idea that the family's behaviors and values may be appropriate *for them*. If he can do that, he should aim at the facilitation of the child's adaptation by working with the family. This process entails his gaining acceptance not as a friend but as someone who can help. Learning the language and values of the family are important because it is the rare middle-class person who fully appreciates the social and personal lives of the lower-class individual. Other suggestions that may be of some use include the following:

(1) Any indications of talking down to the family will reinforce their dislike and distrust of the authority person.

(2) Refusing to state opinions or backing down when confronted by the family will be interpreted as a sign of weakness and interfere with rapport.

(3) Avoidance of some relevant issues for the sake of "being nice" will destroy any respect for the person.

(4) Firmness, not coldness, is the preferred approach.

(5) Programs and suggestions should be geared to the real concerns of the family and not for abstract goals.

(6) Giving the family concrete tools to work with is better than speaking in generalities.

(7) Providing the family with tangible services, if at all possible, will facilitate their cooperation.

(8) Do not expect appreciation, at least in the traditional sense, for these efforts.

Most of these suggestions are self explanatory. Providing concrete suggestions (number six above) is discussed in the next session. An example of a tangible service (number seven above) may be the worker's serving as a go-between for the family and the school.

After the disadvantaged child has experienced difficulties in school, attempts by either the teacher or the parent to intervene are usually viewed as interference by the other party. An increasingly negative series of communications may convince the family, for example, that the teacher is either not concerned or is discriminating unfairly against the child. Subsequent school difficulties may be excused by the parents in such an atmosphere of distrust. Serving as a go-between in this case, the worker can make a valuable contribution by soliciting information from the school and by sharing helpful family data with the teacher. One result of such activities may be to discover that the child, accidently or deliberately, has reinforced erroneous assumptions on the part of both teacher and parents. Regardless of the specifics, however, all parties benefit from this type of interchange which minimizes the defensive maneuverings of all concerned.

The best intentions will not always guarantee success in working with the family, especially one predisposed to suspicion and hostility toward outsiders. The practitioner may well find his contributions are either not accepted or are of limited usefulness. This outcome should suggest another immediate alternative which has proven effective in many instances, namely the use of the community volunteer.

Initial reluctance to use volunteers was a natural reaction from professionals who felt they and only they could understand and deal with delinquents and their families. However, with the failure of traditional therapy approaches and the scarcity of professionals, the use of lay counselors or family workers has gained in popularity. Using volunteers does not remove the responsibility from the worker. Rather, the professional becomes a case manager at a different level; for example, selection, assignment and training of volunteers is essential for the success of a volunteer program. If done correctly, the use of volunteers can be effective even in the most difficult situations. Carkhuff (1971) has described a successful program to train lay counselors indigenous to the inner city, typically regarded as one of the most resistive areas to reach with any services.

THE INADEQUATE FAMILY

One frequently finds families that want to cooperate but seem incapable of handling their children or at least have difficulty with one particular child. Sometimes the family has reared several children without delinquent histories but another child has run into numerous difficulties. This child may be a special child in that he has been sickly, retarded, brain damaged, left alone for a period because of unavoidable environmental circumstances, or for one reason or another has been afforded special status in the parent's eyes. The inappropriate handling of such a child may lead to delinquency in any social class. Patterson, Cobb, and Ray (1970) found that the types of processes in the family leading to delinquent behavior were present in all socioeconomic levels.

Assuming the family does want to help their child or that the worker has prepared them for such involvement, the task of the practitioner is to deliver as quickly as possible to the parents techniques for making successful changes in the child's behavior. For reasons both of efficacy and efficiency, behavioral techniques seem to be the treatment of choice. They are the easiest to communicate, easiest to understand, and have been applied successfully with parents in diverse situations. Using the family itself as an agent of social change allows them to assume primary responsibility for the child which enhances feelings of competence and mastery over their environment. Additionally, the techniques are already being used by the parents but typically in an unsystematic fashion. Minuchin, Montalvo, Guerney, Rosman, and Schmer (1967) discovered that the mothers of problem children in slum areas used reinforcement techniques, but inconsistently and inappropriately for the child's deviant behavior.

Some direct results of inappropriate reinforcement techniques on delinquents have been identified. Delinquents in comparison to nondelinquents, are raised in homes where dependency behavior, approval seeking, and verbalizations of dependent behavior are negatively reinforced (Bandura & Walters, 1959; Bender, 1947; McCord & McCord, 1956). The implications of this extinction of dependency behavior for verbal counseling approaches may explain in part the fact that delinquents do not typically profit from conventional therapy. In fact, Mueller (1969) found that client's behaviors with therapists became increasingly similar to behaviors that occurred within the family constellation.

The strategy of retraining parents to act as more effective behavior modifiers has been successfully applied to parents of disturbed children (see Hirsch & Walder, 1969). The basic idea of using parents as the primary change agents is not only more economical and practical, but Patterson, *et al.* (1970) cited evidence suggesting that it may have a more permanent effect. Their program, in contrast with other attempts, concentrated on changing multiple classes of deviant child behaviors rather than altering a single behavior. Some of their specific techniques and findings have wider applicability for working with parents than their particular study. Relevant suggestions from their program are summarized below.

(1) Having parents simply read programmed texts on child management techniques is of limited value. [As adjunct material, these books may be helpful: *Child Management,* Smith & Smith, 1966; *Living with Children,* Patterson & Gullion, 1968.]

(2) Telling parents what to do is not as effective as the actual demonstration of recommended procedures.

(3) Training of the parent in the home has the advantage of the normal setting but it is a costly procedure. Group training methods are more advantageous once the family becomes involved in the process.

(4) Parents are notoriously inaccurate in remembering their children's early behaviors. Dependable information should be obtained through ongoing recording.

(5) Structuring of home visits is necessary to get an adequate observation of the home. Family members often attempt to avoid the 'intruder' by remaining in an inaccessible location such as the bedroom. It may be necessary to specify requirements of who is to be present and where during these visits.

(6) Observing the behavior of the delinquent by himself is less reliable than watching the behavior of all family members for a period of time.

(7) The verbal behavior of parents (everything is fine now; yes, we understand the problem, etc.) should not be accepted at face value without additional evidence of changes in behavior.

(8) Providing concrete examples of how to apply behavior principles to everyday problems is more easily understood by parents than the supplying of textbook answers.

(9) It may be necessary to become a nuisance to the father in order to obtain his cooperation; i.e. contact him daily, have court personnel call him, etc. The worker should keep in mind that the uncooperative father may be unable to carry out his assigned tasks rather than being deliberately resistive.

(10) The parent's starting with a simple behavioral problem between himself and the child maximizes the probability of a successful experience with the techniques.

(11) One goal of family training is to teach the parents to intercede before the child's behavior becomes extreme and before physical measures are necessary to control it.

(12) Parents should be reassured that an improvement in the behavior of one child does not mean that another child will increase his deviant behavior. Many parents believe this to be true and sometimes are reluctant to initiate change.

THE FAMILY OF THE INCARCERATED DELINQUENT

After delinquency has progressed to the point requiring institutionalization, it is exceedingly difficult to involve the family in rehabilitation of the delinquent. In addition to the predisposing circumstances which may have existed in the family for some time, the incarceration of the child creates additional problems for the family. Many families react very negatively to the institutionalization, preferring to act as if the problem no longer belongs to them. Others use the physical separation as an excuse to justify feelings of rejection that may have originally contributed to the delinquency. Regardless of the underlying factors, it is imperative that staff members attempt to overcome this obstacle to rehabilitation.

Staff time is not sufficient to allow for home visitation, not to mention the expense involved in such activities. Encouraging the family to meet with staff on institutional visiting days has not proven successful. Unless the family is able to afford weekday trips, which would be most unusual, visits mean weekend hours and the resultant absence of key staff members. Moreover, even when all parties are present, family involvement through visits is not regular enough for meaningful interactions to occur. All of these factors add to the communication gaps and lead to misconceptions for both staff and family. The delinquent suffers directly from the lack of family involvement because parental planning is crucial for release programming but more importantly, because the parent's behavior often has been a contributing factor to the delinquent's present situation.

One recent suggestion has been to invite groups of parents of delinquents to the institution for week-long visits (Stollery, 1970). Teams of staff counselors evaluate the delinquent's behavior and plan a unified program for him in conjunction with all family members. This program has the added advantage for low income families of providing a type of family vacation as contrasted with the brief, intermittent visits which may serve as a financial punishment. When groups of parents visit at the same time, it serves to facilitate a sharing of mutual concerns between families. Relaxed communications within the family are stimulated by the structured recreation time and reinforced through the group discussions. Staff as well as family members gain by the family's appreciation for the child's situation, especially pertaining to institutional procedures. Although there are numerous problems inherent in such a program, the results suggest a need for additional innovative attempts along these same lines.

One possible outcome of this type of visitation program may be the family's realization that they are unable to provide the necessary controls for the child. This conclusion is often at odds with their wish for him to remain in the family. After the family accepts their own limitations, they should be much more open to suggestions for new approaches. In this case, for example, a day-care program such as the one described by Post, Hicks, and Monfort (1968) may be appropriate. The child is kept in the home which avoids the guilt or other feelings accompanying removal. However, during the day the child is engaged in a program at a community center which also allows further work with the family. This type of program is less expensive than institutionalization but is more structured than total release to the family setting.

Another possible finding of family evaluation may be that the child cannot be helped by his own family. If the needs of the child can not be met within the natural family, a foster family may serve the purpose. Witherspoon (1966) described the advantages of foster home placements for juvenile delinquents, particularly when removal of the child from the home community is necessary to interrupt the established chain of delinquency. Special training is of course important for the foster parents as well as counseling to prepare the family to relinquish their legal claims to the child.

Both of the above programs provide alternative modes of action which may be necessary in compensating for some family deficiencies.

THE FUTURE

Despite the growing number of attacks on the family, it probably will continue to exist in its present form for some years. Rather than attacking the family with no productive goals in view, society's energies should be invested in researching the family's effects on delinquency and in modifying existing weaknesses with available resources.

Developing typological approaches to delinquency along dimensions other than social class has proven to be a promising research activity. Similarly, identification of types of families that contribute to delinquent behavior in combination with other factors may prove to be productive. Glueck and Glueck (1970) have combined these two ideas in their latest work with their Social Prediction Scale. They identified three types of delinquents and families from which they come: (1) Core type delinquents who have, among other characteristics, inadequate maternal discipline and no family cohesiveness; (2) Intermediate type delinquents who have some family inadequacies but not as many as the core families; and (3) Failures who came from apparently adequate families. This schema definitely is superficial, especially with regard to recent works on typologies by Quay and his associates (Gerard, Quay and Levinson, 1970) and Warren and her colleagues (Warren, 1969). However, it serves as a beginning in a neglected area of research because it does take directly into account the family's influence on delinquency.

Working with the family to effect changes in their behavior has proven to be extremely difficult. Parents seem to be responding to growing criticism of their child-rearing practices by constantly shifting and bending to please the experts or to conform to their child's expressed wishes. Unfortunately, neither society's experts nor their children knows what is best for the family. If nothing else, until answers are available, parents should at least be encouraged to provide a consistent and clear model of what they believe to be appropriate behavior for the child.

REFERENCES

Andry, R. G.: *Delinquency and parental pathology.* London, Methuen, 1960.

Bach, G. R.: Father-fantasies and father-typing in father-separated children. *Child Development, 17,* 63-80, 1946.

Baldwin, A. L., Kalhorn, Joan, & Breese, Fay H.: Patterns of parent behavior. *Psychological Monograph, 58* (No. 3), 1945.

Bandura, A.: Relationship of family patterns to child behavior disorders. Stanford University, Progress Report M-1734, National Institute of Mental Health, 1960.

Bandura, A., Ross, Dorthea & Ross, Sheila: Transmission of aggression through imitation of aggressive models. *Journal of Abnormal and Social Psychology, 63,* 575-582, 1961.

Bandura, A., Ross, D. & Ross, Sheila: Imitation of film mediated aggressive models. *Journal of Abnormal and Social Psychology, 66,* 3-11, 1963.

Bandura, A., & Walters, R.: *Adolescent aggression.* New York: Ronald, 1959.

Becker, W. C., Peterson, D. R., Luria, Zella, Shoemaker, D. J., & Hellmer, L. A.: Relations of factors derived from patient-interview ratings to behavior problems of five-year olds. *Child Development, 33,* 509-535, 1962.

Becker, W. C., Peterson, D. R., Hellmer, L. A., Shoemaker, D. J., & Quay, H. C.: Factors in parental behavior and personality as related to problem behavior in children. *Journal of Consulting Psychology, 23,* 107-110, 1959.

Bender, Lauretta: Psychopathic behavior disorders in children. In R. M. Lindner & R. V. Selinger (Eds.) *Handbook of correctional psychology.* New York: Philosophical Library, 1947.

Bender, Lauretta: Psychopathic personality disorders in childhood and adolescence. *Archives of Criminal Psychodynamics, 4,* 412-415, 1961.

Bennett, Ivy: *Delinquent and neurotic children.* New York: Basic Books, 1960.

Biller, H. B.: *Father, child and sex role.* Lexington, Mass.: Health Lexington Books, 1971.

Brigham, J. C., Rickets, J. L., & Johnson, R. C.: Reported maternal and paternal behaviors of solitary and social delinquents. *Journal of Consulting Psychology, 31,* 420-422, 1967.

Burt, C.: *The young delinquents.* New York: Appleton, 1929.

Carkhuff, R. R.: Principles of social action in training for new careers in human services. *Journal of Counseling Psychology, 18,* 147-151, 1971.

Communications Research Machines Books: *Developmental Psychology Today.* Del Mar, Calif: Author, 1971.

Cooper, D.: *The death of the family.* New York: Pantheon, 1970.

Dole, A. A., & Nottingham, J.: Beliefs about human nature held by counseling, clinical and rehabilitation students. *Journal of Counseling Psychology, 16,* 197-202, 1969.

Douvan, E., & Adelson, J.: *The adolescent experience.* New York: Wiley, 1966.

Fox, V.: Psychopathy as viewed by a clinical psychologist. *Archives of Criminal Psychodynamics, 4,* 472-479, 1961.

Gerard, R. E., Quay, H. C., & Levinson, R. B.: *Differential treatment: A way to begin.* Washington, D. C.: Federal Bureau of Prisons, 1970.

Glueck, S., & Glueck, Eleanor: *Unraveling juvenile delinquency.* New York: Commonwealth Fund, 1950.

Glueck, S., & Glueck, Eleanor: *Toward a typology of juvenile offenders: Implications for therapy and prevention.* New York: Grune & Stratton, 1970.

Glueck, S., and Glueck, Eleanor: *Family environment delinquency.* Boston: Houghton, 1962.

Greenacre, Phyllis: Conscience in the psychopath. *American Journal of*

Orthopsychiatry, 15, 495-509, 1945.

Harlow, Harry: The heterosexual affectional system in monkeys. *American Psychologist, 17,* 1-9, 1962.

Healy, W. & Bronner, A. L.: *Delinquents and criminals: Their making and unmaking.* New York: MacMillan, 1926.

Hertzog, Elizabeth, & Studia, Cecelia, E.: Fatherless homes: A review of research. *Children,* Sept-Oct, 1968.

Hirsch, I. & Walder, L.: Training mothers in groups as reinforcement therapists for their own children. *Proceedings of the 77th Annual Convention of the American Psychological Association, Washington, D. C.,* 561-562, 1969.

Hoffman, M. L., & Saltzstein, H. D.: Parent discipline and the child's moral development. *Journal of Personality and Social Psychology, 5,* 45-57, 1967.

Jenkins, R. L.: The psychopathic or antisocial personality. *Journal of Nervous and Mental Diseases, 131,* 318-334, 1960.

Keniston, K.: *Young radicals.* New York: Harcourt, Brace & World, 1968.

Lipman, H. S.: Psychopathic reactions in children. *American Journal of Orthopsychiatry, 21,* 227-231, 1951.

Liverant, S.: MMPI differences between parents of disturbed and nondisturbed children. *Journal of Consulting Psychology, 23,* 256-260, 1959.

Lynn, D. B., & Sawrey, W. L.: The effects of father-absence on Norwegian boys and girls, *Journal of Abnormal and Social Psychology, 59,* 258-262, 1959.

McCandless, B. R.: *Children: Behavior and development,* 2nd edition. New York: Holt, Rinehart & Winston, 1967.

McCord, W., & McCord, J.: *Psychopathy and delinquency.* New York: Grune & Stratton, 1956.

McCord, J. & McCord, W.: The effects of parental role model on criminality. *Journal of Social Issues, 14,* 66-75, 1958.

McCord, W., McCord, Joan, & Howard, A.: Familial correlates of aggression in nondelinquent male children. *Journal of Abnormal and Social Psychology, 62,* 79-93, 1961.

McCord, Joan, McCord, W., & Howard, A.: Family interaction as antecedent to the direction of male aggressiveness. *Journal of Abnormal and Social Psychology, 66,* 239-242, 1963.

Mead, Margaret: A conversation with Margaret Mead: On the anthropological age. In *Readings in Psychology Today* (2nd ed). Del Mar, Calif.: CRM Books, 1972.

Medinnus, G. R.: Delinquents' perceptions of their parents. *Journal of Consulting Psychology, 29,* 592-593, 1965.

Mennel, R. M.: Origins of the juvenile court: Changing perspectives on the legal rights of juvenile delinquents. *Crime and Delinquency, 18,* 68-78, 1972.

Merrill, Maud A.: *Problems of child delinquency*. Boston: Houghton Mifflin, 1947.

Miller, W. B.: Lower class culture as a generating milieu of gang delinquency. *Journal of Social Issues, 14,* 5-19, 1958.

Minuchin, S., Montalvo, B., Guerney, B., Rosman, B., & Schumer, F.: *Families of the slums*. New York: Basic Books, 1967.

Mueller, W. J.: Patterns of behavior and their reciprocal impact in the family and in psychotherapy. *Journal of Counseling Psychology, 16,* Pt. 2, 1969.

Patterson, G. R., Cobb, J. A., & Ray, Roberta S.: A social engineering technology for retraining aggressive boys. Paper present for H. Adams and L. Unikel (Eds.)., Georgia Symposium in Experimental Clinical Psychology, Vol. II., Pergamon Press, 1970.

Patterson, G. R. & Gullion, M. Elizabeth: *Living with children*. Champaign, Illinois: Research Press, 1968.

Peterson, D. R., & Becker, W. C.: Family interaction and delinquency. In H. C. Quay (Ed.), *Juvenile delinquency*. New York: D. Van Nostrand, 1965.

Peterson, D. R., Becker, W. C., Hellmer, L. A., Shoemaker, D. J., & Quay, H. C.: Parental attitudes and child adjustment. *Child Development, 30,* 119-130, 1959.

Pettit, G. A.: *Prisoners of culture*. New York: Charles Scribner's Sons, 1970.

Post, G. C., Hicks, R. A., & Monfort, M. F.: Day-care program for delinquents: A new treatment approach. *Crime and Delinquency, 14,* 353-359, 1968.

Reiner, Bernice S., & Kaufman, I.: *Character disorders in parents of delinquents*. New York: Family Service Asso. of America, 1959.

Richardson, H., & Roebuck, J. B.: Minnesota Multiphasic Personality Inventory and California Psychological Inventory differences between delinquents and their nondelinquent siblings. *Proceedings of the 73rd Annual Convention of the American Psychological Association,* Washington, D. C., 255-256, 1965.

Riesman, D.: The young are captives of each other. *Psychology Today, 28-31,* 63-67, Oct. 1969.

Rubenfeld, S.: *Typological approaches and delinquency control: A status report*. Washington, D. C. Department of Health, Education & Welfare, 1967.

Sears, R., Maccoby, E., & Levin, H.: *Patterns of child rearing*. Evanston, Ill.: Row, Peterson, 1957.

Shaw, C. R. & McKay, H. D.: *Juvenile delinquency and urban areas*. Chicago: University of Chicago Press, 1942.

Siegman, A. W.: Father absence during early childhood and antisocial behavior. *Journal of Abnormal Psychology, 71,* 71-74, 1966.

Smith, Judith M. & Smith, D. E. P.: *Child management*. Ann Arbor, Michigan: Ann Arbor Publishers, 1966.

Stark, R., & McEvoy, J., III.: Middle-class violence. In *Readings in Psychology Today,* 2nd edition. Del Mar, Calif.: CRM Books, 1972.

Stollery, P. L.: Families come to the institution: A 5-day experience in rehabilitation. *Federal Probation, 34,* 46-53, 1970.

Stolz, Lois M.: *Father relations of warborn children.* Stanford, Calif.: Stanford Univ. Press, 1954.

Updegraff, Ruth: Recent approaches to the study of the preschool child. III Influence of parental attitudes upon child behavior. *Journal of Consulting Psychology, 3,* 34-36, 1939.

Warren, Marguerite Q.: The case for differential treatment of delinquents. *The Annals of the American Academy of Political and Social Sciences, 381,* 47-59, 1969.

Williams, P.: School dropouts. *NEA Journal, 52,* 10-12, 1963.

Witherspoon, A. W.: Foster home placements for juvenile delinquents. *Federal Probation, 30,* 48-52, 1966.

Wood, B. S., Wilson, G. G., Jessor, R., & Bogan, R. B.: Trouble-shooting behavior in a correctional institution: Relationship to inmates' definition of their situation. *American Journal of Orthopsychiatry, 36,* 795-802, 1966.

CHAPTER 4

SOME INDICES OF PREDICTION OF DELINQUENT BEHAVIOR

HENRY RAYMAKER, JR.

- ☐ EARLY DELINQUENT MANIFESTATIONS
- ☐ NEEDS FOR PSYCHOLOGICAL EVALUATION
- ☐ JUVENILE DELINQUENTS AND PROJECTIVE TECHNIQUES
- ☐ NEED TO BE SENSITIVE TO ORGANIC FACTORS
- ☐ SELF-CONCEPT AND THE JUVENILE DELINQUENT
- ☐ COMMUNITY RESPONSIBILITY

A T A TIME when crime rates are increasing, especially the increase in offenses by young people, a review of signs of juvenile delinquency or indices of prediction, along with a review of the contribution that a practicing psychologist can make, is appropriate.

The detection of early signs of delinquency is most likely to occur in the home and school. The loss of interest in school subjects and conflicts with authority figures in the home and school often proceed some acting-out behavior which finally force society to respond and make an official case of juvenile delinquency. It is the sensitivity and motivation of the teachers to make referrals to guidance centers and professionals and the willingness of parents to seek help when these early signs are detected that could lead to a reduction and prevention of juvenile delinquency. Also, parents who are sensitive to early manifestations of delinquent behavior can take corrective action.

EARLY DELINQUENT MANIFESTATIONS

Some of these early signs are resentment of authority figures in the home and school and overt conflicts, resentment of overprotection, resentment of limits and discipline, loss of interest in school subjects and obvious underachievements, confusion associated with inconsistent discipline, impulsiveness asociated with permissiveness, suggestibility associated with peer group antisocial influences, frustration in the child and a need for compensatory behavior, compulsive stealing associated with poverty, involvement with drugs which usually has emotional and social motivations, etc.

There are many ways a child or adolescent may show tendencies toward delinquency. Also, in each case there are different origins, meanings and a matter of degree. The practicing psychologist, counselor, teacher, parent and society are faced with understanding multiple forms of delinquency and multiple causes that require an individual and clinical approach.

NEEDS FOR PSYCHOLOGICAL EVALUATION

To understand a youth and his behavior and formulate predictions a psychological evaluation of the intelligence, achievement, personality and feelings of the youth, along with a family and social history, is necessary. This provides the evidence to determine causes and early signs, needs, frustrations, infer predictions, and plan treatment or guidance.

The majority of young people who come to the attention of psychologists and court workers appear to have normal or average intelligence. Determining this dimension of the youth's profile can make our predictions and placement realistic and will maximize success. We do often see in this population underachievement in school subjects. Evidence that the youth is functioning below his native or potential level such as observing that his achievement scores are often below his I.Q. and grade placement can identify problems which when corrected may prevent delinquency. Many delinquents are functioning below their ability level and are behind in their achievement. One great need which exists on our school systems is to reach these children with remedial instruction and the possibility of these resources existing influences our predictive judgment.

In cases where the juvenile delinquent is mentally retarded and this is confirmed by individual intelligence testing, we can often reduce or control delinquency by removing a major source of frustration by placing the child in a special class within the school system for educable mentally retarded children. This reduces the stress and the feelings of rejection the retarded child shows, which often is the frustration that causes his delinquency or aggression. The success and acceptance the retarded child feels in a special class may meet the need that will modify the behavior pattern and increase conformity. Consistent discipline, structure and appropriate school placement appear to be the treatment needs of the delinquent who is mentally retarded and at the appropriate age referral to the vocational rehabilitation agency is needed. The degree that these resources exist in the community is relative to predicting the behavior of the child.

JUVENILE DELINQUENTS AND PROJECTIVE TECHNIQUES

In the evaluation of the adolescent a sensitive instrument, which provides the psychologist with a sampling of the youth's feelings, attitudes and types of identifications, is the Thematic Apperception Test, or projective technique. The themes and stories which the youth creates on the picture cards in this technique provide meaningful insights into the youth's underlying identifications, feelings and often reveal long felt frustrated needs. Documentation in these areas may identify signs of the degree of the delinquency trend and needs in the youth's personality that are relevant to prediction and management. Experience shows projecting hostility and aggression is often one of the most frequent themes a delinquent develops in the stories he creates on this test.

A second frequent theme is the fact that many youths identify with human figures who are depressed and are moody, introspective, or resentful in areas of authority, restrictions, rejections etc. A third frequent theme is the fact that many youths also project a need to be successful and identify with human figures who are striving for success and recognition. An observation we frequently see in average or bright adolescents who are in custody because of their delinquency is an admission of faults and acts of delinquency and projecting desires to be a better and more successful person. They try to give the impression they have learned their lesson and are going to try to do better.

Sometimes these adolescents show abilities at manipulating. Often, however, their comments suggest an awareness of guilt and a need for help. These are content areas where a majority of juvenile delinquents usually project feelings and attitudes on the Thematic Apperception Test and can be one of the most helpful clinical techniques the practicing psychologist can utilize.

NEED TO BE SENSITIVE TO ORGANIC FACTORS

In the battery of tests used by the psychologist are also measurements that can identify organic brain dysfunctioning where in a small minority of these cases some subtle organic deficit may be partially responsible for aggressive or antisocial behavior. In addition to the tests of intelligence and personality, a sensitive instrument in detecting organicity is the Bender Gestalt test where the child has to copy on paper a series of geometric designs. It is important to rule out organic damage or factors and when identified referral to medical consultation and appropriate treatment and planning may control the aggressive behavior of the child. These awarenesses also help the teacher, counselor and parent to better understand and relate to the child. These determinations are relevant to predictive judgments on the course of the child's behavior and adjustment.

SELF-CONCEPT AND THE JUVENILE DELINQUENT

In predicting the behavior of the juvenile delinquent or estimating response to treatment, it is useful for the practicing psychologist to determine the self-concept of the youth. The delinquent usually shows inadequate self-confidence or sees himself in negative ways or overcompensates for these feelings by being openly aggressive and hostile. The delinquent who maintains a negative self-image may continue to behave accordingly as a way of expressing hostility. It is the analyses of the origin of these perceptions and emotions that often are helpful in achieving self-awareness and insight and permit the delinquent, psychologist, counselor, and others to take steps to resolve and modify these behavior patterns.

The practicing psychologist may be able to infer the self-concept of the youth from the youth's identifications and projections on the Thematic Apperception Test. As a supplement to this, a practical approach to determining these self-perceptions is to ask the youth to write a letter about himself indicating how he sees himself, how he sees his problems and how he feels. Also, it is useful to have the youth complete a sentence completion test as many self-concept projections are revealed by this approach.

Therefore, the practicing psychologist's approach to the problem of juvenile delinquency and the study of prognostic signs is a responsibility to evaluate the intelligence and personality of the child or adolescent, determine his needs, attitudes, feelings, self-concept, review the social history, make recommendations, and be available as a treatment consultant.

It is in the focusing of the recommendations that a sensitivity to the indices of prediction is important as we strive to reduce delinquent behavior patterns. That is, the psychologist needs to make recommendations that may reduce the frustration in the child's life or meet the particular needs in each unique case that will remove the causes of delinquency. It is necessary that the community plan resources that can follow through on these recommendations, which usually include a progressive juvenile court, child guidance clinics, special education classes and consultation with the school system, social agencies such as rehabilitation services, and professional personnel working together in effective communication and coordination.

A psychological evaluation in isolation of the child's environment and continuing influences and resources is an academic exercise. When needs are documented and resources in the community are lacking, then it is the success which we achieve in getting community and social action to develop these resources that will make each community a low predictive or a high predictive environment for success in reducing juvenile delinquency.

In order to formulate or identify signs or indicators which may be used to infer predictions the clinical case method does reveal a pattern or similarities which suggest areas that are relevant in the etiology, treatment, prognoses and prevention of juvenile delinquency. The inferences from this practical experience can offer some indices of prediction. Also, possible warning or early signs in the general preschool and elementary school age population can assist us when parents, teachers and society respond and try correcting problems or meeting frustrated needs before delinquent behavior is manifested or comes to the attention of the court.

COMMUNITY RESPONSIBILITY

It is through a mental hygiene and public health principle of prevention that the magnitude of the juvenile delinquency problem in society must eventually be approached. Juvenile court judges are becoming more aware of the significance of meeting needs, arranging for individual and family counseling and treating the emotional dynamics of delinquency. In this corrective and rehabilitative process the involvement of family, school and supportive service agencies working together can increase the prospect of success as more people see the need for treating causes, frustrations and emotions in contrast to simple removal or isolation of the delinquent from society. It is in the area of social change such as the removal of double standards or the inconsistencies in society that additional progress can be made as often many causes and signs of delinquency are related to poor examples of adults.

A community which is a dynamic society and progressive can cope with problems of juveniles and create a more favorable environment. The worker in this field needs to be involved in social change as behavior is a function of internal and external motivation and influences.

In summary, juvenile delinquency can be reduced by a community sensitive to early signs and indices of prediction of delinquency and can take corrective action. Also, the child who becomes involved in juvenile court action can be evaluated and helped to become a more satisfied and productive person as the sources of his frustrations are removed by planning and counseling.

A forthright approach is for the community to recognize its problems and try to communicate and offer services for this important group of young people, correct its own shortcomings by removing inconsistencies or double standards, provide healthy identifications for youth and provide adequate education, recreation and guidance facilities.

CHAPTER 5

THE JUVENILE DELINQUENT AND HIS ENVIRONMENT

ROBERT G. CULBERTSON AND JEFFREY L. SCHRINK

※◇◇※

- ☐ INTRODUCTION
- ☐ THE FAMILY
- ☐ THE SCHOOL
- ☐ THE PEER GROUP
- ☐ SUMMARY

※◇◇※

INTRODUCTION

"MAN IS THE PRODUCT OF his environment . . . Man is the sum total of his contacts . . . Man mirrors his surroundings." We have heard these and other time worn cliches many times. While we give them a certain credibility, considerable time and energy have been expended looking for various psychopathologies which can allegedly be used to explain an adolescent's delinquent behavior. Some sociologists contend this is a consequence of the power held by psychiatrists, psychologists and other psychiatrically oriented personnel. Hakeem (1957) alleges that psychiatric and psychological explanations are ambiguous and tautological and their research is fuzzy, intuitive and extremely subjective. These allegations are partly correct as there is considerable evidence which indicates that some psychiatric procedures, such as labeling children "pre-delinquent," are arbitrary and whimsical and in some cases may actually enhance the development of delinquent self-concepts and delinquent value orientations.

On the other hand, sociologists have focused their attention on groups and group processes to the extent that they ignore the individual. Writing on sociological explanations, Caldwell (1965) notes that "in the development of their theories they are inclined to inflate the importance of the group until, in some cases, the individual is reduced to a mere shadowy thing that haunts the writer only in his rare moments of uncertainty." Sociologists often portray the delinquent as a "billard ball" propelled back and forth between forces over which he has no control. It comes as no surprise then that many sociological explanations of juvenile delinquency lack empirical support. Finally, because sociologists have concerned themselves with causation, often to the exclusion of treatment, they often have little to offer the practitioner.

Recently there has been greater interaction between the traditional academic disciplines and the resulting programs in criminology, social psychology, clinical sociology and counseling have much to offer. However, these innovative approaches have faced a number of barriers, the most serious of which is the historical boundary lines established by the disciplines which have functioned to inhibit the development of interdisciplinary explanations of juvenile delinquency.

If we are to implement effective treatment strategies we must look beyond the individual delinquent; we must develop the necessary skills to see the delinquent in an environment context. Most competent practitioners in the juvenile justice system support the contention that the adolescent's immediate involvement in delinquent behavior is a symptom of problems in the adolescent's environment. If practitioners intend to become effective change agents, they must examine the adolescent's environment in their effort to develop an explanation of the adolescent's involvement in delinquent behavior. Before discussing the kinds of environmental situations which contribute to delinquency, brief attention should be given to some of the reasons why many practitioners give lip service to the environmental perspective while utilizing individual treatment methods in working with delinquents.

First, we can see the delinquent. The delinquent is an object that can be interviewed, tested, manipulated, counseled and as a result, the treatment strategies take on a highly individualistic approach ignoring the environmental context in which the delinquency occurred. Second, the delinquent is readily accessible. A phone call will bring him to the office and because he is under our legal jurisdiction he can hardly avoid our "treatment." The authoritarian control structures in correctional settings produce the kinds of responses we want and as a result the symptom is treated while the problem is often ignored. Third, focusing on the individual delinquent allows the practitioner to avoid conflict situations with institutions in the adolescent's environment which may be contributing to the delinquent behavior patterns. It is not uncommon for the delinquent to be sacrificed while "professionals" in various agencies or institutions protect their administrative practices which may be dysfunctional for children in general and for delinquents in particular. Fourth, training for work in the juvenile justice system is not always appropriate. As an example some contend that one must hold an M.S.W. degree to be competent in working with delinquents. Amos (1968) and Benjamin (1965) have found no evidence to support this contention. Benjamin contents that social work training may be inappropriate in that it "engenders an attitude of caution or even of pessimism toward those who manifest serious maladjustments or unstable work or family history."

The following discussion of the delinquent's environment will be restricted to those aspects of the environment which can enhance the potential for delinquent behavior: the family, the school and the peer group. This is not to imply that additional aspects of the delinquent's environment are unimportant, or that our discussion is exhaustive. The authors' experience in the juvenile system has lead us to the conclusion that the family, school and peer group are the most important aspects of the delinquent's environment and that it is in these areas where treatment strategies can be most effective.

THE FAMILY

No other aspect of environment is as important to the child as his family. Children raised in instructurally complete and functionally adequate family settings develop healthy self-concepts, learn the necessary skills to engage in social interaction, hold reasonable expectations for themselves, internalize conformist value structures and come to be stable, productive members of society. It is when families fail that we find emergent problems, often in the form of delinquent behavior.

The authors have reviewed considerable theory and research on the family and have concluded that while much has been written the link between theory and practice is often missing. As a result, we have developed a perspective for the practitioner which can be utilized in working with families with delinquent children. Our perspective is not totally original and the practitioner with training in family theory and research will note the inclusion of a number of theoretical positions in the perspective developed here.

It is our position that delinquents often come from families which can be placed on the extremes of a protection—rejection continuum. At each end of the continuum we find some practices which are essential in successful child-rearing, but it is the dominance of one set of behaviors to the exclusion of the other that results in delinquency. At the same time there are some practices at each end of the continuum which are harmful in any family setting.

Protection as used here is meant to include those behaviors and attitudes which function to give the child a feeling of security. Support, protection, love, affection, reinforcement, rewards and defense describe some of these behaviors and attitudes. At the opposite end of the continuum we have used the concept rejection to include those behaviors and attitudes which function to give the child redirection when he violates social norms. Punishment, chastisement, rejection, denial and discipline describe some of those behaviors and attitudes. Delinquents come from families which can be located on the extremes of this protection-rejection continuum. Child rearing in these family structures is not balanced with adequate levels of love on the one hand, and discipline on the other. Below we have cited three situations which personify our perspective. The first involves rejection, the second protection and the third, vascillation back and forth reflecting first one extreme and then the other.

Danny is before the court* for runaway, truancy and auto theft. Danny's natural mother died when he was three, and two years later his father married a divorcee with three children by a previous marriage. At the age of seven, Danny was front page news as police discovered that his stepmother had tied him to a bed while taking Danny's step-brothers to a circus. The child welfare board took custody of the boy and for the following nine years Danny was moved from foster home to foster home, to an orphanage, and back to foster homes. At sixteen, he was returned to his father and stepmother after an exceedingly superficial home investigation by the child welfare board. Within two weeks Danny had left home at least three times, had not attended school and was apprehended by the police for auto theft. Danny prefers the detention facility to returning home and threatens to run away again if he is returned to his father and stepmother contending that an older step-brother has forced him to participate in homosexual acts. The case of Danny personifies the rejection end of the continuum.

James is before the court for theft and consumption of alcoholic beverages. His family is middle class and professes strong religious principles. The boy's mother is very talkative as she nervously rambles about her "good boy who helps at home and has never caused a single problem." James sits rather passively as his mother commences to unfold an alibi for the evening the boy was alleged to have been involved in delinquent behavior, and the father sits calmly as though he has been through this before. James confirms his mother's version of the activities on the evening the theft occurred, contending that the codelinquents who have implicated him are getting even because he refused to go along with the theft. The case of James personifies the protection end of the continuum.

Alan is before the court for chronic runaway and truancy.

---

*The court referred to in this Chapter is the Montgomery County Juvenile Court, Dayon, Ohio, where the senior author worked for more than four years. The judge referred to is the Honorable Farnk W. Nicholas who served the Dayton community for thiry years in the Domestic Relations Division of the Common Pleas Court concentrating on juvenile cases during his last eighteen years of service. Serving one year as President of the National Council of Juvenile Court Judges, and two years as President of the Ohio Association of Juvenile Court Judges, Judge Nicholas is nationally recognized as a distinguished jurist. It is indeed an honor to have been associated with this man.

Alan's mother and father were divorced when Alan was five and because the boy's mother was found "unfit" custody was given to the father. Alan's father and step-mother have been married for eight years and after learning that she could not bear children, they adopted a two-year-old girl. The father outlines a thorough beating administered to Alan, who is now seventeen, for his most recent runaway and the step-mother emotionally tells the probation officer this cannot go on as Alan's behavior is destroying the home they have made for their adopted daughter. The father then describes all the things he has done for Alan. While Alan has been driving for only sixteen months he is now driving his third car, a late sport model. The boy's attire is expensive, his allowance is generous, and the father emphasizes that little is asked as far as work is concerned. The case of Alan personifies vascillation between the protection and rejection ends of the continuum as the boy is beat, then bribed.

A number of psychological and psychiatric concepts could be used to discuss these cases, however, these concepts have proved difficult for the research to operationalize and they are even more difficult for the practitioner to apply to a family crisis situation which demands the practitioner make an immediate response. As a result, the therapeutic strategies which often emerge from these concept are individualistic and focus on character traits in the child and parents, ignoring the situational context in which the behavior has occurred.

Let us examine the case of Danny. The emotional and physical rejection in this case is extreme, but not unique in cases practitioners must handle. The boy's self-concept has been virtually destroyed and the prognosis for success is minimal. The patterns of interaction between the parents have existed for the duration of their marriage and change appears hopeless. Danny's passive father seems comfortable with the step-mother playing a dominant role and Danny has come to be a scapegoat for a range of family problems as he is held out to his siblings as an example of what not to be. The case is made increasingly complex by Danny's refusal to return home, but again, this is not an uncommon problem with which practitioners must cope.

The counseling strategy in such cases is necessarily twofold and includes short-term and long-term goals. The short-term goals are intended to resolve the immediate crisis while the long-term goals are intended to alter the family structure and bring about permanent changes in behavior patterns. Because the accomplishment of short-term goals requires firm, decisive action, there is always a potential that the accomplishment of these goals may interfere with long-term treatment strategies. However, the very nature of delinquency cases often prohibits the use of indirect counseling strategies which may function well in counseling agencies which deal largely with volunteer clients.

In Danny's case the step-mother was advised that her domineering behavior had contributed to the boy's problems and that she must make every possible effort to leave supervision of the boy to his father. Initially she was angered but before the interview ended, she conceded her husband was weak and she was running the household. The issue that she had contributed considerably to Danny's problems was not discussed and she assured the probation officer she would leave the supervision of the boy to his father.

The father was advised that, for whatever reason, he had let his son down and from that point the situation had to change. The father's almost total inability to communicate with his son became obvious as did his guilt about the past and anxiety about the future. Activities were planned and structured which brought the father and son in frequent contact with each other. Danny was then interviewed with his father and an effort was made toward the establishment of positive interaction. All counseling was present and future oriented. Danny agreed to try it at home again and arrangements were made for a home visit the same evening. The father was asked to inform Danny's oldest step-brother that the court was aware of his exploitive homosexual behavior and future activities in this area would likely bring him to the court's attention. The evening counseling session of three hours included the entire family and all discussions were future oriented. The discussion of future goals rather than discussing the past problems enhanced the atmosphere considerably. At the end of the session the family agreed all conversation would be present and future oriented and when they felt the past had to be discussed they would immediately contact the probation officer. The goals, based on the perspective previously outlined, were to bring the family from the rejection end of the continuum to the protection end for the present with future sessions planned to balance the interaction patterns and child rearing procedures.

The case of James posed significantly different problems. Protective forms of behavior had functioned to insulate James from reality. School officials had indicated that James had been a school problem for a number of years and disciplinary action only resulted in strong protests from the mother to the extent that she had demanded the firing of a teacher for failing James in a math class. It was obvious that while the parents were quite upset about James' present behavior, their child-rearing practices reflected exaggerated forms of protection. After about an hour of conversation James asked his mother, "Will you get me out of here Mom?" and her response was a quick "Yes." But she did not, and for what seemed to be the first time in James' life, he was faced with reality as he was returned to detention. The mother first begged, then demanded the boy's release. She approached the judge and made a number of allegations against the probation officer in an effort to enhance the fault of others and to minimize James' delinquent behavior. The judge listened patiently and indicated he would look into the matter and she would be notified that afternoon. After his independent evaluation the judge concurred with the probation officer's decision. To terminate the mother's attempts to manipulate the situation, the judge advised the probation officer to inform the parents that it was his opinion that James was not ready for release. The mother's response was one of anger and she appeared the following morning with her attorney.

In most cases attorneys are helpful and are cooperative with juvenile courts in the development of appropriate responses to an adolescent's delinquent behavior. This was not the case with James' attorney. In an effort to impress his client, the attorney threatened the probation officer with a civil suit and demanded James be immediately released. Again the matter was referred to the judge and again the judge said no but did agree to grant an immediate hearing. After a lengthy hearing the police report was substantiated and James was found to be delinquent as charged. The case was continued for disposition and a social history was prepared with the recommendation to the court that James be placed on probation for an indeterminant period of time.

Judges are seldom trained in the area of family dynamics and delinquency causation and they must rely on the recommendations of their professional staff. However, the practitioner must keep in mind the fact that the judge has the final word. This was to be the case for James as the judge ignored the probation officer's recommendation and James was given a suspended commitment to a state institution without probation and that should he be found responsibile for involvement in delinquent behavior again he would be committed to the appropriate insitution. The parents were equally admonished for their protectiveness and the judge carefully explained to them his reasoning for not placing their son on probation. They were advised that the court did not utilize the resources of the probation department when it appeared that there would be little cooperation. It was adamantly apparent in this case that the parents' protective behavior would continue. James was released and he never appeared before the juvenile court again and at the age of eighteen no further contact with the police had been reported. School officials, after learning James had not been placed on probation, were surprised that he had made significant changes in his behavior and attitudes without the court's supervision.

The case of James demonstrates two important points practitioners should keep in mind. First, as mentioned earlier, the judge always has the final word regardless of the professional recommendation and second, the practitioner must realize that there are occasions where his or her professional services cannot be used. Judges can create a very clear picture of reality for a boy or girl and his or her parents. Oftentimes this is all that is necessary. It requires a judge who has considerable experience in the field of juvenile delinquency, and a judge who will continually educate himself in the area in which he works. While many professionals in the field will perhaps disagree with us, it is our opinion that a judge with experience in handling delinquency cases, and supplemental training through his professional associations such as the National Council of Juvenile Court Judges, is probably more competent in understanding delinquency cases than many professionals. Regardless of how the practitioner feels about the judge, one point must be reiterated—the judge has the final word!

Alan's case is undoubtedly the most complex of the three cases outlined here and it is the type of case that can occupy many hours of the practitioner's time. The judge ordered a psychological evaluation which indicated the boy was generally within the normal limits but that he had developed a set of manipulative skills which were often utilized successfully and that while he was often punished severely, he was more often indirectly rewarded for his delinquent behavior.

Practitioners generally concur with the position that in most cases it is in the child's best interests if he can remain in his home, but this is not always the case. One of the most difficult tasks for the practitioner is to develop a prognosis in a particular case. It is also a task which is often avoided because an unfavorable prognosis may require the practitioner to take action which could have serious implications for the adolescent. However, the failure to develop a sound prognosis and to act accordingly may well result in continued delinquent behavior. The practitioner can easily rationalize his behavior contending that he has a professional obligation to utilize the extent of his skills before removing a boy from his home. As a consequence, some practitioners who rigidly adhere to this philosophy do a disservice to the child as well as the community.

Furthermore, the inability to develop a decisive prognosis in complex cases may well result in institutionalization for the delinquent because of his continued delinquent behavior. It is not unusual for the correctional process to be carried out with great human compassion and little planning. Delinquent behavior continues and not only does the community suffer, but the credibility of the correctional process suffers as well.

Alan's case posed these kinds of problems. It was apparent to the probation officer that the family situation was of such a nature that the father and step-mother would necessarily have to become involved in intensive counseling if their child-rearing procedures were to change. These parents, not unlike a large number of parents of delinquents, saw the problem as child centered rather than family centered. It appeared the father's vascillating behavior had been a part of his relationship with Alan for at least ten years and his habit structure could not be ignored. It was also apparent the

step-mother did not want Alan in their home as her verbalized cooperative statements were contradicted by her continued rejecting
behavior. The probation officer reached the conclusion the prognosis was most unfavorable if Alan were to remain in his home.
The court concurred and Alan was placed in a highly structured
private boarding school.

The decision was a reluctant one but it was based on the assumption that to have allowed Alan to remain in his family setting
would have exposed him to the same kinds of family interaction
which contributed to this involvement in delinquent behavior.
The father and step-mother were extremely resistant and interpreted Alan's removal from their custody as an indictment against
them. While efforts were made to help the parents with their feelings, efforts were also made to help them see the problem in its complexity and how they had contributed to it. The anxiety and guilt
functioned to motivate the parents to seek professional help and
with Alan's removal from the home their relationship improved
considerably. Alan's visits home, while generally successful, demonstrated the difficult problems in changing behavior. The parents
conceded that even though they understood their rejecting and
vascilliating behavior, Alan's presence seemed to stimulate the very
behaviors they thought they understood and could thereby control.
The professional help this family received was by most standards
excellent. In spite of the assistance of counseling from private agencies, the situation never reached the point where Alan could return
home. Subsequent to his graduation from high school he entered
military service and has generally been quite successful.

In our discussion of the family we have intentionally avoided
the use of diagnostic labels for the different situations for two reasons. First, we consider it inappropriate to place labels on an adolescent or his parents when their behaviors are symptoms of problems
which must be examined in the context of the family. Labeling can
be most dysfunctional in the counseling process as it often leads to
our focusing attention on individual behavior ignoring the interactional context in which that behavior occurs. Second, our position on labeling coincides with that of Glasser (1965), Lemert
(1967) and a number of other writers who have noted that when an
individual is labeled in the correctional process, we may well stim-

ulate the behaviors which we consider destructive. The implications of the labeling process will be further examined in our discussion of the school setting.

We believe our approach to family dynamics which utilizes the concept of a protection-rejection continuum has a number of advantages for the practitioner. It is perhaps more difficult in some ways than other approaches because it demands that the practitioner focus his attention on the patterns of interaction in the family setting. However, rather than making subjective judgements regarding states of mind, utilization of the protection-rejection construct can result in more objective judgements regarding the types of behavior which are damaging to the delinquent as well as to other members of the family. Consequently, treatment strategies which are developed from the protection-rejection construct can be based on realistic goals as the practitioner can teach new forms of behavior. There is ample evidence to demonstrate that successful modification of behavior can result in the successful modification of attitudes.

THE SCHOOL

If a child comes from an inadequate family situation, entry into the school system will likely enhance the child's problems. Polk and Schafer (1972) contend that organizational policies and procedures in many schools virtually guarantee the generation and continuance of delinquent behavior. This is indeed a strong position to take when we are constantly reminded by educational administrators that the school system provides the channels to success for today's young people. What these administrators frequently fail to tell us is that the opportunity channels in the educational system are open to some and closed to others. How then does the school contribute to delinquency?

In examining the organizational ideology of the school system it is not uncommon to find a shared assumption that lower income and nonwhite students have limited capabilities and are, therefore, ineducable. The system defies these children as failures before the educational processes being and the children internalize these definitions and come to see themselves as failures. Any learning potential the child may have had is destroyed and the cycle is complete. The concept used to describe this cycle of negativism and failure is the "self-fulfilling prophecy."

Rosenthal and Jacobson (1968) have presented a number of studies demonstrating the consequences of the self-fulfilling prophecy. Pitt (1956) selected a sample of 165 fifth-grade boys, to whom a standardized intelligence test had been administered. The boys in the sample all had IQ scores of ninety-four or higher. The IQ scores were arbitrarily manipulated before they were reported to the teachers. One-third of the scores were increased ten points, one-third of the scores were left the same and one-third of the scores were lowered ten points. The boys were again studied at the end of the school year and the impact on the boys' self-rating were as follows:

> Those boys whose IQs had been fictitiously lowered came to feel that (1) they worked less hard at their school work than did other boys, (2) school was more difficult for them than other boys, (3) their teachers were harder on them in grading than they were on other children, and (4) school was less enjoyable. (Rosenthal and Jacobson, 1968, pp. 54-55)

While IQ scores often shape a teacher's attitudes toward the child other variables are equally important. Jacobson (1966) found the teachers in a school attended by Mexican students saw Mexican students with higher IQs as looking more American. The study presented the possibility that if a Mexican child looked somewhat American, he would be defined as brighter, and the teacher would have higher expectations than if the child were more "Mexican-looking." A number of additional studies cited by Rosenthal and Jacobson support the contention that a child's dialect, race, ethnic background and socioeconomic status are often the determinants of the teacher's attitudes toward the child; attitudes which the child internalizes and makes a part of his self-concept. That self-concept is then reflected in the child's behavior and performance levels.

A second contributing factor to the generation and maintenance of delinquent behavior is the use of irrelevant textbooks and curriculum materials.

Ralph Tyler (1951) has noted:

> The fact that writers of textbooks and teachers have come from a fairly middle class environment may account to a great extent for the

limiting of content of elementary school reading materials and of the books used in other subjects to those aspects of life which are largely middle class in character. Elementary school books do not deal with homes as they are known by a large percentage of American children. The books in use treat business, industry, politics, and the professions usually in the terms of the white collar participants rather than in terms of that which would be most understandable to a large fraction of the children.

It comes as no surprise that many children are alienated from the system that purports to hold the key to success. Frequently, there is little effort to make the materials relevant to working class children and children who come from economically impoverished environments. In fact, it appears at times that elementary and secondary educational systems engage in latent dishonesty. Kvaraceus (1963) describes the situation as a "tragic conspiracy of irresponsible retreat from reality" as the system itself functions to enhance the alienation of youth from education, and perhaps other aspects of society as well, by avoiding the realities of life.

While lower-class youth are most often the victims of these problems, middle-class children are by no means insulated. The conservative, neanderthal mentality which frequently controls textbook and curriculum structures ceates an atmosphere wherein the highly motivated children find little is relevant to the world in which they live. In an effort to define reality the educational system has fostered a bland mediocrity which tends to reward and reinforce the very behaviors and attitudes it has produced.

A third contributing factor is the utilization of inappropriate teaching methods which are seemingly universally applied to very different student groups. When a child fails to learn, denial mechanisms are set in motion as the educational system attributes that failure to the child and diligently avoids examining its own procedures and policies. In appropriate teaching methods function to inhibit learning processes and the development of lower-class and minority group children. When this occurs, boredom sets in, children act out, and teachers spend as much as 80 percent of their time attempting to control the behavior the system has in part produced. Again we see the "self-fulfilling prophecy." Acting out on the part of the child is seen as "proof" that he or she is a problem which justifies more control, which causes additional disruptive behaviors, and the vicious cycle continues.

Betty Levy (1965) states it well:

> I would like to emphasize now the even greater need to train teachers to be able to deal with and attempt to overcome their own "culture shock" and "culture bias." Most middle-class teachers, for example, have little experience, training, or understanding to be able to deal with parole officers, truant officers, social workers, and welfare investigators. Teachers who work in slum schools need to be prepared to work also with these people. They need to be told beforehand that they might have children in their classes who have police records. They need to be prepared so that they can understand and deal with these problems, rather than go in unprepared and be shocked, frightened, and/or resentful of them. They need to be prepared to deal with parents who may be illiterate or partly illiterate, concerned but helpless, or hostile or abusive. More than anything else, I think that teachers who work in slum schools must be helped to become more community minded. They must be made aware of the social and economic backgrounds of the community. They must know the community values, interests, and problems.

A fourth contributing factor is the practice of testing, grouping, and tracking. Intelligence tests do not measure innate ability in any sense because the variable that is measured is itself a reflection of the child's environmental experiences and the opportunities he or she has had. We have ample evidence that intelligence quotients reflect not only the background of the child, but also the situation in which the test is given and the perceived attitudes the test administrator holds toward the child. Some critics contend that intelligence testing should be terminated because of the inappropriate use of the results.

As a result of intelligence testing children are defined as "bright" and "dull," and "ready to read" and "not ready to read," as "achievement motivated" and "unmotivated," and eventually as "successful and unsuccessful." Again the "self-fulfilling prophecy" is obvious. On the basis of some kind of test performance the student's potential is determined. If the child's test performance is low, he or she is grouped and taught with other children who are also labeled as having limited skills and it is assumed they cannot achieve. As a result Hickerson (1966) has noted:

As time goes on the children of the slower group get further and further behind the children of the fast. The rationale for this phenomenon is two-fold: (1) The children in the slow groups are incapable of doing what children of the fast group can do, so why burden them with what they cannot achieve? (2) The less that is offered the poorer becomes their reading in comparison with the other children, until the time comes when their reading levels are so far behind the levels of the fast that they truly can no longer expect to compete with them.

The gap widens at the elementary level and is used to justify placing the child in a low track when he or she reaches the secondary level. The consequences are adverse as indicated in a wide range of studies. Students in lower status tracks find themselves locked in at that level with little opportunity for upward mobility. Teachers' expectations are lowered, the quality of instruction is lowered and as the child's performance falls, the educational system has a built-in justification scheme for denying many children the full benefits according to the more fortunate. The student placed on the vocational preparatory track finds collegiate educational opportunities closed and as a result his future occupational roles are severely restricted. Young adults forced into low status roles in the educational system find ways to compensate themselves, some of which are delinquent.

Polk and Schafer cite the following portion of an interview which demonstrates the direct connection between tracking and delinquency.

You can't get on this, you can't get on that and the girls that were in my class back in the sixth grade—they look at you—"you're in the basic section aren't you." You know, all of a sudden the guys you used to hang out with won't hang out with you no more. They hang out with a new class of people. Like they're classifying themselves as middle class and you're low brow and, you know, you start feeling bad and I said I can prove that I'm middle class and I don't have to go to school to prove it. And so I did. I got out of school. All those kids' mothers buying them nice things in ninth and tenth grades. I said, baby, you ain't talking about nothing—and what your mother has to buy you I can get everyday. I used to sport around. Yeah—I used to show them $125—every day. I used to say—you have to go to school for 12 years and I only went for 9. (How did you get this money?) I'd take it. (How did you take it?) I broke into things. I used to have a little racket set up. I used to have a protection fee—anybody who wants to cross the street, anybody who wants to come into my territory, they had to pay me 25 cents. I gave boys certain areas where they couldn't cross. A cat used to live up there. I say, "okay that's your deadline right there. If you want to go through this way, you give me 25 cents. If I ever catch you coming down through this way, you got a fight on your hands." And they gave me 25 cents.

While you may not find yourself in agreement with the positions outlined by the authors, practitioners often find that delinquents come from educational settings which feature the practices and procedures just described.

As a result, the child is forced out of the very environment that has held out for him the promise of success. Probation and parole officers can attest to the fact that when educational systems learn a child has been adjudicated delinquent, those systems often unwittingly work to reinforce the delinquency label. While the label is often dysfunctional to the child, it is functional to the school because it verifies their initial stereotypes, subsequent treatment of the child, and their contentions regarding his or her limitations. Once the child is labeled delinquent, suspensions are more easily justified as are expulsions.

Wherein does the solution lie? Polk and Schafer are only two of many critics of educational systems as they are presently structured. It is because of the criticism from outside the educational system that we are beginning to see changes and while some of the changes are often symbolic, there are fresh winds bringing new ideas to educational systems. Juvenile court judges, corrections officials and many practitioners are forming and joining groups demanding change and this must be continued. We know too well that social systems have a permanence that is resistant to change and educational systems are no exception.

Unfortunately, the practitioner who must cope with these problems on a daily basis often feels frustrated and views the educational system as overwhelming. A suspension or expulsion can ruin a student for an entire semester and the school has the authority to deprive a child of educational opportunities on the basis of preserving order. What can a practitioner do? He can do a lot. Below we have outlined a number of ideas which the practitioner can use to improve the education experience for his probationers or parolees. These ideas are based on the authors' experience in the juvenile justice system.

The key element is the building of professional and personal relationships with personnel in the educational system. The senior author previously worked in a section of Montgomery County, Ohio, which had a high percentage of Appalachian migrants dating back to the 1930's. The low value placed on education by many of the adults resulted in failure on the part of their children. This, combined with the educational system's refusal to examine certain internal aspects which worked against these children, enhanced their failure.

The change strategy was commenced with a late summer meeting with the attendance officer and various school administrators. Initially, there was a certain level of distrust and at times open hostility as they considered the treatment oriented court to be too permissive and its probation officers too "soft." The communication channels began to open when they understood that the probation officer wanted help in keeping a boy in school and more important, was willing to give help when that boy truanted or was disruptive. The probation officer brought the school officials up to date as to what had transpired in the child's life during the summer, and they shared their problems as well as the child's performance records from previous years.

A plan was developed for each probationer which included careful selection of courses and teachers. As the trust relationship developed, school officials readily admitted that a few teachers actually provoked the complaint of problems. A deliberate effort developed on the part of school officials to steer probationers away from these teachers. In part, because the probationer now had an advocate with an authority base, and in part, because the school system was getting help with their problems, resources which had not been available to probationers became available such as tutoring, jobs and a number of additional opportunities which functioned to enhance the probationer's self-concept and potential for success. While the plans were never perfect because of extremely limited budgets, the effort was obvious as the school came to understand the probation officer's goals and the process was reciprocal for the probation officer.

Alternative strategies were developed to avoid suspensions and expulsions. These strategies were a result of the development of a mutual goal which had emerged out of the probation officer—school relationship which was to keep the child in school. When problems emerged the child in some cases was removed temporarily from the classroom setting and placed in a more restrictive area of the school where he worked independently continually earning credit. If the problem was severe, a setting apart from the school was utilized and whenever possible, a tutor was provided. Again, the school kept the child on the rolls and gave him credit for his work even though he was temporarily placed in another setting. A wide range of alternatives was developed which resulted in no suspensions or expulsions during the second year of the venture.

At the same time a court-school conference committee was established with regular meetings to focus on mutual problems. School personnel from all levels of the educational system visited the court, toured the facilities and engaged in positive interaction with the judge and staff. Ideas were exchanged and disagreements resolved as the schools came to accept the court's position that it would not use its authority to remove from the school or community a child defined as a problem simply because of truancy. It became obvious in a number of instances that minor differences in the past, which were a result of poor communication, had consumed a sizeable amount of energy which could have been used more productively.

There were occasions when cooperation broke down usually because of the school's demand that truants be punished and the court's refusal to comply. The judge stood his ground against committing truants to state institutions and eventually the problems were resolved. This was not the case in all schools and at times educational systems had to be confronted and conflict ensued. The result was not always pleasant but when the educational system fails a child under a practitioner's supervision, the practitioner's responsibility is to the child first. If that responsibility is met, the influence, though sometimes small, will be felt and progress made.

What about the failures, the children who are stigmatized and *forced* out of the educational system and defined by the system as drop-outs? For them, the rejection by the school system leaves one major alternative, that of seeking out a society of peers who are also often products of the same type of educational system.

THE PEER GROUP

Seven boys ranging in age from fifteen to seventeen years are before the court for auto theft. As the case unfolds it becomes increasingly obvious that the boys have been involved in an extremely sophisticated auto stripping operation. The leader described in detail how he and his codelinquents parked a van a short distance from the victim's home and carefully raised the garage door by slowly inflating an inner-tube which had been carefully slid under the door while the victim was asleep in a bedroom near the attached garage. In less than two hours the seven boys had removed the wheels, engine and transmission from a sport car which had been modified for racing. The parts were carefully placed on platforms with rubber tires and moved to the van for delivery to a service station which functioned as a front for a fencing operation. From that point a group of adults who had formed a syndicated operation in several cities took charge buying the parts from the juveniles. Serial numbers were destroyed and the parts were prepared for distribution through both legitimate and illegitimate channels.

Five of the seven boys involved in this sophisticated auto stripping operation were school drop-outs and the two boys who attended school were defined as behavior problems in the school setting. A battery of tests administered by the court psychologist revealed that the boys received scores on intelligence tests which indicated that they were average or above, and the psychological profiles indicated that generally they could be described as normal.

In many ways this group of delinquent boys reflected a number of characteristics frequently found in delinquent gangs. Of central importance is the fact they had developed a detailed justification scheme for their involvement in delinquent behavior which reflected the "techniques of neutralization" concept outlined by Sykes and Matza (1957). Techniques of neutralization are used by delinquents to rationalize and justify their involvement in delinquent behavior, especially when that behavior is condemned by society. As a result of the utlization of these techniques, Sykes and Matza note

that "Social controls that serve to check or inhibit deviant motiva-
tional patterns are rendered inoperative, and the individual is freed
to engage in delinquency without serious damage to his self-image."
In this construct we can note the major function of a delinquent
peer group. The peer group redefines the limits for individual behavior and thereby justifies delinquent behavior for the individual
members of the peer group. The techniques of neutralization include: 1) the denial of responsibility, 2) the dental of injury, 3) the
denial of a victim, 4) condemnation of condemners, and 5) an appeal to higher loyalties.

The first technique, denial of responsibility was easily accomplished for this group as the boys had successfully, in their minds,
deflected responsibility from themselves. Since no one could recall
who initiated the plan, responsibility could not be placed on any
single member of the group. They complained about having nothing to do, they could not find jobs, lots of other people stripped cars
for things they needed and once they got started they could not stop.
These, and other comments the boys made reflected their total ne-
gation of personal accountability as they deflected blame and responsibility to the group and to society.

The second technique, denial of injury was also easily accomplished. No one had been hurt as far as the group was concerned.
They had merely removed automotive parts from one auto for
someone to use on another auto. They emphasized that every pre-
caution had been taken to avoid contact with the owner of the car
and to avoid a possible confrontation and injury. Since no one had
been hurt, no wrong had been committed in their minds.

The third technique, denial of a victim was accomplished by
denying that the owner of the car was the victim. Since the car was
expensive, the victim, if one existed, was an insurance company and
because the insurance company was not a person it could not be a
victim. The victim then became a vague abstraction and nonexistent
in their minds further neutralizing any guilt and responsibility.

The fourth technique, condemnation of condemners reflected
the boys' antagonistic attitudes toward authority systems and individuals holding authority in those systems. In interview sessions the
boys freely expressed their bitterness toward school and police officials, who had allegedly harassed them, while at the same time de-

scribing the indiscrete behavior in which they "knew" these officials had been involved. That the basis for their allegations was heresay and rumor did not diminish for a moment in their minds the credibility of their allegations against those officials who were defined as hypocrites and "deviants in disguise." Even if they had done something wrong the individuals who condemned their behavior were themselves defined as corrupt and could therefore be ignored.

Finally, the fifth technique, appeal to higher loyalties was firmly entrenched. The boys had developed an intense loyalty to the group and its value structure which was more salient to them than laws or any societal norm or value. The conflicts which arose out of the claims of friendship and the claims of law were easily resolved. The value structure of the peer group had redefined the limits society had placed on their behavior and their involvement in delinquent behavior was quickly neutralized by their loyalty to the group and the group's value orientation.

We emphasize this theoretical construct explaining the behavior of delinquent peer groups for several reasons. First, it is our position that the techniques of neutralization used by delinquents to justify their involvement in delinquent behavior are in many respects similar to the rationalizations used by adult members of our society who overtly proclaim their allegience to the law while covertly engaging in tax fraud, corporate theft, industrial and political sabotage and a host of other criminal acts which often go undetected. Second, in at least some respects delinquent behavior may be somewhat more "conformist" than we are willing to concede. When a group of lawyers, law enforcement officials and politicians can justify breaking and entering and burglary, why should we be surprised when delinquent peer groups develop justification schemes for their involvement in illegal behavior. Third, and most important, it is our position that peer group delinquency can be best understood if we see the delinquent behavior as behavior that is the product of a value system which is in conflict with the law, rather than attempting to explain that behavior is an indicator of disturbed personalities.

The practitioner must be aware of the fact that membership and participation in a delinquent peer group can be quite functional for the delinquent in a number of ways. Miller (1958) and others have documented several important concerns of delinquents and the role peer groups can play in meeting these concerns.

The peer group provides "in-group" membership to adolescents who have been excluded from a range of activities society provides for its "conformist" adolescents. To the adolescent, "belonging" is of great importance and the delinquent peer group can fulfill this essential function. Through membership and participation in a peer group, the delinquent gains status and he can develop a reputation which will be admired and reinforced by his delinquent peers. Because the reputation is built on his success in the context of delinquent behavior, the barriers which society might pose are of little consequence.

Through the peer group the delinquent can demonstrate he is "tough" and "smart." He can enhance his reputation and self-image in the group by proving to the other members that he can take care of himself and he can outsmart, outfox, outwit and "con" others without being "conned" himself. "Smartness" as defined by the value structure of the peer group is the ability to achieve valued entity—material goods, personal status—through the maximum use of mental agility and a minimum use of physical effort.

The peer group provides the delinquent with excitement, thrills, risk, danger and the kinds of opportunities to become involved in exploratory behaviors which are not uncommon to many adolescents. Finally, the peer group can provide the delinquent with the feeling of autonomy, freedom from external constraint, freedom from superordinate authority and independence, something against which most adolescents strive to attain.

Returning to the delinquent gang of auto thieves, we find that the peer group is the center of their lives and many of the concerns described by Miller are satisfied by the group. The members are intensely loyal to the group and proud of the reputation they have established for themselves. Success for several months in such a complex auto-stripping operation brought admiration from other peers. Getting caught was one of the risks they were aware of, and the many successes they enjoyed only reinforced their feelings that their present problems with the law were temporary. Their attitudes and behavior clearly reflected the norms and values of the delinquent peer group.

The sexual behavior of the members of the group further reflected the group's value structure. Group sexual activity often referred to as "gang bangs" was justified because the girls had been defined as "street whores" and deserved little better than the treatment they received. The knowledge that one female victim had been placed in a children's psychiatric hospital after one of their exploitive sessions only caused the boys to point to others who had treated her likewise. This along with their contention that she had never really tried to resist was ample justification in their minds that they had done nothing wrong and were not responsible for her ill fate. They were quick to note that they did not treat their girl friends in this way, thereby proving to themselves at least that their behavior was not as bad as it was portrayed to them. Homosexual activities also reflected the excitement theme in the group as they conceded that they had frequented parks where homosexuals were "hustled" for three to twenty dollars. In addition to getting paid for an act which only took a few minutes, it was sometimes necessary to "beat" a homosexual who became too friendly. This aggressive behavior functioned to enhance their self-images as masculine and tough.

The group used drugs on a regular basis but only for excitement and recreation. The members of the group viewed marijuana as many adults view alcohol; social smoking was seen as analogous to social drinking. The justification had a familiar ring in their contention that "everybody's doing it." Drug use is far more conformist in our society than most of us are willing to concede and we should not find it surprising that peer groups find a justification scheme for drug use. More than 100 "mood pills" are consumed per person each year in our society. Geller and Boas (1969) contend that America is a drug-oriented society and adults have set the standard by their own behavior as indicated in the following passage:

> Today's teenagers entered a world in which mood-changing substances were a fact of existence; sleeping pills, stimulants, tranquilizers, depressants and many other varieties of mind-altering chemical compounds had long been absorbed into the nation's pharmacopoeia, and coping pills, swallowing capsules and downing tablets were a national habit . . . They grew up regarding chemicals as tools to be used to manipulate the inner mind. What is a society to do if millions of its young

citizens insist on consuming substances most authorities consider
taboo: when they consider these drugs more appropriate to their life
styles than the drugs their parents use?

It is not our intention to endorse a justification scheme for drug
use; society has by and large accomplished that task. It is our concern that the practitioner be aware of the possibility that drug use
in many cases is not a significant deviation from the behavior of a
sizeable number of adults in our society. Because adults may unwittingly serve as role models for adolescents in this area, drug use is
exceedingly difficult to terminate unless efforts are directed toward
changing the value structures of those delinquent peer groups
which justify drug use.

There is little evidence to support the effectiveness of the professionally training practitioner in working successfully with delinquent peer group such as the group just described. This is due in
part to the practitioner's failure to recognize the value structure
which the delinquent group has internalized, and that the group's
value structure is as important to them as the practioner's value
structure is to him. Furthermore the group's differences with the
practitioner are justified by the members in terms of value differences which supports their contention that since he does not understand them, they do not have to see him as a credible person. The
traditional practice of treating peer groups by establishing probation or parole rules that the members shall not associate together is
meaningless and personifies the practitioner's lack of understanding. For the members of a stable peer group this is like asking them
to leave their "family" for in many cases the delinquent peer group
has functioned as a substitute for the family and has been the primary socializing agent.

One of the most successful strategies in dealing with delinquent
peer groups is the use of paraprofessionals, adults who themselves
have been through the criminal justice system and have been suc-
cesfully reintegrated into society. The practitioner's refusal to note
the important contributions which can be made by paraprofessionals reflects a professional egoism which is based more on a set of
credentials the practitioner possesses than on his success in dealing
with the problem. There is an intense reluctance to concede that

there are individuals in our society who have not been professionally trained who can have a greater impact on the life of the delinquent than the professional. Our professional egoism often functions as a blinder to the successes enjoyed by Alcoholic Anonymous and Synanon, neither of which are operated by professionals.

It is our position that one of the most effective treatment methods in dealing with peer group delinquency is the utilization of group counseling with paraprofessionals serving as co-leaders and leaders in the counseling setting. Only the paraprofessional understands fully the demands of the environment in which the delinquent lives and the consequences of those demands on the delinquent. The paraprofessional has experienced those same demands, succumbed to them and learned to resist them leading a successful life. We do not imply professional training is not important, or that professionals cannot deal with delinquent groups. Rather it is our position that the professional practitioner can be more successful and can better utilize his time in the training of paraprofessionals and functioning as a consultant to those individuals when they face problems that call for consultation and assistance. In not using the paraprofessional we seem to be saying "once a criminal always a criminal" which is contradictory to our treatment philosophies.

SUMMARY

Juvenile delinquency must be seen in an environmental context and not solely as the characteristic of an individual adolescent. While most delinquents are fully aware of the wrongful nature of their behavior, they are much like the rest of us in that they continually search for excuses which function to neutralize their guilt and anxiety. It is indeed unfortunate that they can find in the family context, in the school setting and in their communities examples of behavior which can be used to minimize the seriousness of their own involvement in illegal behavior. The practitioner who treats delinquency as an aberrant, "sick" form of behavior has lost the battle before it begins. As we began, those behaviors which may some times take on aberrant forms are frequently symptomatic of problems in the adolescent's environment. While we cannot lose sight of the delinquent as an individual, we must develop the skills to see him in the context of his environment, because, to not see him in this context is to see only part of him, or in some cases to not see him at all.

REFERENCES

Amos, W.: The future of juvenile institutions. *Federal Probation, 32:*41-47, 1968.

Benjamin, Judith A., *et al.: New Roles for Non-Professionals in Corrections.* New York: National Committee on Employment of Youth, 1965, p. 64.

Caldwell, R.: *Criminology.* New York: Ronald Press, 1965, p. 17.

Geller, A. and Boas, M.: *The Drug Beat.* New York: McGraw-Hill, 1969, p. xvi.

Glasser, W.: *Reality Therapy.* New York: Harper and Row, 1965.

Hakeem, M.: A critique of the psychiatric approach to the prevention of juvenile delinquency. *Social Problems, 5:*194-205, 1957-58.

Hickerson, N.: *Education for Alienation.* Englewood Cliffs, New Jersey: Prentice-Hall, 1966, p. 34.

Jacobson, L.: Explorations of variations in educational achievement among Mexican children, grades one to six. Unpublished doctoral dissertation, University of California, Berkeley, 1966.

Kvaraceus, W.: *Juvenile Delinquency and the School.* New York: World Book Company, 1945.

Lemert, E.: *Human Deviance, Social Problems, and Social Control.* Englewood Cliffs, New Jersey: Prentice-Hall, 1967.

Levy, B.: An urban teacher speaks out. *Harvard Graduate School of Education Association Bulletin,* 1965.

Miller, W.: Lower class culture as a generating milieu of gang delinquency. *The Journal of Social Issues, 14:*5-19, 1958.

Pitt, C. C. V.: An experimental study of the effects of teachers' knowledge or incorrect knowledge of pupil IQ's on teachers' attitudes and practies and pupils' attitudes and achievement. Unpublished doctoral dissertation, Columbia University, 1956.

Polk, K. and Schafer, W. (Eds.): *Schools and Delinquency.* Englewood Cliffs, New Jersey: Prentice-Hall, 1972, p. 200.

Rosenthal, R. and Jacobson, L.: *Pygmalion in the Classroom.* New York: Holt, Rinehart and Winston, 1968.

Sykes, G. and Matza, D.: Techniques of neutralization: A theory of delinquency. *The American Journal of Sociology, 22:*664-670, 1957.

Tyler, R.: Can intelligence tests be used to predict educability? In K. Eells *et al. Intelligence and Cultural Diversity,* Chicago: University of Chicago Press, p. 45, 1951.

CHAPTER 6

RUNAWAY YOUTH: CAUSES FOR RUNAWAY BEHAVIOR

RICHARD E. HARDY AND JOHN G. CULL

- ☐ INTRODUCTION
- ☐ REJECTION AND RESENTMENT
- ☐ THE SELF-CONCEPT
- ☐ IMPORTANCE OF PEER GROUPS AND ROLE MODELS
- ☐ RELATIONSHIP BETWEEN RUNAWAY BEHAVIOR AND DEVELOPMENTAL TASKS
- ☐ SUMMARY

INTRODUCTION

THE RECENT DISCOVERY of the sadistic slayings and secret graves of twenty-seven boys in Houston, Texas, has helped in focusing much needed attention of parents, professional helping persons, policemen and others on problems of the teenager who leaves home in what has been called "runaway." The number of young runaways has been estimated to total anywhere from six hundred thousand to one million a year (Parade Magazine, 1973).

Anthropologists tell us that the most persistent institution in the history of mankind has been the family unit which has been traced as a phenomenon back to the dawn of man. The family has seemed almost impervious to external pressures which threaten it or external pressures which impinge upon the individuals within it; however, we are now seeing increased evidence within our culture that the family is no longer immune to pressure and change. In fact we are now seeing many types of pressures which are weakening its solidarity. Family disharmony seems on the increase as divorce rates soar, not only in our country and culture but across the world. Perhaps the most persistent attacks on the family unit have centered around questions relating to the effectiveness and purpose of the family. The family now serves a weakened role in inculcating the social and moral values of our society. Other institutions have assumed responsibility for this role and an increased emphasis in molding the opinions and attitudes of young persons has been taken on by their peers. The attacks on the viability and practicality of family units commenced with lower classed families; however, the questions of the efficacy of a family unit has spread to the middle and upper classes so that now it is a generalized concern among sociologists, anthropologists, psychologists and marital counselors.

More and more social scientists are confronted with clients whose basic problem is that of a deteriorating family unit. The spectacle of the deteriorating family is depressing. Figures now show approximately fifty percent of delinquents come from broken homes, the fact that families are increasingly being broken by desertion and divorce are of immediate concern and even among those family units which remain intact, there are exhibited many problems of a social and emotional nature. Alcoholism, other drug addiction, crime and suicide are now rampant.

The family frequently has been cited as the villain of many social evils but with regard to delinquency and runaway behavior there has been a substantial agreement that the family is to blame. The difficult and puzzling stage of adolescence brings about many profound problems. As Mead has aptly stated, "Parents have been rearing unknown children for an unknown world since about 1946" (Mead, 1972).

REJECTION AND RESENTMENT

The rejection of either or both parents by the child is certainly an important factor in demonstrated aggressive behavior on the child's part. Many children feel rejected and react with overt aggression toward parents and the family units. Rejected children generally show a marked tendency toward an increased resistance and quarreling in relationship with adults. They also show considerable sibling rivalry.

Many family members who are confronted with a child's hostile, progressive or delinquent behavior react very negatively. In addition to the problems of financial or social misfortunes, the family as a unit is generally ill-prepared to deal with these situations. Often there are real communication problems because there are definite differences in values, especially between the outside peer culture and the individual's family.

There are some early signs which can indicate possibilities for runaway behavior. Some of these include resentment of authority figures in the home and school, resentment of over protection, open conflicts, resentment of discipline, loss of interest in school subjects, impulsivity associated with permissiveness, heavy influence of juvenile peer group, antisocial attitudes, general frustration and need for compensatory behavior and involvement with drugs.

THE SELF-CONCEPT

It is important for parents and others to understand the concepts related to self-esteem. Often persons who are prone toward runaway behavior show inadequate self-confidence and see themselves in negative ways. An individual who maintains a negative self-concept often continues to behave in accordance with this concept by way of expressing hostility. Counseling sessions with a social worker, rehabilitation counselor, psychologist or other helping profession person can be a real help if this helping individual is keenly tuned into the subculture of youth and current mores and patterns of behavior. Professional service workers and parents must be willing to look into the conditions that produce attitudes toward runaway behavior. These include the environment of the home and the interrelationships between the individual runaway and his parents and peer associates. Every effort should be made to get children inclined toward this behavior to become involved in meaningful activities, if not possible within their home, at least within their community areas. Projects in which students can find meaning through helping others are often of sufficient and substantial value in modifying negative self-concepts and poor attitudes toward the community, home and society in general. If at all possible, families should attempt to have joint projects of mutual interest. These can help in maintaining and improving relationships among family members. Projects should be selected by the family team and not forced upon younger family members by parents or older relatives or siblings.

Another helpful resource is that of grandparents or other relatives who are at least one generation removed from the youth. Since they are less closely associated, there is less ego involvement. Children often can go to such persons and find considerable positive regard and acceptance. In some cases grandparents may be able to be very helpful in that they constantly reinforce positive self-appreciation and more on the part of the young person.

The parent also may wish to consider allowing the young person to get a job in order to become more self-sufficient. This can improve concept of self and cut down on amounts of time which are often used negatively. It should be remembered that most young people get quite bored with themselves, their friends and family units. This is partially due to the large amount of time which many of them use unproductively.

Rapid Social Change and Its Influence on Youth

Institutions such as the church, the family governmental structures of service, the university, and other educational systems are changing so rapidly that many persons are losing their anchor points for emotional stability. Parents look around them and find little or no certainty in their jobs, in their family life, or in traditional and religious beliefs formerly held sacrosanct. All of us are deeply influenced by the effects of the mass media such as television. These media to us depict what the outside world seems to have. The outside world seems to have so much more than so many think they have.

Diminishing Value of Work

In the early days of the development of this country, the Protestant ethic played a most important part in bringing about advancements in agriculture, technology, and the social services. The amount of hard work which an individual did was a direct indication in many cases of his status in the community. Work for work's sake was highly respected. The Protestant ethic is now much less on influencing factor on attitudes of persons toward work than it once was. In fact, by the year 2000 it may well be that family attitudes in teaching children such characteristics as dependability and diligence related to work may be drastically modified. Society is moving toward a much greater leisure time involvement. At the present time the effects of this accelerating movement away from the Protestant ethic are being felt. This means that convincing persons the way to success is through hard work of an honest nature is becoming even more difficult. Even vocational specialists such as vocational rehabilitation counselors in state and federal agencies are now talking about de-emphasizing vocational aspect of rehabilitation services which in itself indicates some drastic changes in the philosophy of many persons in the social service area on vocations and work.

There seems to be a definite emphasis toward getting what we want the easy way. This emphasis is perpetuated and reinforced by many white collar workers who are able to "get around the law" by various methods. An example is the landlord who puts enough pressure on tenants to receive monthly payments for rent but does not maintain his buildings according to city ordinances. Youth often see different applications of the law applied according to socioeconomic status of the individual accused. Sentences can vary enormously according to whether an individual brings an attorney with him to court, whether the offense is a traffic violation or a more serious one. These societial problems greatly influence attitudes of youth.

IMPORTANCE OF PEER GROUPS AND ROLE MODELS

Pressures for conformity come from all sides. Persons in the ghetto feel pressure to conform to the ways of behaving of persons of the ghetto. These behavior pressures are particularly strong among the adolescent groups and especially influential among adolescent boys. The emphasis seems to be on beating the "system" somehow, and this attitude should not be considered an unhealthy emphasis. It represents the wish of most Americans—to somehow get established and find happiness within a social system which is now in constant turmoil and within a society which is in many ways unhealthy.

In order for the person from the ghetto, for instance, to beat the system, he must either "fake out" some bureaucratic program such as the Deparement of Public Welfare and get on the public dole, or behave as two different persons. He must demonstrate one type of behavior which will secure his position within his own peer group and demonstrate another type of behavior which will allow him to secure employment in the outside world. His only other alternative is to leave his peer group and those things which he has felt important in order to enter another man's world. It is much easier for all of us to remain in a world which we have known and adjusted to than it is to modify behavior in order to become members of a different society. Think how difficult it would be for most of us to move into a culture different and distinct from our own. The same types of problems and equal in complexity exist for persons who are from improvished areas, either rural or urban, when they face finding employment and security in the world of work. These problems cause considerable ambiguity among both parents and youth.

Another problem which often leads to crime and runaway behavior is that of the lack of sufficient role models for individuals to follow. One of the earliest influences on all persons is that of the parents and much of the early child's play involvement is concerned with the work behavior of adults. When adults within the family are not able to work, children simulate the behavior which they exhibit and this behavior is often characterized by frustration and idleness.

Many youngsters who find themselves in trouble at home need to understand their own motivations—reasons for their behavior. The most prevalent reason, for instance, for difficulty on a job is that of inability to get along with fellow workers. Certainly one of the prime causes of runaway behavior is the inability to get along with others within the family constellation, members of the individual's peer group and members within the community at large. This is often due to personal immaturity. When there is a basic lack of understanding of human nature—the weaknesses and strengths of all of us—there can be a real tendency to misunderstand that behavior which most of us demonstrate most of the time—that of self-centeredness. "Rap sessions" held in various community centers and under the auspices of various community groups may be of substantial value to young persons and to family members also who wish to come into a group situation in order to discuss problems which they may be having. In addition, they will find support and interest in them as individuals which they may have never found before. Many youngsters who exhibit runaway behavior are involved in this type of action in order to gain attention or recognition, having failed in other areas of life in the highly competitive society of today. Quite often runaway behavior is an effort on the youngster's part to have the family stop and take stock of what is happening within the family.

Idleness and hopelessness can be the handmaidens of behavior which can be characterized as crying out behavior, that is, the individual is crying out for attention, recognition or concern. When youth attempt time and again to find acceptance within their families but can find no point of basic interaction and no acceptance and must remain from their point of view on the outside of a warm interactional relationship within the family, runaway behavior often results. The hopelessness of many youth is profound, especially in ghetto areas where they must sit for hours on porches or in apartments with inadequate facilities and are unable to join in meaningful activity. However, runaway behavior is not the sole province of the ghetto family or the lower socioeconomic class family. Runaway behavior is becoming more and more prevalent among middle-class families and upper-class families, especially when the parents become so involved in activities outside the family they are unable to establish warm meaningful relationships with their children. Many youth are unable to find meaningful activities for themselves outside their family constellation. Many youth are just plainly bored. When activity opportunities are lacking and when the ties within the family are weak chances for runaway behavior and delinquent behavior are compounded.

RELATIONSHIP BETWEEN RUNAWAY BEHAVIOR AND DEVELOPMENTAL TASKS

Much behavior of individuals can be explained and better understood through the concept of developmental tasks. Havighurst (1957) has outlined the developmental tasks according to age groups of life. He breaks the life span of individuals into six areas. Infancy and early childhood, middle childhood, adolescents, early adulthood, middleage, and later maturity. Runaway behavior is generally confined to the period of adolescence which runs roughly from age twelve years to eighteen years. According to Havighurst (1957) there are ten specific tasks within this age frame of adolescence. These are:

1. Achieving new and more mature relations with age mates of both sexes.
2. Achieving a masculine or feminine social role.
3. Accepting one's physique and using the body effectively.
4. Achieving emotional independence of parents and other adults.
5. Achieving assurance of economic independence.
6. Selecting and preparing for an occupation.
7. Preparing for marriage and family life.
8. Developing intellectual skills and concepts necessary for civic competence.
9. Desiring and achieving socially responsible behavior.
10. Acquiring a set of values and an ethical system as a guide to behavior.

Many of the causes of runaway behavior among contemporary youth can be tied directly to individual failure of one or more of these developmental tasks of adolescence. Failure to achieve new and more mature relations with age mates leads to a severe social frustration. The individual who failed in this task soon sees that he is out of step with age mates. Successful members of the peer group who are achieving this maturity in their relations with other members of the peer group adjust well and feel more comfortable in social situations. However, the individual who failed in this task feels isolated, alone and has no sense of belonging to the peer group. This is a key factor in precipitating runaway behavior.

Related to the developmental task of achieving new and more mature relations with age mates of both sexes is the task of achieving a masculine or feminine social role. It is at this point that the youngster must assert his identity in the social role and must have a clearly defined self-concept of masculinity or femininity. Again, if he is unable to achieve this level of identity he will be out of step with the peer group and again will feel isolated and rejected. The third developmental task again is related to the first two but is even more specific in its requirement of adjustment. The task of accepting one's physique and using the body effectively is a very difficult task for adolescents since this is a period of gangliness and lack of muscular control. Therefore, the individual is clumsy, unfamiliar with his body, unfamiliar with its potential and feels strange with himself and with others. Until he can become adjusted to himself he cannot become adjusted to his peer group.

Perhaps the key developmental task which relates to runaway behavior is the need to achieve emotional independence of parents and other adults. If the individual is not able to achieve a masculine or feminine role and declare himself an adequate, separate, competent individual and sever the emotional ties which have bound him to the parents and have rendered him a child, he will experience extreme frustration. He will feel thwarted in many areas and will feel the only solution to this thwarting and isolation is to escape from the environment. This results in runaway behavior.

Often runaway behavior results when the individual feels the requirements of maturity and requirements of "the establishment" start impinging on him to the extent he feels socially suffocated. In this situation the individual is striving to retain his immature status and is rejecting the damands for maturity. The few developmental tasks as outlined above help to create the drive for runaway behavior in this instance. For example, when the youth who is reluctant to relinquish his maturity is forced to consider achieving economic independence, selecting and preparing for an occupation, preparing for marriage and family life and developing skills and concepts necessary for civic competence, he will feel that again if he escapes from the environment which is impinging on him, he will be able to delay relinquishing the immature role with which he feels so comfortable. So failure on these developmental tasks will also provide a clue to predicting runaway behavior. The individual who exhibits runaway behavior totally rejects developmental tasks of achieving socially responsible behavior. In fact, runaway behavior generally is characterized by socially irresponsible behavior. It is an attempt to reject participation as a responsible adult in the life of the community and in the life of the family. However, by rejecting this role, the individual is unable to adequately meet the last developmental task, that of acquiring a set of values and an ethical system as a guide to behavior. For only when an individual is able to function in a socially mature and responsible manner can he get adequate feedback which assists him in developing his own personalized set of values and ethical system which will guide his behavior in a socially responsible manner.

SUMMARY

In summary, runaway behavior is characterized by a panic situation of the young person. He feels he must escape from the environment in which he is functioning for several reasons. However, all of them tend to be a crisis situation within the family or within the community. There are pressures which are impinging on him which are unacceptable pressures and demands are being made which he feels he cannot meet. Therefore, if he runs away he escapes from the reality system which is so unpleasant at that period of time. There is very little foresight or insightful decision making prior to runaway behavior. If runaway behavior characteristics can be identified by family members or guidance counselors, school teachers, ministers, etc. within the community prior to the decision of the youth to run, counseling can be very effective to solve the problems of this youth. Pressures in the environment which are so unacceptable can be relieved, demands can be eased and the youth can grow and mature socially and psychologically from a learning experience such as this. However, if the environment becomes so difficult the individual elects to exhibit runaway behavior this becomes a habit pattern which may be reinforced throughout life resulting in an aversion on the part of the individual to face up to any adversity and attempt to conquer the negative aspects of the environment.

REFERENCES

Havighurst, R. J.: *Developmental Tasks*, 2nd Edition, New York, Longmans, Green and Company, 1957.

Mead, Margaret: A conversation with Margaret Mead: on the anthropological age. In *Readings In Psychology Today*, Ted. Bell, Mar, California, CRM Books, 1972.

Parade Magazine, October 7, 1973.

CHAPTER 7

THE EFFECTS OF MOOD ALTERING DRUGS: PLEASURES AND PITFALLS

PAUL L. ROSENBERG

- □ INTRODUCTION
- □ HALLUCINOGENS
- □ OTHER HALLUCINOGENS
- □ STIMULANTS
- □ NARCOTICS
- □ DEPRESSANTS
- □ INHALENTS
- □ CONCLUSION

INTRODUCTION

WE LIVE IN AN AGE where a nation of young people have been cast adrift, cut off from their elders, to search alone for meaning in a world that often does not make sense. The normal rites of passage have been ruptured. Our children no longer seem able to use the old cultural norms as a yardstick. These valuable traditions, which tie us so richly to the world, are being stripped of their meaning by the increasing speed of social change. Without a cultural inheritance, a young person is forced to grope for direction at a time in his life when his adolescent attachment to utopian goals and his desperate struggle for independence cloud his ability to make mature judgments. In this confusing market-place of growing up are many drugs, some old, some new, which are able to profoundly affect the depth, intensity, and meaning of our experience of reality and of ourselves.

Nursed by the inpersonality of the television set, taught to hide behind the masks of conformity that have become caskets for many of their parents, our young people have been cut off from exper-iencing their own wholeness by the blast of our mass culture. Afflu-ence can have an emptiness as profound as that of a ghetto. People at all levels are starving, searching desperately for anything that al-lows them the chance to feel better. Drugs, like alcohol, often ap-pear to offer a way out. Drugs can increase one's sensitivity to feel-ings or they can depress one's internal experience of one's self. They can alter the boredom and plainness that is so much a part of life. But the more you depend on a pill to feel alive, the less you can feel yourself. The drug becomes a device for stimulation, like mastur-bation, which gets you away from the real thing. Suddenly, the drug takes over: you become automatized by the need for artificial assist-ance which diminishes your control over your own world. Reality is not heightened sensitivity. In the confusing search for something real, people often mistake more intense experience for the deeper realities of intimacy and communication. We must avoid trying to frighten people away from the world of drugs. Rather, we must il-luminate the problems that drugs create. Then we must trust our youth to explore, experiment and eventually choose their own way, which is indeed the process of growth and maturation.

Drugs are not good or bad. They cannot be eliminated from the American scene. We must face the reality that they are here to stay. This means that we must avoid trying to educate our youth to resist all drugs as evil. In a world where drugs are ubiquitous, we must rely on the ability of youth to choose for themselves, for we cannot protect them. When presenting the facts about drugs and their ef-fects, we must be very careful to point out why drugs are so pop-ular, acknowledging their pleasures as well as their pitfalls. Thus, the viewpoint we present will be realistic and will help to make sense out of the confusion of the drug scene. Our children are desperate for someone they can trust. In focusing on the negative aspects of the world of drugs, in an attempt to protect by feat, we alienate the very ones we want to help. It is only with humility and honesty that we can help to convey the kind of information about drugs that will help others find their own way in the difficult world of growing up today.

HALLUCINOGENS

LSD (Lysergic Acid Diethylamide)

LSD is chemically derived from ergot alkaloids. These compounds are found in a fungus of the genus *claviceps*, that occasionally infected wheat in Central Europe. When bread was prepared from this grain there were outbreaks of ergot poisoning with temporary psychotic behavior. Albert Hoffman, a Swiss chemist, who synthesized LSD in 1937, accidentally ingested some in 1943 and discovered its ability to produce severe distortions of consciousness. LSD remained relatively unknown in the United States until 1959 when a religious group on the West Coast began using it for the induction of mystical states.

Timothy Leary's work at Harvard on LSD began in the early 1960's. Previously, he had been an outstanding psychologist whose personality evaluation procedures are still widely used. His LSD research broke the normal boundaries of academic propriety and led to his expulsion from Harvard. He helped to promulgate the widespread use of LSD, providing many with guidelines on how to handle this powerful psychedelic drug. Concomitantly, the use of marijuana and other drugs increased dramatically, particularly among the white, middle class. LSD was felt to be a kind of salvation. Adolescents of many ages headed for San Francisco's Haight-Ashbury in the summer of 1967 when the vision of salvation peaked in the world of flower children. Initially, the love culture seemed possible. But soon the pressures of too many mouths to feed and too much hostility turned the once peaceful hippie scene into a dangerous, desolate ghetto. Some users began to demonstrate the poor judgment and mental disorganization that can result from the excessive use of LSD. The drug that *turned on* so many people could also destroy, both by horrifying bad trips and gradual mental deterioration. It is fortunate that of the many millions of Americans who have experimented with LSD, only a few appear to have been seriously damaged by it.

The Acid Experience. An LSD trip can be of a magical or mystical nature, giving one's environment the quality of paradise or it can turn the world into a raging, terrifying inferno. Not only are there altered perceptual effects, but the very meaning of our existence can be called into question. A single LSD trip can totally alter one's direction in life.

The intensity of an LSD experience is dose-related. The drug produces hypersuggestability. Thus, one's emotional state when taking the drug as well as the environment or setting in which the drug is used are extremely important in determining what kind of trip one has. You can never be sure where you are going. LSD is always a voyage into the unknown. Sometimes a trip begins slowly, with gradual changes in one's perceptual awareness. The intensity of color seems to radiate with greater vividness. The whole world may seem enriched. At other times the experience may start with an explosive force and drop into a mystical, magical, delusional world, where reality changes swiftly. Perceptual alterations, which are usually predominant, involve distortion and changes in perspective rather than true hallucinatory phenomena. At higher doses, hallucinations are more common. Synesthesias, where one sense seems to flow into another, often are reported. Music may seem to touch your body. Depth perception may alter. A plaster wall may seem like mountainous terrain and solid objects may appear to undulate to the rhythm of the music. Sexual orgasms may be experienced in multiple modes.

The ability to estimate the passage of time is altered. With the rapid flow of experiential events, the individual on LSD feels a great deal of time must have passed. Five minutes may seem like hours. Thought processes are loosened during and often following the LSD experince. Associations may become more fanciful and one's judgment is seriously impaired by magical, illogical thinking. Ego integration may dissolve, causing extreme panic states. Parts of traveling safely with LSD involves being able to tolerate new states of ego disorientation without fear. One needs the ability to stay calm, while feeling a loss of connection to the body and normal ego boundaries.

Beyond the usual acid trip is the possibility of religious experience. Mystical states occur spontaneously and have been reported since Biblical times. LSD sessions occasionally have similar, if not identical, transcendental qualities. People describe seeing the Godhead or the golden radiance of God. Usually the experience is related to one's religious background and is remembered as a deeply moving religious event.

Panics and "Bummers." The increased intensity with which LSD allows us to voyage into our innermost feelings also can carry us to the depths of terror. Frequently during an LSD trip, there are brief periods when one feels afraid. If the response to this fear is running away or increased anxiety, one can create a terrifying and overwhelming crisis. For those who have taken LSD numerous times, the first encounter with the extreme terror of an LSD *bummer* frequently motivates them to stop taking the drug permanently.

Panic experiences of ego disorganization are sometimes somaticized; it is as if one is dead, that the rest of the world is dead, that one's body is coming apart, or magically bleeding to death. *Bummers* are experienced both interpersonally and intrapersonally. In a group, the heightened suggestability of the LSD state may cause one to feel that unrelated movements of others are meant as signs of an impending attack. The paranoia may grow rapidly until it involves everything. Feelings of depersonalization or unreality become overwhelming. The more one fights or flees from the paranoia, the more frantic and intense it becomes. Suddenly there does not seem to be any hope. Out of this desperation comes the frantic terror and panic of an LSD *bummer*. Often people are severely shaken and are left with intense anxiety for weeks following a bad trip. A person can often be talked down from a *bummer* by an experienced guide. Getting an individual to focus on his breathing helps to orient him and reassure him that his body is still intact. One can remind him that he is taking a drug which accounts for the experience he is having. The firm, commanding, reassuring voice of an experienced guide, helping the individual to understand what is happening, is enough to bring most people down. When someone cannot be talked down in such a manner, any of the major antipsychotic tranquilizers are rapidly effective. Some researchers have suggested that the use of tranquilizer may increase the likelihood of flashbacks.

Changes in Direction. One's conception of what is important in life is developed in our early years, matures in adolescence and usually remains stable throughout our adult life. These assumptions are rarely thought about and remain as unconscious determinants of what we want and how we behave. LSD can cause rapid and major changes in these basic feelings which can change totally the way a person chooses to live. To illustrate this, let us briefly review two case histories.

Tom, when brought into a county hospital by his parents, was a nineteen-year-old young man who had been going to college. For the past year and a half he had been taking LSD during weekly beer parties on the beach with his fraternity brothers. He continued to go to school, did better than average work and lived at home. His parents were unaware of the fact that he was taking LSD. His lifestyle remained unchanged. Approximately six months before he was brought to the hospital, he was picked up while hitchhiking by a group of hippies. He accompanied them to their commune where he took LSD. On his first trip with this familial group, he experienced profound new sensations. Their caring and sensitive relationships gave him his first deep awareness that he wanted more intimacy than he had known previously. When he returned home, he quit college which he now saw as a useless waste of time. He gave away his clothes and refused to wear shoes. His parents felt desperate as he was planning to leave home permanently to join his hippie friends.

His family never had a great deal of internal cohesiveness. They were relatively stable but rarely related emotionally. Tom had never had any of the important experiences at home that he was able to have in his new relationships. Though he was unrealistic, he was not psychotic. He had changed his values so enormously that he could no longer remain within the sphere of his earlier upbringing.

In another case, a young *straight* salesman took LSD for the first time with his girlfriend. During his first and only trip, this isolated young man experienced such tremendous warmth and tenderness from his girlfriend that he was overwhelmed by previously unknown feelings of love and affection. He decided that his past way of life no longer made sense. After the trip, he quit his job, and went to work for a community organization which assisted young people who were having problems with drugs.

Such enormous changes in lifestyles do not always occur. Less pronounced changes are more common. Some individuals attempt to maintain their LSD heightened level of awareness after their trip. This leads to bizarre or unusual behavior, expressing their dissatisfaction with normal, comparatively mundane reality. In their search to reestablish the beautific vision experienced on LSD, some may temporarily lose their ability to make appropriate judgments. They act as if the world had been transformed and they may place untenable demands on the people around them. They may ask "why? Why do I need a car, or new clothes, when simple things are really enough?" This is indeed simplistic thinking, but one cannot challenge it with ordinary logic. People are very willing to give up a job or a way of life for a vision of something that seems much more important.

This has happened to many. It may be one of the reasons for the dramatic change of values we see in the counter-culture. And perhaps, in the long run, we might be wise to consider where the mad rush of progress is taking us; whether the natural pleasures of seeing the world in fresh, simple ways are not sometimes missed by our sophisticated, appliance-using society.

Flashbacks and Psychoses. The dangerous consequences of post-LSD reactions are rare. Considering the tremendous power of the LSD experience this is quite fortunate. Yet for the few who go through the terrors of repeated flashbacks or who become psychotic, an LSD trip can spell disaster. Most people recover from these sequelae, but some will remain in our state hospitals for long periods of time.

Flashbacks occur when unresolved psychic trauma is partially brought to awareness but incompletely dealt with during a trip. It is like opening Pandora's Box just a bit and not being able to seal it tight again. Later, some event jars the box just enough to open it briefly. With the dread contents exposed to awareness, even in the unconscious mind, the disorientation of the LSD state flashes back suddenly. Eventually, one's psychological defenses return and normal reality is reestablished. Flashbacks can be treated by psychotherapy by repeated use of LSD in a treatment setting or by major tranquilizers. Insight-oriented psychotherapy is the treatment of choice but may take a number of years. Flashbacks frequently cease spontaneously. Flashbacks can occur with fullblown psychotic hallucinatory effects or they may appear as only mild perceptual changes. Marijuana and other drugs can precipitate them as can emotional experiences and anxiety. Other post-LSD reactions include depression, chronic anxiety states, prolonged visual effects, and paranoia.

Psychotic reactions requiring hospitalization are a consequence of using LSD in only a very small percentage of cases. Such individuals most frequently have schizophrenic decompensations or, more rarely, prolonged hallucinosis. Usually such psychotic states resolve slowly with therapy. LSD is most likely to cause psychotic reactions in individuals who have rigid defenses which are crucial to their stability or who have had previous schizophrenic illness. Well-integrated individuals almost never have any of these prolonged disastrous effects despite the fact that they too can have frightening LSD *bummers*.

One syndrome that is similar to an LSD flashback is the repeated experience of being *stoned* (i.e. confused, anxious and disoriented) which occurs in some individuals who have rigid defenses against their angry and destructive impulses. If they have any drug experience, from LSD to marijuana, which loosens their defensive control of their enormous anger, they become unable to tolerate even the mildest of anxiety-producing or threatening situations. They feel *stoned* or dazed as they attempt to control their unacceptable feelings. It is much the same feeling of overwhelming confusion and disorientation that normal individuals might have brieflly in reaction to a catastrophe. This feeling of being *stoned* is persistent and may last with variable intensity for years. It is aggravated by the omnipotently demanding passive-aggressive personality style that is most frequently seen in this syndrome. Psychotherapy for this condition is often prolonged and difficult.

It is a wonder that so many severely disturbed people who have taken LSD and other psychedelics have not become more bizarre or disturbed. Perhaps, the accepting, loosely structured, undemanding quality of the underground community allows disorganized individuals to function without drawing attention to themselves. It is not clear why LSD will increase the mental disability of some individuals and not others.

Physiologic Considerations. LSD is one of the most potent chemicals known. Merely twenty-five micrograms of this drug can cause a change in one's inner awareness. Usually, doses range from 100-500 micrograms, although intake of up to 2-4,000 micrograms have been reported. The trip lasts from six to twelve hours with its peak occuring during the first two to four hours. For most people, tolerance will begin to develop after a single dose and may take four to eight days to wear off. Cross tolerance exists between most psychedelics including LSD, mescaline and psilocybin. Experiments have shown that these drugs cannot be distinguished experimentally by experienced users.

LSD has many sympathomimetic effects, most pronounced of which is pupillary dilation of up to six millimeters. Minor elevation in blood pressure and temperature occur, as well as muscular weakness, numbness, tremulousness, tachycardia and mild hyperglycemia. The nonspecific stress of the LSD state produces increased adrenocortical steroids. Eosinophilia and leukocytosis also can be observed. Electroencephalographic tracings show diminished amplitude and low voltage fast waves with increased desynchrony. Periods of dreaming during sleep are prolonged for the twenty-four to forty-eight hours following an LSD experience.

The mode of action of LSD remains speculative. Naturally occurring neurologically active amines such as serotonin and norepinephrine show chemical structures similar to most of the psychoactive drugs. Hallucinogenic agents may compete with and block or possibly facilitate synaptic transmissions.

LSD has been involved in a great controversy involving possible chromosomal damage. Unfortunately, these studies have utilized subjects who have had multi-drug exposure. Nevertheless, there is clear-cut evidence that LSD does increase the number of chromosomal crossovers. Chromosomal changes appear three times more frequently in LSD users than in control groups. These changes are similar to those induced by radiation, viruses and other mutagens. There is evidence suggesting that LSD can cross the placenta increasing the chromosomal changes in the fetus. However, from the epidemiological point of view, LSD only rarely has been implicated in congenital birth defects. The effects on germ cells still have to be evaluated. We can conclude only that we do not know the consequences of the chromosomal changes that are observed with LSD use. We must proceed with caution until adequate data are available.

Clinical Uses. Research work on LSD remains in its infancy. A number of studies already have shown some promise for LSD as a therapeutic agent. Patients on the verge of death after a protracted and painful illness, such as cancer, usually experience a great deal of anxiety and terror. With proper preparation, an LSD session can substantially change their perspective on their impending death. Most feel more accepting about the inevitability of death. Additionally, LSD has been shown to decrease pain in chronically ill cancer patients and to increase the effectiveness of opiates.

LSD has proven to be of some value in the treatment of alcoholics. More than half of the alcoholics treated with one to three high dose sessions of LSD have shown improvement. Reports from Eastern and Western Europe and the United States suggest that LSD may be a useful adjunct in insight-oriented psychotherapy. Combined with regular therapy sessions, LSD experiences inhibit ego defenses and allow for the recall of primitive fantases and traumatic memories not usually available to the conscious mind. LSD enhances emotional abreactions. Reports from psychoanalytic researchers using LSD suggest that even the earliest of traumas, the pain of being born, has somatic traces which can be re-experienced. Claims have been made for the value of LSD in treating both schizophrenic and neurotic patients. These experiments bear further study as LSD could well become an important addition to the armamentarium of psychotherapy drugs.

OTHER HALLUCINOGENS

Mescaline (3,4,5,-Trimethoxyphenylethylamine)

Mescaline, one of the alkaloids present in the peyote cactus which grows in the Sonoran deserts of the American Southwest and Mexico, has long been used by Indians as a part of religious rituals. In these ceremonies the adult men of the tribe sit through the night after chewing peyote buttons, having visions and singing peyote songs.

Mescaline, the active alkaloid of peyote, is chemically related to epinephrine. It was studied in the early 1950's and received much popular attention. Peyote has an intensely bitter taste and often causes nausea and vomiting. Trips on peyote tend to last twelve to twenty-four hours while mescaline lasts six to eight hours. Many drug users feel that mescaline produces a psychedelic experience that has more colorful, gentle somatic qualities than LSD and is less likely to be terrifying. In contradiction, research work has shown that people are unable to differentiate between the effects of most psychedelics.

Psilocybin and Psilocin (dimethyl - 4 - phosphoryltryptamine and dimethyl - 4 hydroxyltryptamine)

The psychoactive alkaloids found in the Mexican mushroom, *psilocybe mexicana heim,* is also used by Indians in Mexico to produce religious visions. Psilocin is slightly more potent than psilocybin. Both produce states indistinguishable from LSD but have a duration of approximately three to six hours. They are rarely, if ever available on the street, although preparations of other substances are frequently sold as psilocybin.

DMT (dimethoxytryptanine) and DET (diethyltryptamine)

DMT often has been called the businessman's acid trip as it produces rapid hallucinogenic effects which last ten to thirty minutes. It is inactive when taken orally. Usually people smoke DMT, either by heating the crystals and inhaling the vapors or by diping marijuana into a solution of DMT. It has a strong, acrid, metallic odor. It can be sniffed or injected. Intramuscular injections can cause a tight, choking sensation in the chest and brief periods of unconsciousness followed by intense hallucinations. DMT occurs in the seeds of *Piptadenia peregrina* which are used in South America to make *Cohoba* snuff. DMT has autonomic effects similar to LSD. DET is a synthetic preparation whose psychoactive properties resemble DMT.

Lysergic Acid Amide

The wild American morning glory has four species which produce seeds containing lysergic acid amide and isolysergic acid amide. The potency varies with each batch of seeds. The seeds are pulverized and taken orally, often producing a lethargic, dreamy state with frequent nausea and vomiting. Hallucinations occur at high doses to the point where ergot toxicity is observed.

STP (2,5,dimethoxy-4-methylamphetamine)

STP is a synthetic hallucinogen that recently has come directly from the experimental laboratory into street use. It was alleged to precipitate frequent *bummers* and last one to two days. However, larger than normal amounts were used, probably accounting for these misconceptions. It is thought to be about as potent as psilocybin.

The Peace Pill-PCP

PCP is an animal tranquilizer known as phencyclidine (Sernyl). First making its appearance in the summer of 1967 as *the peace pill* in San Francisco, PCP received a lot of attention and was known to cause frequent bad trips. Some find it enjoyable at first, but there have been repeated reports of acute paranoia and *bummers.* Known as *angel dust* it is sprayed on marijuana or parsley and sold as an hallucinogen. It usually produces a greater disorganization of the thought process than LSD. Feelings of unreality are also common. It can be identified frequently by the heavy chemical odor that lingers in the air when it is smoked. A cheap chemical, which apparently is easily obtained, it is frequently sold as LSD, mescaline, or THC. At times it may be added to other drugs to boost their effect. The quality and potency of drugs obtained on the street are always unknown. Strychnine and other poisons have been found both alone and as contaminants of such drugs.

Marijuana and Hashish

Marijuana is the common name given to the dried leaves and flowers of the hemp plant, *cannabis sativa.* Hashish is made from the dried resins of the same plant, or the Indian variety, *cannabis indicus.* Hashish is more potent but contains the same active chemical, tetrahydracannabinol (THC). It can be classified as an hallucinogen since, in adequate amounts, THC produces hallucinations.

Historical Considerations. Cannabis indicus has been used in India for centuries for religious, pleasurable, and medicinal purposes. In 1839, W. B. O'Shaughnessey published an article, "On the Preparations of the Indian Hemp," which first introluced the therapeutic possibilities of cannabis into Western medicine. O'Shaughnessey had been serving with the British Army in India. He suggested that hemp might be useful in producing analgesia, as an anticonvulsant, and as a muscle relaxant. His report generated a great deal of attention. By 1860 the Ohio State Medical Society's committee on *cannabis indicus* reported success in treating pain, childbirth, coughs, psychoses, and insomnia using this new drug. In 1889, E. A. Birch reported in *Lancet* that Indian hemp could be used in treating opiate addiction. A year later, in 1890, J. R. Reynolds reported in *Lancet* on thirty years of clinical experience using cannabis. He observed that cannabis was useful as a sedative and was valuable for various neuralgias, migraine headache, and numerous nervous conditions including depression. He warned against overdose, noting the necessity to adjust the quantity given to each patient. Even the great American physician. William Osler, in his 1916 edition of his textbook of medicine wrote, concerning migraine headaches, "*Cannabis indicus* is probably the most satisfactory remedy."

Indian hemp was used extensively by physicians throughout the latter half of the nineteenth and early part of the twentieth centuries. Hemp was a frequent component of over-the-counter nerve and cough cures. In 1937 the marijuana tax act put an end to the common use of cannabis for medicinal purposes. This occurred over the objections of the American Medical Association who protested that it was a useful drug.

Since the 1920's, the use and distribution of marijuana through the fringe or criminal element of our society has given it a reputation for being associated with criminal behavior and violent crimes. The La Guardia report and many recent studies have disproved this associated. Yet there remains a widespread misconception that the use of marijuana presages a moral degeneration and eventual addiction to heroin.

Why Do People Like Marijuana? The tremendously rapid in-

TABLE 7-I.

DRUG USED	PHYSICAL SYMPTOMS	ACCOMPANIED BY	DANGERS
Glue Sniffing	Violence, Drunk Appearance, Dreamy or blank expression	Tubes of glue, Glue Smears, Large paper bags or handkerchiefs	Lung/Brain damage Death through suffocation, or choking, Anemia
Heroin, Morphine, Codeine	Stupor/Drowsiness, Needle marks on body, Watery eyes, Loss of appetite, Blood stain on shirt sleeves	Needle or hypo-quet-string Cotton Tourni-qupet-string Rope, Belt, burnt bottle, Caps or spoons, Glassine envelopes	Death from over-dose
Cough Medicine containing Codeine and Opium (Romilar)	Drunk appearance, Lack of coordi-nation, Confusion. Excessive itching	Empty bottles of cough medicine	Causes addiction
Marijuana, Pot, Grass	Sleepiness, Wander-ing mind, Enlarged eye pupils, Lack of coordination, Crav-ing for sweets, in-creased appetite	Strong odor of burnt leaves Small seeds in pocket lining Cigarette paper, Discolored fingers	Inducement to take stronger
LSD, DMT, STP	Severe halluci-nations, Feelings of detachment, Inco-herent speech, Cold hands and feet, Vomiting, Laughing. and Crying	Cube sugar with discoloration in center, Strong body odor, small tube of liquid	Suicidal tenden-cies, Unpredict-able behavior, chronic exposure causes brain damage
Pep Pills, Ups, Amphetamines	Aggressive behavior, Giggling, Silliness, Rapid speech, Con-fused thinking, No appetite, Extreme fatigue, Dry mouth, Shakiness	Jar of pills of varying colors, Chain smoking	Death from over-dose, Halluci-nations

crease in the use of marijuana throughout all levels of our culture is surely the most striking drug phenomenon of the past decade. Studies have shown that from 50%-80% of our college students have used or use marijuana. Of course, only a few use it daily. Yet, more and more people seem to find it an enjoyable and relaxing pastime. One young man describes his feeling this way, "The thing about it is that it makes me feel whole; grass is like a wholeness where you can still function but still have that all-in-one enjoyable feeling." Many have found that marijuana is a valuable tranquilizer. It can take away the feeling of emptiness and insecurity. It can create a delicious timelessness in which the mind seems more awake and the world particularly vibrant and meaningful.

TABLE 7-II.
COMMON SYMPTOMS OF DRUG ABUSE AMONG TEENAGERS

Change in school attendance, discipline and grades
Change in the character of homework turned in
Unusual flare-ups or outbreaks of temper
Poor physical appearance
Furtive behavior regarding drugs and possessions
Wearing of sunglasses at inappropriate times to hide dilated or constricted pupils
Long-sleeved shirts worn constantly to hide needle marks
Borrowing of money to purchase drugs
Stealing small items from school
Finding the student in odd places during the day such as closets, storage rooms, etc. to take drugs

During their first encounter with marijuana, some individuals experience nothing out of the ordinary. Anxiety about smoking grass for the first time can completely shut off the effects of the drug at moderate dosage. For others, the intensity of the new perceptions can be overwhelming. The changes in time and spatial dimension, the clarity and depth of feeling that are often reached are profound experiences Marijuana and hashish are usually smoked but they can also be taken in the form of an alcohol extract, or, more frequently, mixed in foods such as brownies or cookies.

Usually marijuana is used as a means to foster social communication, much as alcohol is used socially. By passing a *joint* around and turning on together, an immediate comradship is established. Under these circumstances people often find it easier to relate and be involved. As people become more intoxicated, they tend to become increasingly withdrawn into their fantasies and reveries, thus cutting down on interpersonal communication. When alone, people tend to use the drug to decrease anxiety, to speed up their mental processes and to enjoy its somatic effects. The ability of the marijuana high to ameliorate feelings of anxiety, emotional pain and loneliness perhaps best explains why so many repeatedly turn to this drug experience. Marijuana is likely because it helps in feeling better; it is replacing alcohol as the drug of choice of today's young people.

Physiological Effects. The ability of marijuana to produce psychological and physiological effects varies with its THC content. The percentage of THC usually present in marijuana available on the streets is less than 1 percent. Panic, hallucinatory and dissociative reactions can occur when more preparation are available.

Initially, the drug causes drowsiness, dryness of the mouth and weakly dilates blood vessels producing injected conjunctiva. Tachycardias, slight decreases in blood pressure, and pupillary dilation are common. Transient hypoglycemia often causes a craving for sweets. This hypoglycemic response may disappear with more chronic use. At higher doses there is a diffuse depressant effect on the central nervous system. A dreamy, lethargic state occurs where inhibitions are decreased. Impairment of immediate memory, increased suggestibility, shortened attention span, fragmentation of thought, synesthesias, altered sense perceptions and moderate ataxia are all aspects of the *high* of marijuana intoxication. This hypnogogic state has qualities similar to the sedative experiences during the induction of anesthesia as well as the psychedelic experience with LSD. Coordination studies in driving automobiles have demonstrated that intoxication with moderate doses of marijuana does not impair driving skills. Higher drug levels cause difficulties with attention and perception that makes driving hazaradous.

Partial tolerance develops with chronic marijuana use. Tolerant individuals often find their *high* periods shortened with fewer perceptual changes. However, the timeless tranquilizing and comforting qualities usually remain. Tolerance disappears three to five days after drug use stops. Marijuana is not addicting. Severe psychological dependence results when individuals depend on grass to relieve their anxiety and frustrations. There are no problems in withdrawing from marijuana. Only occasional heavy users have periods of restlessness and anxiety. Most people use it in their spare time to induce a mild euphoria. With this kind of use, psychological dependence usually does not become a problem. Morning hangovers are infrequently encountered. Yet some individuals may have these regularly. They report fatigue, lethargy, mild to moderate confusion and dissociative feelings. No fatalities have been reported from an overdose of marijuana. The drug, when smoked, is automatically self-titrated. If the user becomes excessively intoxicated, he finds himself unable to continue smoking and thus discontinues his drug intake.

Psychological Changes. During a marijuana high, one experiences a rapid flow of thoughts and associations. Often one is able to hear or feel impulses from different parts of one's self that are normally repressed. The vicious, silly, childish, or self-disapproving voices within may be clearly heard. Often one takes the role of a spectator looking at one's own feelings and reactions. There is a general enhancement of the prevailing mood. Hostile or angry feelings are usually modified or lost entirely. An individual who is *stoned* may be aware of the intensity with which he is able to perceive the external reality. There is a change in the quality of reality, as if the veil of one's anxieties were lifted and perception were sharpened. Alternatively, one may feel cut off and fragmented, producing severe paranoia.

The marijuana high can be focused both externally or internally. One can go from the internal to the external experience rapidly. Frequently, people state that they have had to respond to external reality such as a knock on the door or being stopped by a policeman. They note that they can appropriately orient themselves except when extremely intoxicated. This control is an unusual quality of marijuana intoxication.

It often has been stated that marijuana acts as an aphrodisiac. Basically this is true, although it does not appear to be in itself a sexual stimulant. Instead, the aphrodisiac qualities of marijuana seem to be due to its ability to remove inhibitions and allow one to focus intensely on the pleasures of sexual sensations.

The syndrome of the heavy marijuana abuser is only beginning to be understood. He tends to be an individual who feels very inadequate and uses intellectual defenses to avoid his painful feelings. The prolonged use of marijuana creates a kind of distance from the world. One observes what it happening rather than participating with feelings and reactions. This withdrawal includes a loss of interest in others as well as a lessened concern for the propriety of social norms. The chronic marijuana user has a sluggish, even flowing, almost mechanized walk that can be identified by a keen observer. He tends to neglect his body and there is a loss of general alertness. He seems to be far away and often demonstrates clearly confused or loosened thought process. Delusional or obsessional ideation may be present. No longer does it seem meaningful to hold a job or complete school. This lack of involvement has been called the amotivation syndrome. Most of these symptoms are reversible when the individual stops abusing marijuana.

Adverse Reactions. Varying degrees of mind paranoid or fragmented feelings are commonly reported. These disappear as the drug wears off and require no treatment. Acute and chronic psychoses develop only rarely; they develop most frequently in rigid, schizoid individuals. These may require long-term psychotherapy and tranquilizers. In chronic psychoses, particularly with marginal but functioning individuals, it may be difficult to get them to give up using marijuana. They have come to rely on its tranquilizing effects and do not connect their disorganization with the use of the drug.

STIMULANTS

Amphetamines

Amphetamines are a class of drugs which act as stimulants of the central nervous system. Their use and abuse extends throughout all levels of our culture, from the truck driver who takes a *bennie* to stay alert on the road to the housewife who needs her morning diet pill to keep up with the rapid pace of everyday life. It is little wonder that the youth subculture has adopted amphetamines as a frequently used, though less frequently abused, form of stimulation.

Amphetamines were prepared first in 1887 but did not become

clinically available until 1930 when the sympathomimetic effects of amphetamines began to be compared to those of epinephrine. They were not used frequently until the second World War. There are a variety of them, including amphetamine (Benzedrine®), dextro-amphetamine (Dexedrine®), meth-amphetamine (Desoxyn® or Methadrine®). Combinations such as Obetrol® are used to decrease the unwanted side-effects of nervousness and irritability.

Pharmacological Effects. Amphetamines function as a stimulant of both the motor and sensory aspects of the central nervous system. They produce an alert, awake feeling of confidence and potency and facilitate task oriented behavior for four to six hours. Amphetamines stimulate heart function with the heart rate increasing proportionately to the dose of the drug. Increased irritability and increased perception of auditory stimuli are also dose related. At high doses, toxic psychoses develop with visual and auditory illusions, delusions and hallucinations having extremely paranoid characteristics. Sexual interest often is increased on the intellectual level but the physical ability to perform may be reduced.

The pharmacological evidence suggests that amphetamines act through multiple pathways involving catecholamine metabolism, monamine oxidase inhibition and by direct intrinsic effect. The dose of amphetamines needed to produce toxic psychotic effects varies tremendously. Chronic oral or intravenous use of 100-500 mg. per day usually precipitates psychosis but individuals have tolerated well over 1,000 mg. per day without toxic signs. While not addicting, amphetamines are extremely habituating, producing profound psychological dependence. Withdrawal from the drug produces tenseness, tremors and anxiety culminating in moderate to extreme depression. People develop rapid tolerance to the effects of amphetamines so that the drug no longer remains effective unless the dose is constantly increased. With large repeated doses taken intravenously damage and loss of brain cells occurs. It is surprisingly, however, that despite tremendously heavy amphetamine abuse, most individuals ultimately show only minimal functional brain damage. There are recent reports of a new syndrome where inflammation and damage to blood vessels are seen in association with intravenous amphetamine abuse. There is a significant increase in cerebrovascular accidents (strokes) in these patients.

The rate of metabolism of amphetamines is relatively slow. Usually the body takes two to three days to eliminate a single dose of the drug. Much is excreted unchanged in the urine which facilitates detection when a question of toxicity arises.

Amphetamine Syndromes. The mildest form of amphetamine abuse has been common throughout all levels of society, from students to housewives. It is usually iatrogenic and consists of the daily use of low dosage of amphetamines from 10-60 mg. per day. Physicians have been in the practice of prescribing amphetamines for weight gain and other symptoms of depression. Amphetamines reverse mild depression for a time, but due to the rapid tolerance that develops, individuals who begin using moderate or low doses of the drug must soon find that this does not meet their needs. Slowly, they must increase the amount they take to get the same kind of effect. Many overlook the basis euphoria and sense of powerfulness that goes along with amphetamine use, believing instead that they are taking the amphetamines for weight reduction, or because the doctor prescribed it. As increasing amounts are used, insomnia often results. Fatigued in the morning they again have to increase their intake to get through the next day. As they begin taking higher and higher doses, suspicious feelings erupt into their consciousness. They believe that people are against them. Numerous frightening perceptual experiences occur which are interpreted in a paranoid manner. There is a tremendous lability and frantic mood swings. Thus, the physician who prescribes amphetamines freely can unwittingly convert a patient's mild depression into a toxic psychosis. At best, he can help his patient become habituated to amphetamines rather than dealing with their underlying depressed feelings.

Intravenous use of amphetamines is relatively rare. It is restricted to a very small group of individuals whose feelings of inadequacy are so extreme that they leave the individual with a total sense of powerlessness. The experience of an injection of intravenous amphetamines gives such an individual an incredible sense of power and potency. They rapidly become habituated. Usually the drug is taken in *runs*, lasting several days, in which the person does not sleep, rarely eats, and takes the drugs as frequently as possible, usually every two to six hours. As the drug is injected, the user experiences a sudden euphoria (a flash or a rush) which is felt as an explosive orgasmic aliveness of the body and mind. It is an extremely pleasurable sensation to feel alive when your normal state of existence is one of helplessness and apathy. Most users feel that their intellectual functioning is dramatically increased. Some write great poetic pieces, songs or long drafts of manifestos to save the world.

Usually, amphetamine abusers take this drug intravenously in small groups. Often, after the initial rush there is a great deal of talkative communication and activity. As the abuse continues, this activity takes more bizarre and paranoid forms. One *speed freak* couple had strings throughout their apartment forming a kind of spiderweb on which they would hang pictures of various objects. Their paranoia caused them to lock their door with six different locks. Like other habitual users, they tolerated a great deal of filth in their *pad* and took very poor care of their bodies.

When amphetamine abusers appear for help, they often are either acutely paranoid or seriously depressed after a long run. They may be suffering from vitamin deficiency and malnutrition. It is both this neglect and the physiological damage to the body and brain that is responsible for the well-known slogan "Speed Kills."

Treatment Considerations. Toxic psychosis with hallucinations require the use of antipsychotic drugs. Panic reactions or anxiety attacks can usually be treated with sedatives or minor tranquilizers such as Valium®. Usually, amphetamine abusers have not had sufficient nutrition for a long time and require vitamins and a well-balanced diet. The depression that follows abuse of amphetamines is best treated with regular exercise and rest. Amphetamine abusers are extremely difficult to rehabilitate because of their severe personality problems. Until they can develop a sense of competence and usefulness, they frequently return to amphetamines as a way out of their intolerable emotional world.

Cocaine

Cocaine is a potent stimulant. It was used by the Incas of South America as a stimulant for runners in their postal system. By chewing coca leaves, the couriers were able to stimulate their physical abilities much as trainers today use amphetamines to push athletes or horses to greater performance. Cocaine, often called *snow,* is a preferred drug by the upper-middle-class drug players of today's scene.

The use of cocaine to treat morphine addiction began around 1880. Even Sigmund Freud in 1884, recommended cocaine for neurasthenia and morphinism, insisting that cocaine was nonaddicting. As one story goes, Freud was apprehensive when going to social gatherings and would often take cocaine to increase his sense of well-being. This continued only briefly until he observed its addictive potential.

Physiologic Effects. Cocaine stimulates the central nervous system. It appears to potentiate sympathetic nervous functions, perhaps by inhibiting the uptake of norepinephrine at transmitter sites. It is a potent local anesthetic of the eyes, nose and throat.

Cocaine is addicting but less rapidly than opiates. Its potential for creating a feeling of competence leads to psychological dependence more rapidly than physiological addiction. Although addicting, withdrawal symptoms are more like those of amphetamines rather than heroin. They include tenseness, muscle ache, mild nausea, general somatic discomfort, anxiety, restlessness and depression. Heavy cocaine abuse, which occurs rarely, often produces severe paranoid psychoses in which the abuser frequently feels that there are small animals or bugs which he must continue to pick off his skin.

Cocaine is a well-loved drug by many who enjoy its ability to induce a sense of power and excitement that is difficult to obtain even with amphetamines. The problem users have with cocaine is that its effects are very short lasting, usually only thirty to sixty minutes. Then there is a prolonged come-down period of three to six hours during which there is mild to marked somatic discomfort.

The Use of Cocaine. Cocaine is rapidly absorbed through the nasal mucosa. Many sniff this drug, often using a dollar bill rolled up to form a narrow tube which allows them to inhale the cocaine crystals past the hairs in their nostrils. The effects are felt rapidly but without a *rush.* With extended use, vasoconstriction produces damage to the nasal mucosa. Eventually, a hole in the nasal septum may occur due to the slow erosion of nasal tissue.

Intravenous use of cocaine produces a flash of sexual and physical excitement which is extremely intense. It is a fantastically pleasurable sensation. However, the flash and high are brief so that repeated doses are needed to prevent the uncomfortable comedown. For this reason, cocaine is often combined with other drugs, frequently heroin. This combination is called a *speedball*. It has both the stimulatory euphoric effect of cocaine while it has the softening and soothing qualities of heroin.

NARCOTICS

Smack (Heroin), A Seductive Curse

Heroin is the king of drugs. It is the seductive but miserable mistress for the many people who have to hide from the depression and anguish of their own experience of themselves. Heroin is king because it leaves you floating on a calm sea where nothing seems to matter and everything is okay. It is the beatific world of peaceful fantasy where your mind swims in the warm, comfortable, somatic sensation of being held, without pain, and protected from the concerns and worries that make up your life. Suddenly the emptiness disappears. The great, gaping hole that hurts, which you had to hide from everyone, is gone; the terrible gnawing inadequacy has vanished. And in its place is the power and comfort that is called confidence. No one can get to you when you keep *nodding*.

Heroin is not a harmful drug. It can be taken for years with almost no physically deleterious effects. Its major side-effects are constipation and, for some men, impotence. It is the great seducer because it makes one feel so good. It feels better than psychotherapy or sexuality. It creates a state unlike reality where there is total safety. But heroin, like any narcotic or depressant, is an anesthetizer. It depresses the feeling world and erases from experience the very sensations which are needed to touch life. For many people whose pain is intense, heroin, they feel, is the only way to maintain a constructive lifestyle. Musicians and artists often have turned to heroin to avoid their agony and thus continue their productiveness. Many manage to continue in good health and remain employed for many years. Indeed, if it were not for the intense prejudice against the drug, the rapid tolerance that develops, the dangers of overdose, and for the consequences of nonsterile intravenous injections, heroin might well become the tranquilizing drug of choice for those who suffer from incapacitating anxiety. Unfortunately, the major traumatic effect of heroin is the problem of obtaining it in our society. Having to score daily, with their arms eating up countless dollars, causes the addict to be a slave to his body's craving for heroin.

On first exposure, heroin usually produces nausea. By the second or third dose, the nausea disappears. Then heroin is pure pleasure, at least for a while. Pleasant dreams and fantasies obliterate life's difficulties. Within a few days, tolerance develops so that more heroin is needed to get high. Soon, each day is spent trying to *cop* enough stuff to stay normal. Rarely, if ever, is heroin encountered whose quality and supply are good enough to really get off. The desperate slavery causes the gradual erosion of self-respect. This loss is often bespoken by the ease with which an addict will relate the one thing he hasn't done; it is with this that he retains his last glimmer of self-respect. He has lied, cheated, conned and maneuvered, but perhaps he has not stolen or she has not been a whore.

It is the economic pressure of the heroin scene that causes so many to lose their souls. As slaves in an environment where heroin is expensive and illegal, a whole generation of young addicted people are being forced by their society and their addiction to become criminals. It is an unfortunate sign of our culture's callousness that so many of us look on sick, dependent, disordered addicts as evil degenerates.

The English experience of giving drug users carefully supervised maintenance programs of heroin has proved that heroin itself is not necessarily a detrimental drug. They have shown that narcotic addicts can be stablized with the official administration of this drug. Americans are beginning to experiment with methadone maintenance which is proving enormously successful.

Whether we like the moral consequences or not we must consider the fact that there are large numbers of people in our country who feel so desperate that they go out of their way, often destroying their entire lives, to take heroin. Normal habits are essential to our functioning. We get into the habit of getting up early to get to work on time. Habits are hard to break. Once someone has become habituated to living in a world where pain is not confronted and experienced, it may be impossible for him to return to the often uncomfortable realities of life. Perhaps we must learn to accept the continuing need for maintenance therapy as a necessary compromise.

A Habit Is Getting Off. With a rope, tie, belt or old nylon stocking you stop the circulation from your shaking, sweating arm. You decide which of your well-scarred veins you have a chance of hitting; then you slip in the needle attached to the eyedropper with the rubber bulb on the end. Releasing the pressure lightly from the bulb you anxiously look for the red glob of blood in the bottom of the dropper which means you've got a *register*. You've got to be sure you're in the vein before you inject the stuff. If you miss, you get another abscess. The sickness hurts in your bones, your nose is running and you hurt so much you almost wish you were dead. With a slow push it's in and within a few seconds you're beginning to feel normal again. Your dilated pupils become very small. Your confidence is back; you're all right for a few hours before the sickness begins to come again.

Most addicts rarely get high from heroin. Their increasing tolerance to the drug usually prevents them from getting enough to get them off. Their shooting just prevents them from feeling sick. Most addicts could withdraw in five to ten days if they really wanted to. This rarely happens because of their fear of being sick, as well as their lack of commitment to getting clean. Most have become so accustomed to using heroin to avoid problems and have so little to look forward to that they really do not want to give up the relief of their addiction. Moreover, today's street heroin is so diluted that most addicts are addicted to minimal amounts of heroin and have, objectively speaking, mild withdrawal problems.

The variability in the quality of street junk exists in all types of drugs. If an addict scores a few bags of *pure shit* he can accidentally overdose himself causing severe respiratory depression and death. The variety of substances used to cut junk, which then get injected intravenously, add to the dangers of heroin abuse.

It is important to understand that there are many kinds of heroin addicts. In today's drug world we are seeing more of the young addicts whose heroin experiences are recent (under two years) . Such an addict usually has a greater chance of returning to the social world he came from, not having burned the many bridges that the chronic, long-term addict has already destroyed. The young addict of today is occasionally able to give up heroin with relative ease. He has a nonaddicted lifestyle he has not completely forgotten.

It is hoped that the rehabilitative process will take into consideration the relatively new phenomenon of today's *young addict*. There is a need for withdrawal and support facilities for young people who can return to a nonaddicted way of life. The more severely addicted or chronic addict usually needs long-term maintenance therapy. Occasionally, after years of rehabilitation, a stress-producing situation may trigger an addict's need for heroin. Habits return with lightening speed. Just shooting a day or two is enough to revive the intense need for heroin that initially took two to three weeks to develop. An important part of treating addiction is to provide addicts with withdrawal assistance when they have reverted to heroin in a period of stress. We must be willing to help the addict in times of crisis, offering him the kind of support that will enable him to find better ways of handling stressful feelings.

DEPRESSANTS

The Red Devils

Barbiturates, particularly secobarbitol (Seconol® or reds) , are frequently abused drugs, particularly in the ghettos. They offer a similar kind of relief to that of heroin. They depress feelings so that you do not have to know how hard it is to be alive. When you come from a ghetto, you are depressed most of the time. Even though you may stagger around with slurred speech and slowed thought processes, it may still feel better than being aware of how unpleasant life can be. Besides, when you are *stoned,* you do not notice how poorly coordinated you are.

Reds are readily available in ghettos and relatively easily obtainable by adolescents at all socioeconomic levels. They are sold in rolls and can be bought at almost any school in the country, particularly in urban areas. They are addicting and can be very dangerous.

Accidental overdose or suicide can occur, particularly in individuals who take sleeping pills and have developed a tolerance to the sedative effects of the barbiturates. With their sensorium clouded by the drug, not yet to the point of unconsciousness, depressed and sleepless people have continued to take sleeping medications until lethal doses have been ingested. Alcohol, which potentiates the effects of barbiturates, sometimes contributes to this process.

Withdrawal from barbiturates can be extremely dangerous. Even with the most painful withdrawal from heroin, death is not a serious risk. In withdrawing from barbiturates, the body becomes tremulous. As time passes, there is hypotension, fever, vomiting, uncontrolled tremors, and eventually grand mal convulsions, delirium and hypothermia. The probability of grand mal seizures increases with the amount of the drug taken daily. Since withdrawal from barbiturates represents a potentially life-threatening situation, it is essential that this be done under medical supervision. Usually doctors withdraw an individual by decreasing their maintenance levels by approximately ten percent every day or two. Convulsions can occur up to one or even two weeks after sudden withdrawal. This sometimes occurs to individuals in jail who have been separated from their source of drugs. Unfortunately, medically supervised barbiturate withdrawal is rarely, if ever, available in our local jails.

Research has shown that barbiturates change the normal EEG patterns during sleep, reducing the usual amount of rapid eye movement (REM) time. Dreams, which are important in maintaining emotional equilibrium, occur during the REM phase of sleep. Thus, barbiturates may help to create emotional tension. With nonbarbiturate sedatives available, perhaps the excessive use and availability of barbiturates will decrease.

INHALANTS

Among the very young, children of elementary or junior high school age, there remains the intermittent fads of the inhalation of very toxic substances. These include glues, gasolines, and aerosols. All of them are very dangerous, potentially causing damage to numerous body organs.

Airplane Glue, Plastic and Rubber Cement

When these substances are inhaled initially the effects often are similar to those of early alcohol intoxication, including light-headedness, euphoria, giddiness and exhilaration. Occasionally, vivid colorful hallucinations occur which may last up to twenty to thirty minutes. Other reactions include loss of muscular control, slurred speech, blurred vision, drowsiness, stupor, and gross mental disorientation. In some cases, coma and death have occurred.

The main ingredient is these products is toluene. This organic solvent and others like it are extremely dangerous when repeatedly inhaled. Damage occurs to the brain and central nervous system, as well as to the liver and kidneys. Depression of the blood forming elements in the bone marrow has been reported. Although not addicting, the body rapidly develops a tolerance to toluene. Repeated or ragular use of organic solvents can produce severe or permanent damage.

Gasoline, Paint Thinner, Solvents, Kerosene and Lighter Fluid

These hydrocarbons are very toxic, producing distortions similar to that of alcohol intoxication. In addition, ringing or buzzing in the ears and reverberation of sound are common. Prolonged use of these drugs can cause seizures, delirium, hallucinations, coma and in some cases, death.

Aersol Sprays

Widely used in the American scene, aerosol sprays pour out everything from whipped cream to oven cleaners. They contain propellants which, when inhaled, cause pronounced effects. These usually last only five to ten minutes and include dizziness, uncontrolled laughter and varied hallucinations. Since it is often difficult to seperate the propellant from the spray, concomitant inhaling of deodorants or paint often produces long term damage. Freon, when inhaled too rapidly, can freeze the larynx causing edema and death by suffocation.

Asthmador

The belladonna alkaloids can be extremely valuable in pharmaceutical agents, as well as being extremely dangerous or deadly hallucinogenic drugs. Old fashioned asthma preparations, such as asthamador, contain belladonna and in many places are still available over-the-counter. An asthamador trip is usually a tremendously frightening, overwhelming experience. There have been reports of an asthmador trip lasting as much as seven or eight days with periods of blindness and extreme confusion.

CONCLUSION

Those involved in drug rehabilitation are necessarily caught in a double bind. As they represent our society's orthodox view that sees all illegal drugs as *bad* they must present a limited orientation. On the other hand, rehabilitation specialists often realize that they lose the trust of their clients if they take an attitude which morally disapproves of all drugs. It may be difficult to be nonjudgmental. Our role as counselors is to help people differentiate between harmful drug abuse and tolerable drug use. The final decision must rest with the individual.

CHAPTER 8

JUVENILE OFFENDERS AND THE DRUG PROBLEM

STEPHEN CHINLUND

≋≋≋

☐ GENERAL REMARKS
☐ CAUSES OF DRUG ABUSE
☐ PROCESS OF DRUG INVOLVEMENT
☐ TREATMENT
☐ A NOTE ON RUNAWAYS
☐ A PLAN FOR WORKING IN SCHOOLS
☐ CONCLUSION

≋≋≋

GENERAL REMARKS

THE HISTORY OF DRUG ABUSE has presented us with a flow of changes through the years. More recently, since 1965, the flow has become a flood. This need not frighten us. In fact there are many persisting underlying themes in the pattern of drug abuse since ancient times. Probably even prehistoric man discovered that there were some leaves and weeds which produced desirable changes in his consciousness. This presentation will concern itself with those persistent themes.

In concentrating our attention on young people, there is a benefit for those of us who are interested in a wider clientele

139

group. In my experience, young people bring into relief the problems which are more subtle as they present themselves in adults. There certainly are exceptions but, generally, young people reveal the real problems behind their drug abuse more openly than adults.

This does not mean young people are easily able to answer the question, "Why do you abuse drugs?" Almost invariably, young people confronted with that question either give superficial answers or honestly admit that they themselves do not know the answer. The material below is offered out of hundreds of conversations with addicts. They have been most helpful on the question of causality as they look *back* on their years of addiction having achieved a plateau of months or years of abstinence. They are even more able to reflect on the causes which were obscure while they were in the midst of drug abuse.

CAUSES OF DRUG ABUSE

There is a broad underlying cause behind all of the particular causes for drug abuse listed below. This basic problem is one of proportion: the balance between felt strength and felt challenge. As an individual, I feel I have the capacity to achieve certain goals and to enjoy certain dimensions of life. For example, I may feel that I have the intelligence and the training and the skill to complete a college education. I may feel that I have the sensitivity, patience and the liveliness to be a good friend. In these cases, my felt strength is up to the felt challenge of college work and friendship.

On the other hand, I may look years ahead and be anxious about my potential as a parent. Similarly, I may worry about my capacity to hold a job or to be a high level supervisor. In these cases, there is a great distance between my sense of my own strength and a remote challenge.

Faced with this gap between strength and challenge, I may do one of many things:

a. Take steps to develop my strength further.
b. Lower the sense of challenge by aiming for different goals.
c. Some mixture of (a) and (b).

d. Postpone the time of facing the challenge.
e. Take some sort of drug which will give me the illusion that my strength is great enough to meet the challenge.

This last alternative is, of course, the critical one. It can apply to a bright young person who is valedictorian of his class; the most popular youngster in town with everything going for him. This youngster may feel he must become President of the United States. Nothing less will satisfy his parents, his own sense and his own awareness of his great gifts and privileges. If he is only seventeen years old, however, this may come as an overwhelming challenge. He may then turn to drugs to fill the gap.

Precisely the same problem applies to another seventeen-year-old youngster who has no friends, a tangled, violent family, has dropped out of school and has no working skills. For him the challenge of any kind of satisfaction at home, at work, in school, in sex or with peers seems as uncertain as does the presidency for the youngster in the first example. He, too, with the same fervor, may seek to use drugs.

Following are several examples of particular causes or challenges lying behind drug abuse. It must be borne in mind that any youngster can manage these challenges if he can be aware of them as appropriate to his strengths and gifts.

Adventure-seeking

All young people, to a certain extent, enjoy excitement. They like going to movies or listening to stories that are scary. They may, in many cases, like to be frightened, within limits, more than our security-oriented culture allows. Protective parents, who have grown up knowing fear as a welcome companion, seek to minimize the fearfulness of life and, in some cases, overdo it. This surely is a healthy aspect of life for a young person. If we all avoid frightening situations, we would never try to make new friends, take new jobs. Indeed, we would not even risk falling in love. If the normal options for adventure seem to be closed, then drug taking becomes more attractive.

This type of drug taking is particularly applicable to the very young. Glue sniffing and other types of experiment are an internal desire sought by many youngsters who feel the other avenues of adventure are closed.

Peace-seeking

For young people who have suffered great turbulence in their short lives this is a particularly attractive reason for using drugs. They are unaware, in many cases, of ways by which they can satisfy their desire for tranquility apart from drug abuse. For some this leads to smoking marijuana, the use of tranquilizers, sleeping pills and even heroin.

Young people vary in their need for peace. Some exist quite happily with fighting at home between brothers and sisters, between parents and with peers. Radios and televisions go full blast while the sounds of traffic, police sirens, fire bells and ambulances scream in the streets. Others are unable to tolerate easily even that which would appear to be an average level of turbulence. There is no norm here. There are only felt needs.

Friendship-seeking

Making friends involves some skills. For most people those skills come fairly easily. For many, many others they come with great difficulty and, in some cases, never come at all. The loneliness experienced by those who have fewer friends than they would like, or more superficial relationships than they would choose, is painful almost beyond describing. Then loneliness leads those individuals to desperate acts. One of the mildest forms of despair is the taking of alcohol or marijuana in order to smooth the inhibitions obstructing the seeking of friendship. For many, this relatively mild form of drug taking becomes a lifetime habit without any apparent destructive consequences. It is a benign catalyst in the friendship seeking process. For others, it can be the beginning of a spiral downward into alcoholism and use of more serious drugs. Unfortunately there is no guaranteed way a youngster can know ahead of time how it will be for him.

This desire for friends as a drive of life which can lead, if thwarted, to the taking of drugs, knows no age limit. Even the very young may be tempted to drown their loneliness in any drug that will do the job.

Power-seeking

All people, including those who are quite young, want to have some sense of their own strength. Playing King of the Mountain can be a very serious game even for little children. One of the reasons children take drugs is to provide the illusion of strength while there is very little in fact. This can lead to the early abuse of amphetamines and cocaine in particular. In a mass society where youngsters spend a great deal of time in large groups, it is often the case that a particular young person never feels he is the best in anything. It is important that he have this experience by having groups be small enough and his own skills and competence recognized.

Needless to say, this continues to be a problem as life goes on. Many individuals who have struggled several years feeling they were just one fish in a big pond finally felt some satisfaction in jumping into a smaller pond.

Aesthetic-seeking

This tends to be characteristic of young adults but it also can be a problem for those in the upper age limit of our concern. The bored middle-class student is particularly vulnerable to invitations to use mescaline, peyote, LSD and other ever-new inventions because of the promise of new awareness of color, texture or mass. It has taken artists months and years of discipline, in many cases, to build the quality of awareness which seems to come instantaneously for these drug takers. Since mescaline and peyote seem to have little continuing dangerous effect, according to present research, the fad of their use has continued since the mid-1950's. Some serious problems can result but this has not impressed itself sufficiently on college students to prevent use.

Sex companion-seeking

This differs from friendship seeking only in the specifically sexual concern. It is a well known but complicated fact about adolescence that youngsters are beginning during that time to discover a sexual identity. For young people who develop sexually at an early chronological age, the changes can be particularly bewildering. Even for those, however, who develop in an average way, the experience often is an upsetting one. Boys and girls are afraid of their possible inability to be attractive to each other. Both fear the possibility of being homosexual. Boys, in particular, worry about their capacity to perform according to some abstract ideal of male sexuality. Girls sometimes are afraid of becoming pregnant. Both are anxious about the unknown range of modulation in sexual expression. For all of this a variety or drugs appear to offer some relief. Cocaine and amphetamines continue to enjoy some false reputation as aphrodisiacs. Marijuana has a mildly inhibition reducing quality which makes it appear to be a similar type of drug. Alcohol, though essentially a depressant, may be experienced in a similar fashion.

Whatever the drug abused, the question of sexual identity is one which has led many young people into the downward spiral of deepening involvement in chemical abuse.

Transcendence-seeking

In the early '70's it became much clearer that many young people were seeking an experience in drugs which can only properly be called mystical or religious. Critics of this impulse may disapprove and choose to describe it as escapist. Others, and I would include myself, see it in a much more positive light. Man's hunger for some sense of life which is transcendent and unitive appears to be ultimately sound. Many of those claiming such an experience have been our most dynamic, moral, spiritual and even political leaders. The fact that churches have tended to become heavier in their rationale has contributed to the flight of young people. Their dissatisfaction with the pedestrian offerings of institutional religious forms has led them in two different directions. One is toward the movement presently characterized as "Jesus people" (loosely organized groups of teenagers and young adults bound together only by their faith) and, two, drug taking. The impulse towards transcendence varies greatly from one youngster to the next. In those for whom it is a strong impulse it simply must be satisfied somehow.

PROCESS OF DRUG INVOLVEMENT

The peer pressure for and against the use of various kinds of drugs provides a heightened sense of life. It can be a powerful force and, in most schools in the early '70's it has been a powerful drama involving two conflicting forces. This has been helpful as an arena for young people to make choices about life. In those situations where the pressure is all in the direction of getting involved in drugs, the arena, of course, has been destructive. Only the strongest young people have been able to think of it as a place for choosing.

There is one positive dimension involved in the process of drug taking which adults underestimate only to their peril. That dimension is one which I must call communality. As young people sit around a circle sharing marijuana, passing it from hand to hand and getting high together, they may be experiencing a sense of togetherness which goes much deeper than anything else offered by the adult world. We may be upset about this but it certainly has been a fact for many youngsters. For some of them, this has been a way of expressing their protest against what seems to them to be an overemphasis on private property. In the drug world there have been gentle eddies and backwaters where young people have floated comfortably. They were happy to be out of the tide of the rushing ambition of twentieth century America. By no means all have succumbed to drowning in deeper drug abuse.

Another piece of the process which should be mentioned is that there are youngsters so deeply ripped by life that they have started taking drugs with suicide either consciously in mind or just below the surface. Certainly for those injecting any substance directly into their veins suicide is a significant motivation.

TREATMENT

In this section some attempt will be made to offer a course both of prevention and treatment which is addressed to the individual causes listed above. It is intended to be seminal rather than prescriptive. It will serve its purpose only if readers adapt it to their own needs.

Adventure-seeking

The opportunities for adventure grew apace in the America of the mid-'70's. The increase in the various wilderness groups, mountain climbing and outward bound camps is most heartening. There is no question in my mind that this speaks directly to the need for adventure, particularly for the very young, but also for the rest of us, adults of all ages.

There is some element of adventure, however, in all the material listed below: making friends, exploring sex, testing power and trying mystical or contemplative exercises can all be enormously adventurous. Indeed, I would question the proportions of any efforts in those areas that appear to be risk free.

Peace-seeking

Searching for peace is something which most young people find difficult to do alone. They need reassurance and encouragement from grownups whether they are parents, or teachers, or other important people in their lives. Individuals working with young people need to encourage them to seek out the help and the strength of adults who can provide them with important reassurance as they continue in life.

They also need to know how to provide peace for themselves. Developing the skill to find out why they are anxious, why they are sleepless, why they are jumpy—this is a skill which even very young people are able to acquire if they have the right kind of help. Even youngsters under ten are able to isolate a problem, think of alternative action to take in response to the problem, make a choice and proceed. They also are well able to understand that some problems simply must be borne, but that in bearing them consciously they can be more peaceful than they would be if they were simply fighting the problems.

Friendship-seeking

This is perhaps the most important of all. I believe much in the value of groups such as those described by Doctor William Glasser in his book, *Reality Therapy*. Young people desperately need friends as much or more than in other age groups. In order to have friends they often need a lot of help. Settled in a group, where they can be encouraged to face someone, look him in the eye and say, "I would like to be your friend." is an enormous benefit. If the group has the courage and the honesty to let the person addressed respond in a candid way, this is even more helpful. Similarly, having the group committed to help each of its members can be an enormously constructive phenomenon. It will not happen by itself. There must be good leadership but I see it as absolutely critically important.

Power-seeking

There are those who have looked at me with disbelief, after working for ten years with some rough drug addicts from the streets of New York, when they have heard me recommend a particular prevention/treatment device for power-seeking drug abusers. I have recommended the scouting program, 4-H Clubs and the Camp Fire Girls. The reason for this is that these organizations have provided ways in which young people can feel important and realize they have made important achievements. The fact that they have been culturally out of touch with some segments of the society does not alter the importance of this central fact. A cadet program in the Minisink Settlement House in Central Harlem has offered a variation on this same program. I am convinced they have saved many youngsters from drug involvement because of the dazzling status they have legitimately achieved as cadets.

Aesthetic-seeking

This is perhaps one of the most difficult areas to address directly. Probably it only is a matter of special skill. Where an individual art, dance or music teacher has been able to encourage youngsters, the possibility of drug involvement simply evaporates. This tends not to be a routine aesthetic experience however. Rather, it is a passionate, committed, dedicated, disciplined schedule of work. The benefits come from the work itself as well as the final product. For many visionary young people this is the only subject which will successfully encourage them.

Sex companion-seeking

There has been much creative work done in the past ten years to meet the needs of adolescents in being clearer about their sexual identities. There are more and more trained group leaders who meet with youngsters in both single-sex and coed groups for the purpose of discussing physiology, including the variety of physical appearance, emotional development, including range of physical attractions and also values.

School programs have tended to be lamentably reticent about the question of values. It is not necessary to promote a particular point of view in order to discuss homosexuality, premarital sex, and promiscuity. Much could be said about the variety of life experiences involved in each of these dimensions of life. They can be discussed openly with benefit to everyone as can chastity and monogamy.

Young people across the nation have welcomed these new opportunities to be open with each other about their fears and hopes, their anger and their tenderness. Many in my generation wish we had been afforded similar opportunities to avoid the avoidable traps in the road of discovering our sexual identities.

Transcendence-seeking

Formal church programs are increasingly aware of the willingness, in many cases even the eagerness, of young people for distinctly spiritual experiences. No longer are ministers so shy about suggesting the possibility of young people praying together and worshiping together. In the '50's young people would attend chapel services as a "prize" for attending a dance. Today a whole new set of values prevails. Dating in the old (1950's and before) sense of the word is uncommon. Young people move much more freely as groups than they did then. Expression of sexual attraction is more relaxed and they, therefore, have more psychic energy for the more transcendent dimensions of life.

Besides the formal church institutions, many young people meet together informally or with only the least formal structure to satisfy this deep need. Adults in the community would do well to examine these movements with care. Some of them are enor-

mously idealistic, positive and should be given every opportunity
to blossom as they will. It is only rarely that they are characterized
by demonic leadership such as shocked the country in the person
of Charles Manson. Transcendent religious experience can be
positive and critically important for many young people who
would otherwise look for that experience in drug taking.

A NOTE ON RUNAWAYS

The runaway youngster has become a major national problem.
Some of them are very young indeed. It is possible that the impulse to run has come from anyone of the problems listed under
Causes. The probability is that there was a high interest in adventure. Another possibility is that conditions at home had become so psychologically turbulent that, in fact, the major impulse
would better be described as peace-seeking. These are two normally contradictory impulses. The greatest care should therefore be
taken to listen as is indicated in the material which follows.

Basic Principles for Action by Individuals in Small Agencies

Be aware of your own limits. If someone is seriously addicted
to heroin or barbiturates or is heavily habituated to the use of
amphetamines, it is usually necessary to offer massive help, more
help than one person can give. Well meaning teachers, clergymen
and even physicians have tried to help young people who were
headed pell-mell down the spiral of increasing drug abuse. This
note is not so much an abmonition not to try; rather it is a warning to be aware early when one reaches one's own limits. At that
time, it may be necessary to seek civil commitment, some sort of
hospitalization, or a therapeutic community rather than try to do
the whole job alone.

Consider the whole context of force operating on the youngster: home, school, friends, work, the variety of community pressures as well as the internal emotional forces. Anyone of them
may be the critical matter. There is a great danger in oversimpli-
fication, the tendency to see a single cause as the whole problem.

Most important is the need to listen carefully. In fact, many
young people want no more than that. They want to be seen for

the individuals they are, they want to be recognized as having their own special feelings and hopes. In many situations it is enough simply to hear them out carefully, get them to describe their own alternatives and encourage them to make their own choices.

Where it is not possible to achieve such a simple, rapid resolution of the problem the seven Causes might be considered, at least in the mind of the counselor, as a way of focusing on the problem. In most cases there will be a combination of two or more causes conspiring to lead the individual to take drugs. I think it is helpful to see the Causes as described above in basically a *positive* form. The counselor then becomes the ally of the individual youngster in seeking legitimate positive goals. He avoids becoming an enemy in the eyes of the young person, a meddler who simply wants to cut him off from the drugs which come to mean a great deal to him. This positive emphasis can be critically important.

As the 1970's run on there is a mood of exaggerated liberty in some circles of young people. Some of them have asked me, with tears in their eyes, if it is ever OK to say "No." This is the reverse of the old puritan ethic. Before, nice young people were expected to say "No" virtually all the time to drugs, sex and many other even milder matters. Now, there is a mood in the subculture which says one must always say "Yes." They feel, therefore, as if something is wrong with them if they want to say "No" to a new drug experience, a new sex experience, an illegal action or some other ill conceived adventure. Adult counselors need to be aware of this need and develop the skill and timing to be able, appropriately, to suggest that it is desirable, sometimes, to say "No."

A PLAN FOR WORKING IN SCHOOLS

The primary purpose of the program would be the achievement of a sense of control and cooperation shared by students, teachers and the administration. The main factor leading to drug abuse is the sense of helplessness and despair facing a young person. All the structure below is aimed at healing that sense of futality.

Student meetings

There would be groups for student leaders. These would include the most positive students, those who seem to be emotionally strong enough to lead others and persuade them of the value of creating the best possible school program.

There would be meetings with the fence sitters. Students who are neither leaders nor clearly into the drug using world need to have the support and encouragement of each other. They would be defined by the fact that they are not chronic truants or obviously using drugs nor are they the most promiment among class leadership.

Some attempt would be made at crisis intervention for the most negative of the student body. It is extremely difficult to plan and implement formal groups for this segment of the school population since they are so despairing that they tend not to come to group therapy sessions.

Teacher groups

There would be meetings for the teachers who are simply interested in better cooperation with the students. These would be relatively low-key meetings and cannot be called therapy per se.

There would also be more intensive types of meetings in which teachers would share their deepest feelings particularly as they relate to the work. Anxiety about their own middle-class background and values as they encounter ghetto culture is important to encourage.

Family-Student groups

The pattern of these meetings would be the combination of five students and such family members as could be persuaded to come. This multifamily therapy pattern has proven to be invaluable in reducing tensions for the partially intact family.

Student-Teacher groups

These groups would combine the most positive students and the teachers. They would deal with the difficulties having to do with leadership roles. The pressures can be tremendous and they need an appropriate arena for relief.

CONCLUSION

Every encouragement should be given to appropriate individuals seeking to work with young people who are seriously involved in abusing drugs. The one aspect of the work which I would like to emphasize in conclusion is this:

There is a primary need for adults to be as open and honest as they possibly can be in work of this sort. Cool, detached caricatures of the professional attitude is definitely counterproductive. Overheated, distorted involvement is no help either. In between, however, young people are seeking grownups who will meet them as fellow human beings with problems and satisfactions of their own as we work together to find real solutions for our struggles. There is no substitute for honest, open expression of concern.

SUGGESTED READING

Hardy, Richard E. and Cull, John G.: *Climbing Ghetto Walls*. Springfield, Charles C Thomas, 1973.

Hardy, Richard E. and Cull, John G.: *Drug Dependence and Rehabilitation Approaches*. Springfield, Charles C Thomas, 1973.

Vedder, C. B. and Somerville, D. B.: *The Delinquent Girl*. Springfield, Charles C Thomas, 1970.

CHAPTER 9

THE "HIPPIE" DRUG ABUSER

MELVIN COHEN

〰〰〰〰〰〰〰〰〰〰〰〰〰〰〰〰〰〰〰〰〰〰〰〰〰〰〰〰〰〰〰〰

- □ THE YOUTHFUL DRUG ABUSE SUBCULTURE
- □ POPULATIONS STUDIED
- □ DEGREE OF MULTIDRUG ABUSE
- □ THE FAMILY AND DRUGS
- □ TREATMENT OF MULTIDRUG ABUSER

〰〰〰〰〰〰〰〰〰〰〰〰〰〰〰〰〰〰〰〰〰〰〰〰〰〰〰〰〰〰〰〰

THE TITLE OF THIS CHAPTER IS, in several ways, a misnomer, for the lack of clarity of what is a "hippie" and for use of an outmoded term. The term "hippie" has been used and misused to describe diverse individuals at different times and at different places. Historically, as Hamburger[1] has indicated, the "hippie" movement began in the winter of 1963-64 in Greenwich Village in New York City and a few months later in the Haight-Ashbury section of San Francisco. The influx of new people into these areas continued for several years and reached its heights in the late 1960's. Then things began to change and those who were known as the "flower people" began to disappear. The "hippies" have now virtually disappeared from these areas and what is left of the "hippie" movement now exists primarily in communes and other scattered areas. But while

---

[1]E. Hamburger, Contrasting the hippie and junkie. *Int. J. Addictions.* Vol. 4 (1969), p. 121-135.

they were around, they made a large impact on our society, and were the forerunners of today's youthful drug culture.

"Hippies" were identified outwardly by their mode of dress, length of hair, and mode of residence. Inwardly, there was a self-identification with a deviant subculture and philosophy of life which advocated love and intimacy, the welfare of the group, and rejection of and alienation from the dominant culture of their parents. Another mark of identification was the acceptance of drugs as necessary to attain certain inner states and to expand one's consciousness.

There have been a number of studies which investigated the problem of who these "hippies" were, where they came from, their family background, educational status, and, more specifically, which drugs they used and why. In New York, Holmes and Holmes[2] investigated drug use and drug users in the major East coast "hippie" enclave, the East Village area. Briefly, the group identified as "hippies" (using the criteria of self-perceived alienation from society, self-identification, and life style—including dress, abode, and identification with the "drug scene") came from middle or upper class families, were high school or college dropouts, were politically "left," used a variety of drugs, and were sexually promiscuous.

Drug use was reported as primarily a peer group phenomenon. Initiation into drugs was through close friends. Attitudes about drugs came about from peer groups' opinions and not from parents, mass media, or other establishment institutions. Marijuana was the first drug used in most cases and was reported as being extremely pleasurable. Although fifteen percent of marijuana users and thirty-six percent of LSD users reported having bad trips, this was not a deterent for further use of drugs.

The "hippies" studied in the Haight-Ashbury area of San Francisco by Pittel, *et al*[3] were similar but more extreme. Whereas in the New York sample there were more native New Yorkers and

[2]D. Holmes and M. Holmes, Drug use in matched groups of hippies and non-hippies. Center for Community Research Final Report, (1971).

[3]S.M. Pittel, V. Calef, R.B. Gryler, L. Hilles, R. Hofer, P. Kempner, and R.S. Wallenstein. Developmental factors in adolescent drug use: a study of psychedelic drug users. *J Am Acad Child Psychiat*, 1970.

East Coast people who became involved in the "hippie" culture, in the San Francisco group the majority were people from different states and different areas of the country. There is evidence that they were also psychologicaly more pathological than the New York group. The primary drugs of abuse were marijuana, LSD, and amphetamines.

But, the "hippie scene" that previously existed is virtually gone. Without going into specific reasons for the rise and fall of the "hippie" culture, suffice it to say that talking about "hippies" in the original sense of the term is not applicable, nor necessary, when discussing drug abuse among today's youth. The adolescents and young adults of today may physically look like yesterday's "hippies" with their mode of dress and length of hair, but they do not necessarily share the common philosophy nor self-identification of the "hippies" and their use of drugs and reasons for drug use are also different.

Furthermore, drug use has become so widespread among today's adolescent and young adult population that it is parochial to discuss drugs among any one specific group. "Youthful drug abuse" is the name of today's game, regardless if it occurs among "hippies," or "straights," black or white, lower class, or upper class. It is those young people of *today* from their early teens to their mid-twenties, who comprise a counterculture and who abuse drugs, that will be the primary focus of the remainder of this chapter. But this is not to forget that the adult population still refers to today's drug-using, long-haired youth as "hippies," thereby giving this term a wider meaning than it originally had.

THE YOUTHFUL DRUG ABUSE SUBCULTURE

It has long been a historical fact in western culture that adolescence is the age of peer groups and the breaking away from parental influence. Friends begin to have greater influence over one's behavior and attitude than parents. Adolescents develop their own slang and "in-group" language as a means of declaring their independence. They adopt, or create, cultural phenomenon that are rejected by, or not a part of the adult culture—e.g. rock music, new dances, social causes, idol worship. They also want to understand

and to experience fully the world about them. It is a time of giving up the old for the new—new values and attitudes, new friends, new causes, new interests.

The peer group now becomes one's social reality. The adolescent "hangs around" with his friends. Certain physical locations become "hangouts"—pizza parlors, candy stores, suburban shopping centers, coffee shops. Two of the major areas of discussion are what to do and where to go. Part of this is related to the fact that our society does not actually provide much for adolescents to do or places to go. They hang around and become bored—they want to do something that will give them excitement and establish their own identity apart from the adult culture. What they do depends on what is "out there" in the physical world for them to select. If it is not "out there" in the first place, if it does not exist in the culture, then it would never be available to the youth subculture.

And so we come to drugs. Drugs exist in our culture—both "good" drugs and "bad" drugs. The "good" drugs are those which are considered as medically useful—cures for physical and mental illnesses. The "bad" drugs are those which are not sanctioned by the larger culture and which supposedly have a limited medical function. But the distinction between good and bad drugs becomes fuzzy because good drugs can be abused or used by people for other than medical reasons.

The original hippie cultists espoused the use of specific drugs, marijuana and LSD (and other hallucinogens), for making one more sensitive and aware—expanding one's senses. In a way, they introduced drugs into the youth subculture. They added a certain "glamour" to drugs which was not present before (except for the use of drugs like marijuana in certain groups—e.g. musicians and artists).

But many drugs were available even before the hippies glamourized them. They have been an accepted part of western culture for many years. Drugs were and are manufactured and marketed for all of one's ills, particularly as a regulator of emotions and emotional problems—barbiturates for sleep, amphetamines for fatigue, tranquilizers for anxiety, antidepressants for depression and so on and so forth. Adults were using them, doctors were prescribing them, and so they must be alright. The adult society's use of legal drugs, plus the hippie cult's glamourization of illicit drugs, (plus a host of factors unknown or too numerous to discuss) must be considered as having played a significant role in making drugs a part of today's youth culture.

But not all of our youth use drugs and a smaller number abuse them or use them illicitly. There have been numerous studies showing differing amounts of drug use reported by adolescents and young adults. Surveys of drug use among students and nonstudent populations, for example, range from 5 percent use to 80 percent use.[4] Most of those who use any drugs usually report using, or having used, marijuana. Smaller numbers report using hallucinogens, amphetamines, barbiturates, glue, etc. An extremely small number report having used heroin. One problem of investigation is to determine those variables which differentiate the drug users from the nondrug users.

Blum[5] has compared high school and college students who used both legal and illicit drugs with those students who never used any drugs. Nonusers of drugs tended to be the satisfied, close-to-family, moderate, religiously active, idealogically stable, and technologically oriented students. Those who were drug users tended to show less religious involvement, more political interest, in opposition to parents and conventional values. The greater degree of drug abuse, the more the students showed evidence of being "deviant," very dissatisfied with things in general, dropping out of school, and having considerable faith in drugs as tools to achieve a variety of personal and interpersonal purposes. The student drug users tended to use a variety of drugs rather than using only one drug. There was also a positive relationship between students and parent's use of drugs. The greater the parent's use of drugs, like barbiturates and amphetamines, the more likely their son (or daughter) would also use these drugs.

In a number of studies, involving middle-class high school and

---

[4] D.F. Berg, Illicit use of dangerous drugs in the United States. Bureau of Narcotics and Dangerous Drugs, United States Dept. of Justice, (1970).

[5] R. Blum, *Students and Drugs.* (San Francisco, Jossey-Bass, 1969).

college students in Vermont, Steffenhagen, and his colleagues,[6,7,8] found a positive relationship between drug use and emotional instability for rural and urban high school marijuana users. Among college students, there was a strong relationship between the degree of multiple drug use and pathology (as measured by the MMPI) and between the degree of social participation with drug users and frequency of marijuana smoking.

Freedman and Brotman,[9] studying a population of students in a private high school, report nonusers tended to come from intact homes to a greater degree than did drug users, and their homes were characterized as more close-knit. Identification and practice of religion were lower among the users than in the nonusers, and the users had a less favorable attitude toward school, fewer planning on going to college. All of the drug users had friends who also used drugs, whereas this was true for a little over 60 percent of nonusers of drugs.

These authors describe the process of initiation into drug use as facilitated by drugs being defined as desirable and by a widespread interest in the use (both legal and illegal) of mood-altering substances. The drugs which the students reported using were marijuana amphetamines, glue sniffing and some hallucinogens. The instrument of initiation into drug use was usually a close friend who was admired by the individual, and who has had prior drug experience himself. This latter point is extremely important, because it emphasizes the *social* factor in drug abuse, and has been reported over and over again in the literature. The youthful drug abuser is *not* an isolated or solitary person. Drug use is a social phenomenon —one must have contacts to obtain drugs and most drugs of abuse today are taken in the presence of others, as a group experience. Smoking pot is more fun when others are smoking with you, and

[6] R.A. Steffenhagen and P.J. Leahy, A study of drugs use patterns of high school students in the state of Vermont. (Report from the University of Vermont, 1969).

[7] C.P. McAree, R.A. Steffenhagen, and L.S. Zeutlin, Personality factors in college drug usage. (Report from the University of Vermont, 1969).

[8] R.A. Steffenhagen, C.P. McAree and L.S. Zeutlin, Some social factors in college drug usage. (Report from the University of Vermont, 1969).

[9] A.M. Freedman and R.E. Brotman, Multiple drug use among teenagers: plans for action-research. In *Drugs and Youth-Proceedings of the Rutgers Symposium on Drug Abuse.* (Springfield, Illinois, Charles C Thomas, 1969).

very few people take an "acid trip" alone.

Grinspoon[10] writes of the initiation to drugs of students on a campus where drugs are used. The student who enters into such a campus climate begins to experience pressure, sometimes subtle, sometimes overt, to try drugs, usually marijuana at first. Many of his campus friends use marijuana, and not to use it becomes deviant within this important peer group to the new student. He, or she, wants to be a part of the youth "scene"—the subculture in which marijuana use is an expected mode of behavior along with styles of music, dress, politics, sex, etc. This is related to the adolescent's strong need for belonging and is obviously not restricted only to the campus situation.

In an early study of drug abuse among young middle-class psychiatric patients,[11] we found that those who had a history of heavy involvement with illicit drugs differed from moderate users and nondrug using patients in that they were more intelligent, spent much time away or lived away from the parental home, were diagnosed as character disorders rather than psychotic and if female, were more sexually promiscuous. These findings suggest a specific adolescent and young adult subculture which encourages the use of drugs and promiscuous sexual activity.

In a study of eleven adolescent middle and upper-class psychiatric patients, ten of whom were multidrug users, Milman[12] found that those who had been treated and diagnosed prior to drug usage were all seen as having personality disorders. Following drug usage, all patients were diagnosed as having acute or chronic schizophrenia. These patients were characterized by chronic social disability, including failure to complete school, delinquency, and participation in a drug subculture.

Hensala, *et al*[13] compared twenty psychiatric patients using LSD

---

[10]L. Grinspoon, *Marijuana Reconsidered.* (Cambridge, Mass.: Harvard University Press, 1971).

[11]M. Cohen and D.F. Klein, Drug abuse in a young psychiatric population. *Amer J Orthopsychiat* Vol. 40 (1970), pp. 448-455.

[12]D. Milman, The role of marijuana in patterns of drug abuse by adolescents. *J Pediatrics,* Vol. 74 (1969), pp. 283-290.

[13]J. Hensala, L. Epstein, and L. Blacker, LSD and psychiatric inpatients. *Arch Gen Psychiat* Vol. 16 (1967), pp. 554-559.

with an age-matched control group of nondrug using patients, on various clinical and demographic factors. The LSD patients, hospitalized for several psychiatric disorders in which drug use was not a precipitating factor, were white, young (median age twenty-two), had histories of multidrug use, showed chaotic and sexual behavior, responded to intrafamilial conflict with antisocial and dyssocial behavior and had poorer work histories than control patients. The authors concluded that the clincal picture of the LSD-using patient is the same as that of habitual multidrug users.

In a study of twenty-three young male patients admitted to a psychiatric hospital as a result of LSD ingestion, Blumenfeld and Glickman[14] found that eighty-eight percent had used other drugs. Over seventy percent of the drug patients had previous psychiatric treatment, and the patient's difficulties antedated the use of drugs. Thus, drugs seem to have been the effect, not the cause, of the patient's psychiatric problems.

POPULATIONS STUDIED

Several of the studies reported and discussed in this paper are based on findings relating to "normal" populations of high school and/or college students, and others are based on findings relating to "deviant" populations of psychiatric patients. Many of the psychiatric patients studied may have at one time been considered a part of a school population and, conversely, subjects in the "normal" school population may some day become part of the psychiatric population. In terms of drug abuse, the patients may be seen as a population who used drugs as a way of coping with their psychological problems and either their psychological problems or drug use became too difficult for them to handle, and they required hospitalization. The "normal" drug users may be those who are able to more adequately handle their problems and/or their use of drugs. Shearn and Fitzgibbons[15] compared the drug use patterns of a group of young psychiatric inpatients with those of college and uni-

---

[14]M. Blumenfeld, and L. Glickman. Ten months experience with LSD users admitted to county psychiatric receiving hospital. *New York State J Med* Vol. 67 (1967), 1849-1853.

[15]C.R. Shearn and D.J. Fitzgibbons, Patterns of drug use in a population of youthful psychiatric patients. *Amer J Psychiat* Vol. 128 (1972), pp. 65-71.

versity students and found the patients showed a much greater involvement with drugs, both in number of drugs used and frequency and length of use.

These authors consider the hypothesis that drug use is for the adolescent and young adult, "a readily available technique for attempting to cope with life difficulties, and intrapsychic stress. Rather than proving to be an effective way to coping, however, the use of drugs, because of their effects on the physiology of the body and because they place the user in a deviant position with regard to social standards, adds further stress to an already overstressed organism. At some point a professional observer decides that the person is in sufficient distress to require hospitalization."

Along with the increase in the use of habituating and addictive drugs—amphetamines, barbiturates, LSD, marijuana, etc.—among middle-class adolescents and young adults, there has been an increase in psychiatric hospitalization of young patients with a history of drug abuse. At Hillside Hospital, a private, voluntary psychiatric institution in New York City, we have found that the percent of admissions under twenty-five years of age who had a history of drug abuse was five percent in 1960, thirty-one percent in 1967, and sixty percent in 1969-1971. Most of the drug users had used a variety of drugs, and were high school and college dropouts.

THE DRUGS

Let us now examine more closely which drugs are being used and/or abused in the youth culture. Without a doubt, the most widely used drug is marijuana. It is probably the only drug that is used by over ninety percent of all multidrug users. Although marijuana is the drug of initiation for most individuals, glue, amphetamines, and barbiturates have also been reported as drugs of initiation. When age is considered as a factor, there is a higher incidence of glue sniffing reported as the first drug used by those who started drug use at an early age (eleven to fifteen years of age). After a certain age, about sixteen to seventeen, virtually no one first "turns on" with glue.

In a survey of 117 hospitalized drug users, we found one hundred percent of the males and ninety-seven percent of the females had used marijuana. It was the first drug used by the majority of patients, males starting to use marijuana at an average of $17\frac{1}{2}$ years of age and females at an average of $16\frac{1}{2}$ years of age.

The use of marijuana was followed closely by the use of amphetamines, seventy-nine percent of males and eighty-five percent of females using this drug. In terms of percent of use, hallucinogens were third, eighty-four percent of the males and fifty-five percent of the females having used some form of hallucinogen (LSD, STP, DMT, peyote, mescaline, etc.). For barbiturates, sixty-one percent of the males and forty-six percent of the females reported using this drug. Thirty-four percent of the males and twenty-two percent of the females used heroin at least one or more times. Glue sniffing was reported by less than twenty percent of each group and only by the younger patients.

Many of those who report amphetamines as their first drug of abuse, started by using their drug for "legitimate" purposes, such as weight reduction or staying up to study for an examination. They find the drug has pleasurable features other than for the reasons originally taken. Barbiturates may have been started also for 'legitimate" reasons, such as to induce sleep, and then continued for the psychological relaxation and "drunkenness" feeling it provides.

When asked directly about reasons for initiation into drug use, subjects report a variety of reasons, the predominant ones being curiosity and peer group pressure. Reasons for continuing to use drugs vary from group pressure to enjoyment of "getting high," to acknowledgement of the pharmacological properties of the drugs. For example, in our work with young multidrug abusers in a psychiatric hospital, patients were asked the reasons they had used particular drugs. The primary reason given for marijuana was to "get high." Those who also used amphetamines report using this drug either to relieve depression or to work and/or study better. Patients who had used barbiturates gave as a primary reason the drug's actions as a relaxant. Hallucinogenic users reported curiosity and "getting high" as the main reasons for using a variety of hallucinogenics. Those patients who also used heroin reported several reasons, the major ones being "getting high," relieving tension and stress, and relaxing.

An important fact to consider is that over ninety percent of these subjects used at least two different types of drugs and about eighty percent used at least three different types of drugs. The subjects were clearly multidrug users. An extremely small number of these subjects had fixated on only one type of drug (e.g. barbiturates, amphetamines, marijuana). This is not to say that using marijuana, for example, leads to the use of other drugs—but that it is the most widely used drug among those who use a variety of drugs.

Similar findings were reported by Shearn and Fitzgibbons,[15] also using a population of young psychiatrically hospitalized drug abusers. Most subjects tended to be multidrug users, seventy-three percent having used marijuana, sixty-two percent amphetamines, and fifty-two percent hallucinogens, plus other drugs (twenty-six percent of all subjects tested did not use *any* drugs). These authors also reported that using any drug before the age of fifteen accurately predicts future serious drug involvement (i.e. the eventual use of barbiturates and narcotics).

In our study of age of onset of drug abuse among psychiatric patients,[16] drug abuse is related to future drug use differentially for males and females. For males, the earlier the onset of drug use (ages twelve to fourteen), the greater the likelihood of becoming heavily involved with a variety of drugs, *excepting* heroin. Males who start using drugs *after* age fourteen tend to become involved with heroin use. For females, the earlier the age of onset of drug use, the more likely they are to become involved in all drugs, including heroin.

Furthermore, from reviewing patients' histories, one gets the impression that among the older drug users (eighteen years of age and older), both male and female, there was a tendency towards a "mod" or "hippie" style in which drugs might possibly have a more philosophical or value-related role. For the younger patients (ages twelve to fourteen), particularly the younger females, drug use does not seem to be related with a bohemian or "hippie" style of life, but appears to be peer-group oriented, antisocial or acting-out behavior. The older drug users started their drug use primarily away from home, usually at college, whereas the younger ones started and continued drug use primarily while living at home.

---

[15]*Ibid.*

[16]M. Cohen and D.F. Klein. Age of onset of drug abuse in psychiatric inpatients. *Arch. Gen. Psychiat.* Vol. 26 (1972), pp. 266-269.

DEGREE OF MULTIDRUG ABUSE

In our initial study of drug use among young, middle-class psychiatric patients[17] we found patients who had a history of heavy involvement with illicit drugs differed from moderate users and non-drug using patients in that they were more intelligent, spent much time away, or lived away, from the parental home, were diagnosed as character disorders rather than psychotic, and, if female, were more sexually promiscuous. These findings suggested a specific adolescent and young adult subculture which encourages the use of drugs and promiscuous sexual activity.

The classification of drug use by degree of involvement with drugs has important implications. Many studies have "lumped together" as drug abusers those who have used drugs only one time with those who are chronic and habitual users. This type of breakdown gives you two groups—those who have *never* used illicit drugs and those who have used them at least once. A subject would go from one group (nonuser) to the other group (user) by merely puffing on one marijuana cigarette or taking one amphetamine tablet.

Although you would probably find significant differences between the two groups mentioned above, the differences would be important more in terms of defining and/or describing the non-drug user than the drug user. In such a breakdown, no use versus any use, we would probably find the nonusers to be a distinct group and the users to be a pretty "mixed bag" of people.

Rather, it is more important and meaningful in studying youthful drug abusers, to distinguish between different levels *within* the drug abuse category. Someone who used marijuana and amphetamines once a month for a year should not be considered the same as someone who used these drugs several times a week for over three years. Involvement with drugs and the drug culture is quite different for both. And the potential outcome or result of drug abuse is also quite different for both.

Severity of drug use, as a concept, is multidimensional, and may be interpreted in many ways. For example, among psychiatric pa-

---

[17]M. Cohen and D.F. Klein, Drug abuse in a yocng psychiatric population. *Amer J Orthopsychiat* Vol. 40 (1970), pp. 445-448.

tients it may be interpreted as indicating a poor prognosis, a negative reaction to psychiatric treatment, producing deleterious psychiatric effects, etc. The definition of severity we have worked with is not concerned with psychiatric effects or treatment *per se,* but rather with drug use as an indicator of an individual's degree of rejection of social roles and willingness to engage in dangerously illegal practices, as well as the possibility of habituation or dependence on a drug or drugs. A regular user of heroin should be considered a *severe* drug user not only because he is likely to become addicted to the drug, but because he is also likely to get arrested. A person using marijuana regularly is not as likely to get arrested and runs a lower risk of physiological and/or psychological dependence.

At Hillside Hospital, we have developed a scoring method for determining severity of drug abuse among patients.[18] The method takes into account the *number* of drugs used, the *frequency* of drug use, and the overall *length* of time each drug was used. According to their scores, patients were placed in one of four groups—nonusers, mild, moderate, or heavy users. These groups were then studied to see what happens to them six months after they left the hospital.

Controlling for variables such as diagnosis and sex, we found that those patients who were nonusers or mild and moderate drug users prior to hospitalization did fairly well after a period (average of six to seven months) of psychiatric hospitalization. They were working, going to school, and using drugs minimally. However, those patients who had been rated as heavy drug abusers prior to hospitalization, did very poorly after a similar period of hospitalization. Most of them went back to heavy drug use, and were not working or going to school. This was true regardless of their behavior in the hospital. They might have been considered as good patients in the hospital, but after they were discharged they again became heavily involved with drugs. Thus, a rating of heavy drug abuse yields a negative prognosis, whereas a rating of mild or moderate drug abuse has a good prognosis. One problem which has yet to be solved is which variables differentiate those indivduals who are mild or moderate drug abusers and whose drug use never progresses

---

[18]M. Cohen and D.F. Klein, A measure of severity of multidrug use. *Int J Pharmacopsychiatry,* in press. (1972).

beyond that point from those mild and moderate drug abusers who eventually progress to heavy drug use.

Drug users have also been categorized as "tasters," "experimenters," and "heads," roughly comparable to the mild, moderate, and heavy drug abuse breakdown. The "tasters" are those who try several drugs one or two times just to satisfy their curiosity. The "experimenters" are those who use drugs as a way of modifying their emotional and intellectual states and are willing to try anything, but usually do not get that involved to become psychologically or physically addicted to these drugs. The "heads" are those who become dependent on drugs (or on a particular drug), and must use them constantly. It is possible to become psychologically and/or physically addicted to amphetamines, barbiturates, opiates (narcotics etc.), and several others. The question of addiction or habituation to marijuana and the hallucinogens is still debatable, but the inclination is towards psychological habituation to these drugs.

THE FAMILY AND DRUGS

Another variable studied in relation to adolescent drug abuse is parental use of drugs. Smart and Fejet[19] have studied this problem and found a positive association between parental use of psychoactive drugs (amphetamines, barbiturates, tranquilizers, etc.), as reported by students, and students' own use of marijuana, LSD and psychoactive drugs. The authors suggest that adolescents modeled their drug use after parental use and one way to reducing adolescent use would be to reduce parental use of drugs.

The role of the family has been implicated in other ways. Wilmer[20] indicates there was serious discord in the families of the drug abusers he studied. Parents tended to reject their children or give them "contingent love." The children perceived this as sham and, during adolescence, they rejected the moral and ethical values of their parents. Their behavior and values became antithetical to those of their parents, drug abuse being one of the outcomes.

[19]R.G. Smart and D. Fejet, Drug use among adolescents and their parents: closing the generation gap in mood modifications. *J. Abn. Psychol.* Vol. 79 (1972), pp. 153-160.

[20]H. Wilmer, Drugs, hippies and doctors. *JAMA.* Vol. 206 (1968), pp. 1272-1275.

In our own research on psychiatric patients, we compared the self-reported social values of drug users with a nondrug using control sample.[21] The subjects were all from middle-class backgrounds, and it was hypothesized that the drug users would be more rejecting than the controls of traditional middle-class values represented by their parents. The results showed that the drug users tended to reject the values of family, religion, moderation, discipline, and work, but they were not more rejecting than the nondrug users of other societal values such as education, money, marriage, and a secure job. What they may have been rejecting was the Protestant ethic of hard work, restraint, and discipline; however, they were not rejecting ways of "making it" in society, such as education, money, and job security.

TREATMENT OF THE MULTIDRUG ABUSER

The treatment of the youthful multidrug abuser is far from solved. Currently, there are more methods and programs dealing with the heroin addict than with the nonaddicted multidrug abuser. For the heroin addict there are three basic types of programs—methadone maintenance, detoxification, and drug free social programs based on the Phoenix House-Daytop therapeutic community concept. The methadone maintenance and detoxification programs are primarily for narcotic addicts and could not be applied to a nonaddict population. Thus, most current programs aimed at treating the youthful multidrug user have been either traditional psychiatric care involving inpatient hospitalization or outpatient therapy, or drug free social programs similar to those for narcotic addicts.

The effectiveness of any of these treatment modalities have not yet been proven, primarily because efforts at evaluation have been minimal. We do have evidence, however, of the relative ineffectiveness of traditional phychiatric hospitalization in the treatment of heavy drug abusers. As stated previously in this paper, we have found that those who were heavy drug abusers prior to hospitalization do very poorly after they leave the hospital and re-enter

[21]M. Cohen and D.F. Klein, Social Values and drug use among psychiatric patients. *Amer J Psychiat* Vol. 128 (1972), pp. 131-133.

the community. They return to heavy drug abuse and show a general decline in overall psychological functioning. Their work and/or school progress is minimal. It is obvious the psychiatric care they received, which has been reported as quite beneficial to nondrug and mild and moderate drug abuse patients, was not sufficient nor effective in helping the heavy multidrug abuser reverse a downward trend.

The drug free social programs use confrontation group techniques, peer group pressure, role-playing techniques, etc., to treat the heavy multidrug abuser. Some of these programs are day programs and the client otherwise lives at home except for the time he spends in the program. Other drug free social programs are residential, in that the client actually lives at a treatment facility for a period of time. The major critique of the drug free social programs is that clients stay in treatment for long periods of time (one to three years) and become too dependent upon the treatment facility. However, the effectiveness or ineffectiveness of these programs have yet to be properly evaluated.

CHAPTER 10

A THERAPEUTIC APPROACH TO THE REHABILITATION OF THE YOUTHFUL DRUG ABUSER THE SEED

JOHN G. CULL AND RICHARD E. HARDY

- ☐ APPLICATION CRITERIA
- ☐ BACKGROUND OF THE PROGRAM PARTICIPANTS
- ☐ SERVICE DELIVERY SYSTEM
- ☐ STAFFING AND TRAINING
- ☐ IMPACT AND RESULTS
- ☐ SUMMARY

APPROXIMATELY TWO YEARS AGO, the SEED was founded in Fort Lauderdale, Florida, by Art and Shelly Barker. The basic design of the program is the general treatment model developed by Alcoholics Anonymous; however, there are several modalities which are peculiar to the SEED. The description which follows is basically an outline of the goals and methods of the program; however, certain intangibles which are difficult to describe exist in the program.

The SEED was developed because of a desperate need for help which existed for young people in the Fort Lauderdale area as a result of the heightened incidence of drug abuse. It was felt that new approaches to the problem were needed; therefore, the SEED concept evolved. The SEED program's concept was based on the premise that man can change his behavior and can live and cope in his environment. The young people who seek help from the SEED program learn that they can no longer *cop out* with drugs; but that they have daily problems and must learn to live with them. At the SEED, they obtain a sense of belonging to something meaningful along with the knowledge that they can find purpose in their lives with the extra ingredient—a sense of dedication toward helping themselves and helping others to help themselves. The primary function of the SEED program is to provide rehabilitative services for the young person who has become a drug experimenter, user, abuser, or addict.

APPLICATION CRITERIA

The SEED is made available to anyone needing help. The addict who must have some sort of maintenance—such as Methadone—to assist him in achieving detoxification will not be accepted by the SEED until such time as he is able to tolerate a truly *cold turkey* program of abstinence. Since its main program is not detoxification, the aim is to work with the experimenter, user, abuser, or addict who has used drugs less than ten years. Because of the age range—nine years to early twenties—parental consent of the majority of applicants is needed.

Anyone seeking help from the SEED and is in need of detoxification treatment is referred to the appropriate facilities. Those applicants who are in need of medical attention are referred to appropriate hospitals and/or their private physicians. These young people then come back to the SEED program once they are considered to be in sound medical health. Other than these selected criteria, the SEED makes no distinction concerning participation in the program.

Physical discomfort of *withdrawal* is at a minimum among participants. Even those young people who have used heroin for two or more years and have $200-a-day habits (this is equivalent to $60 to $65 in New York) take only approximately three days to pass through the withdrawal symptoms.

BACKGROUND OF THE PROGRAM PARTICIPANTS

A unique factor of the SEED program is that it reaches into the schools. In this community, estimates show that between seventy and eighty-five percent of the children are experimenting with, using, or abusing drugs. The SEED has been successful in reaching young people through referrals made by principals, teachers, and counselors of the various schools in Broward County. The apparent change in students using drugs such as the decline of grades, failures, and dropouts, along with attitude change has added to the frustration and dilemma of educators. Due to the referrals made by educators to the SEED program, the majority of the young people destined to become delinquents and burdens on society have been able to continue in school education and to aid teachers in understanding the drug problems of the young. The young abuser is of considerable help in helping other drug abusers since he understands not only the values but also the language of the drug culture (Hardy and Cull, 1972).

Many young people, no matter how well they progress, have environmental backgrounds which are quite impossible for them in terms of adjustment. If there is no reinforcement from the family, the young person will meet constantly with disappointment and discouragement. For those young people in this particular situation, the SEED has been able to assist with the cooperation of either the courts and/or various agencies (vocational rehabilitation, family services, etc.) in obtaining foster homes and has been successful in continuing to work with them in their new environments.

SERVICE DELIVERY SYSTEM

The first phase of the SEED's program consists, in most cases, of a two-week program of intensive group discussions but is expandable when needed. During this two-week period, the group discussion sessions average approximately twelve hours per day. In these sessions, the participant is aided in gaining insight into what he is and what he has done to his life by taking drugs; but more importantly, he learns what his life can be for him and the impact he can have on others if he is *straight*. These two weeks represent the equivalent in time of the participant's going to a psychologist and/or psychiatrist for a period of three years on a one-hour, once-a-week basis. The fourteen day intensive group sessions provide a radical and comprehensive change which facilitates the learning process of the participant. The SEED is operated on a continuous seven-day week basis. The participant in this fourteen day program is at the SEED from 10 a.m. to 10 p.m., during which time he is involved constantly in *rap* sessions under the supervision of staff. These rap sessions are carefully guided and the intensity is maintained at a controlled, effective level. When necessary for certain individual needs, *rap* sessions also are held on a one-to-one basis with a staff member.

Upon successful completion of this first phase, an additional three-month period ensues which requires the participant to attend four group sessions a week. This phase of the program offers practical application of his learning processes. He learns to function and coe in his environment while returning to the group involvement. The criteria of success of this program are based not only on the fact that the young person is drug free, but also on his attitude change toward life; that is, there is a love of self and others, community and country, and a sense of dedication to help his fellow man.

Due to the age of participants, they can adjust well to change. The amount of attitude change in the individual seems to indicate that the three-month period is quite effective. In some instances, individuals require either an extension of the two-week period or an extension of the three-month program. Periodic follow-up is done to see how the participants are doing.

If the participants learns well and grasps the meaning of honesty, love, respect, discipline, and affection, there is no need for him to go back to drugs. For the young people who are found to have deep-rooted psychological, or serious physical problems, the SEED makes referrals to medical doctors, psychologists, and/or other community programs. This is true particularly during the individual's participation in the two-week intensive program.

Up until his introduction to the SEED, the *druggie's* best, most reliable friend has been the lie that he speaks and lives in order to mislead his parents and his teachers. This same lie directed to a staff member at the SEED is guaranteed to trigger a *choicely worded* verbal barrage not soon to be forgotten. Why? Because the staff member is a former *druggie* himself and can *smell* a lie that you or I would accept as fact!

Because it is tough to lose an old friend—and the lie has been his *best* friend—it must be replaced with something of at least equal value. This is where the SEED asserts its true strength and individuality. Just after the above-described verbal barrage, the staff member will close the one-on-one session by saying to the thoroughly deflated recreant, "I love you." No one who has heard this shopworn phrase as it is spoken at the SEED can fail to be deeply moved by the sincerity and purpose behind its use. The reinforcing effect of true concern (love) is quite awesome.

The success of the SEED program also depends largely on family participation. The families are encouraged to attend two meetings a week to participate with the young people. Through this participation, the parents can get an overall picture of what the SEED is about and can see the gradual improvement of not only their own children but also those of other parents. They also can acquaint themselves with these other parents.

The group participation of parents and children, particularly those parents who are deeply involved with the program, has produced remarkable results in that the family unit is brought closer together and gains a better understanding of the dynamics of its problem. Also, with the family, it has been observed that a greater level of love and compassion evolves within the family.

Fundamental to the continuing success of the SEED's program —especially during the period immediately following the two-week initial phase—is a highly effective intelligence network put together by Art Barker which is composed of ex-druggies, teachers, police and concerned friends. If an apparently rehabilitated participant is seen even talking with an unreconstructed acquaintance, Art knows about it in a matter of minutes and is able to get to the offender for further therapy before recidivism sets in.

STAFFING AND TRAINING

The SEED has been able to train group leaders and help them develop talents of leadership. It also has been successful in encouraging these group leaders to continue more intensively in all endeavors to help combat the drug problem in the Fort Lauderdale area.

The SEED is strictly a paraprofessional organization with its group leaders and staff coming from the program. Because of its uniqueness, the quality of staffing can be maintained only on this basis. Art Baker is responsible for the overall operation of the program and for seeing that the outline and guidelines which have been developed are followed and the objectives fulfilled. He is also responsible for seeing that the other personnel maintain a high level of proficiency in meeting their obligations and fulfilling job requirements. Additionally, he is a liaison officer with other agencies in the community to effect cooperation and coordinate efforts that benefit the community maximally without duplicating existing services.

There are four senior group leaders whose responsibility it is to maintain group supervision when groups are in session. They assist in training new group leaders and junior group leaders. The junior group leaders are individuals who have gained some insight into the working of the SEED program, but as yet have not developed the maturity or had experience which would prepare them to take a major responsibility for the conduct of either the initial intensive group sessions or the latter therapeutic group sessions. As they gain responsibility, they move on to being senior group leaders and assume a role of deeper responsibility. The staff of the SEED program, twenty-five paid and fifteen volunteers, can effectively handle the approximately three hundred active participants in the program.

IMPACT AND RESULTS

The SEED has had a demonstrable impact in the Fort Lauderdale area. Its program has reached into the courts, the jails, the minority ghetto areas, and the schools of Broward County. The Broward County Personnel Association officially has adopted the SEED as its 1971 drug project and is assisting in obtaining employment for the successful young people while in, as well as when leaving the SEED program. The district supervisor of the Florida Parole and Probation Office and his staff have been playing a vital role in the rehabilitation of these people during and after their participation in the SEED program. The SEED also uses resources such as Broward General Hospital, Henderson Clinic, Family Services, Community Services, Vocational Rehabilitation, and adult education on an emergency and a referral basis. The SEED recently became a member of the Cooperative Area Manpower Planning System (CAMPS) which is sponsored by the local city governments of Fort Lauderdale and Broward County. CAMPS is attempting to create a force of local agencies to effectively coordinate and cooperate in employment-developing opportunities. One role of the SEED is that of rehabilitating young people to enable them to become employable and constructive members of society and their community; therefore, involvement with these other social action agencies is essential.

It is interesting that the professionals who visit the SEED to observe the program seem to elevate different factors to prominence. One man might be struck by the obvious affection which permeates relationships between staff and participants; another by the sense of discipline displayed; and a third by the basic honesty of the program.

We feel the most effective factor influencing the youthful drug abuser at the SEED is peer pressure. The youthful ex-drugee is a potent influence in exerting conformity behavior. Cull (1971) has shown that peer pressure is influencial even among schizophrenics who have rejected interaction with the social world in a manner somewhat similar to the members of the drug culture. Social roles are changing rapidly. No longer do the elders in our culture exert the impact on behavior and judgments they did in the past (Cull, 1970); consequently, the SEED has turned to the group which can exert sufficient social pressure to change behavior—the youthful "ex-drugees."

The drug dependence problem is one of the most pressing in the country, and Broward County is no exception. This is evidenced primarily by arrests, particularly of the youth between ages thirteen and twenty. The SEED's records substantiate this age span and document the fact that many youths start on drugs at an early age and advance from marijuana to hard narcotics within one year. In an effort to combat the drug problem, the SEED was founded approximately two years ago. The basic model for the program is the general treatment program developed by Alcoholics Anonymous, with some very important modifications.

The counselors or staff members are rehabilitated drug offenders. After having gone through the program themselves, they have been judged to have the necessary skills and motivations to assist in helping others. These skills consist basically of the ability to develop an empathic relationship with others, the presence of strong desires and a dedication to help others and themselves, and finally, the ability to become skillful and successful group leaders.

The group sessions may be categorized loosely with the more formal Guided Group Interaction and Transactional Analysis type groups. In the sessions of the SEED, both formal and informal group pressures are brought to bear upon the individual members by other members and leaders. As may be expected, it takes a very skillful leader to know when and how to apply pressure to any particular member or any particular segment of the group. This leader also must know how to channel the group's pressures to effective and fruitful endeavors. The group leaders are extremely adept at reading the character of each member and then applying or halting the pressures. Having once been drug offenders themselves, they are able to pierce the protective shell which each drug offender throws about himself. The group leaders refuse to fall into the verbal and the cognitive traps which the drug offender erects. In the language of *Transactional Analysis,* the leaders see the games drug abusers may be playing and refuse to play them.

They then point out to the individual how false ideas have led him to his present state of affairs.

The atmosphere where this guided group interaction takes place contains simply *affection, empathy, discipline,* and *love.* This *love* is a powerful tool in the hands of skilled leaders. In social power terms, the leader has been endowed referent power by the other members of the group. While at no time will he deny any group member, he does, however, skillfully manage the application of power. He uses his power to maintain motivation by reassuring those members who may have just received the brunt of a group session.

The above-described atmosphere of love has been coupled with the skillful handling of guided group interactions to form the SEED's unique and highly successful program. A new member attends two full weeks of twelve-hour sessions. If he has not made adequate progress, he may continue for two more weeks. Once a member has shown that he is responding, he is then allowed to return home. Prior to this he has stayed in the home of another participant and has gone to school or work from that home. After finishing this period, he returns to SEED for further group sessions every night for three hours and all day Saturday. This process lasts for three months. The member is then *straight* and attends only once or twice a week from then on.

During the day, there are two separate groups—one for males, the other for females. Particular problems are discussed and solutions found. In the evening, there is a general session which every member attends. The staff members take turns leading the discussion and help each other whenever necessary. Twice a week there is an open session in which parents, friends, teachers, probation and parole officers, and concerned others participate. At the open meetings, there are usually about 250 members and up to four hundred visitors.

An essential element in the success of the SEED is the amount of community participation and aid. Referrals to the SEED program come through many channels. Some are self-referrals, others come because of parental or peer pressure. The various courts are probating individuals to the SEED and sometimes send an individual to it for a pre-sentence diagnostic type study. Many individuals, of course, come because of the attention of concerned adults such as relatives, teachers and police officials. The SEED, because of its unique method and unequaled success ration (now claimed to be over ninety percent), has managed to gather full community support.

SUMMARY

In summary, the SEED is an organization of former drug offenders who are dedicated to helping others. Its president, Art Baker, is a truly rare individual who has somehow combined great skill and genuine concern to the ability to teach and treat drug offenders. Its program of guided group interaction, honesty, concern, and understanding seems to have meshed into a workable method. The testimory of parents, doctors, friends, teachers, prison officials, members of school boards, and others all point to the fact that the SEED is a viable, dynamic program.

REFERENCES

Berne, Eric.: *Transactional Analysis in Psychotherapy.* (New York, Grove Press, 1961).

Cull, J. G.: Age as a factor in achieving conformity behavior, *Journal of Industrial Gerontology.* (Spring, 1970).

Cull, J. G.: Conformity behavior in schizophrenics, *Journal of Social Psychology,* 117, (July 1971).

Hardy, R. E. and Cull, J. G.: Language of the drug abuser. In Hardy, R. E. Cull, J. G.: *Drug Dependence and Rehabilitation.* (Springfield, Thomas, 1972).

Urbanik, Richard: Report on the SEED: a working drug treatment program in Fort Lauderdale, Florida, Department of Correction, State of North Carolina, (1971) (unpublished).

CHAPTER 11

CASE STUDIES OF YOUTHFUL DELINQUENTS

Compiled by

John G. Cull and Richard E. Hardy

J. A. S.

White—Female—eighteen

Single

High School Graduate

Drug abuse characterized by an inability to adjust vocationally and socially.

Referral Source:

Miss S. was referred to the Department of Vocational Rehabilitation by Dr. B. of the Adolescent Clinic City Hospital. She is presently being followed at the Adolescent Clinc for adjustment reaction to adolescence, characterized by drug abuse. She has been in the methadone program and has received guidance and counseling.

Social Data:

Miss S. is an eighteen-year-old white female. Her family background is less than ideal. Her parents have recently divorced, and since then she has been on her own a great deal. Her father is an alcoholic now living out of this state. She is the youngest of three children all of whom have experienced problems in living. She feels that her mother is not very concerned about her actions and cares very little about her. She and her mother argue almost constantly.

Miss S. was arrested for drug abuse. She was caught using heroin. She is presently out on bond and has been referred for a physical examination and evaluation of her drug dependence before she goes to court. She was placed on probation with the stipulation that she enter a drug treatment program. Before the arrest, she had used heroin regularly for the past six months. She has used a variety of drugs including cocaine, marijuana, LSD, heroin. She had been exposed to hepatitis two weeks before her arrest. One of the boys she and her friend were sharing their "works" unit with had hepatitis. In spite of all her troubles, she did manage to graduate from high school by going in the summer.

Medical Data:

Miss S. was seen by a clinic physician for a general examination and for determination of a physical addiction. She states that she feels fine with no physical complaints. She has been exposed to hepatitis through the use of a friend's dirty needle. 10 cc. of gamma globulin were given as a prophylaxis. Her general appearance is that of a thin, healthy, adolescent female.

General Physical Examination:

HEIGHT   64 inches   WEIGHT   117½
VISION   normal
SKIN—Color   normal   PALLOR   no
   ERUPTIONS   mild   ICTERUS   no
EYES   Normal
NOSE—OBSTRUCTION   no   SINUS TENDERNESS   no
MOUTH AND THROAT   ORAL HYGIENE   poor
                                 GUMS—Caries present
                  TONSILS   normal
LYMPH GLANDS   normal
THORAX   normal
LUNGS   clear to auscultation
HEARING   o.k.
EPISTAXIS   no
HAY FEVER   no
TOOTHACHE   no
CHEST PAIN   no
COUGH   mild
APPETITE   fair
ABDOMINAL PAIN   no
DYSURIA   no
B.P.   120/70
HEART RSP   normal

ABSOMEN   soft
GENITALIA—stage of development—stage V
NEUROLOGICAL   gait—good   pilonidal sinus—normal
                            strength—good   coordination—good
                            balance—good   reflexes—normal
FEET   normal
FEMININITY
PERSONALITY TRAITS   tense   restless

Positive findings revealed needle scars on both arms. It was the opinion of this physician that she is physically addicted, needs psychiatric referral and at some time gama globulin as a prophylaxis for possible hepititis. The physical impression is that of a young, healthy female with the exception of needle marks. It is also recommended that she be placed in the Methadone program.

Educational Data:

Miss S. has not done well in school, especially in high school. Her grades were below average—D's and F's; however, she did manage to graduate from high school by attending summer school to make up for credits lost during the regular year. A transcript of her high school performance indicated that Miss S. was not involved in any extracurricular activities.

Psychological Data:

Upon completion of the medical, Miss S. was referred to the Guidance Clinic for psychiatric therapy. A battery of tests consisting of the Wechsler Adult Intelligence Scale, Bender-Visual-Motor Gestalt Test, Wide Range Achievement Test-Reading Section, Tree-Person Drawing, and the Rorschach Test were given.

Miss S. is a thin, brown haired, brown eyed girl who was pleasant and responsive and who had a tendency to talk in a dunning fashion and to play with her rather greasy, straight hair. She presented a rather dull, uninteresting physical appearance in that she was dressed somewhat sloppily in brown, short culottes, a short brown suede jacket and loafers. However, upon closer inspection, she was actually a rather pretty girl with pretty eyes and a pleasant smile which seemed all too infrequent. Miss S. sat sprawled in her chair and seemed unaware of her bare thighs being exposed, yet she was overly anxious to keep her chest covered up with her jacket; she almost seemed to make a "thing" out of keeping her jacket closed. She appeared to enjoy the testing, and as time went on became more comfortable and was able to laugh; at such times her eyes sparkled and she was a very attractive girl. She talked at length about wanting to leave her mother and go out on her own but at the same time feeling guilty since she was the last child.

She thinks her father is a "nice guy" but does not like living with him. She snickered and became evasive while talking about her father; and gave the impression that there is far more involved here than meets the eye. She spoke of her feelings of depression, her having been caught and her sexual experiences with various boys in a curiously detached, depersonalized way. She rationalized having been caught as "the vice squad is corrupt," and that "this city is too big and unfeeling." She considers the people where her father lives as being "warm," friendly, loving and judging people for their "inner self." She further says that people who take drugs because of nothing better to do are much like her.

Miss S. is able to function on the bright normal level of general intelligence according to her full scale I.Q. of 117; her verbal score of 114 and her performance scale of 122. She has difficulty in those areas which require concentration and synthetic ability on visual-motor tasks; her concentration has a tendency to come and go with the results that the quality of her performance fluctuates. On the other hand, she was able to demonstrate superior social comprehension and judgment in a hypothetical situation. Her "gifted" score on the subtest which involved attention to environmental essentials suggest that she is overly concerned with things rather than people. Other areas tested generally fell in the bright normal range. Certainly this is a very bright girl whose intellectual functioning tends to be somewhat erratic because her intellectual energies are being dissipated by emotional concerns. Miss S. is presently reading on the 10.2 grade level, which gives her a standard score of 103 and places her in the fifty-eighth percentile for one of her age group. This is considerably below her level of intellectual functioning and is an example of her problem with utilizing her intellectual ability in every day living situations. At this time there does not seem to be any indication of a central nervous system dysfunction. Her test results are those of a bright, sensitive, withdrawn, immature, and somewhat regressed individual who is maintaining a passive-feminine orientation in her approach to her world as a defense against inward strivings toward destructive fighting and sadistic impulses which actually terrify her. She is one who feels depressed, constrained, and trapped and has a sense of not being alive and of watching life pass her by at this time. Actually, she feels unable to participate in life and goes to great lengths to project the blame on others, circumstances, places, etc. so that she will not be forced to recognize her depressed, inadequate state. She entertains many feelings of inner emptiness and futility.

This is a girl who has much sex-role confusion and who appears to be experiencing panic over a sexual identity crisis. She is confused about who and what she is, is frightened and guilty of her narcissistic and auto erotic urges. She often provokes situations such as seducing the male in order to later resent and blame him for the predicament in which she finds herself. When she deals with the male, it is in terms of her feelings of intense hositility, and her tendency to deal with males as well as people in general in a sneaky, self-centered and manipulatory way. She does have some feelings of panic concerning the male inasmuch as she has a tendency to project on to him her intense sadistic, destructive, aggressive and annihilating impulses.

Miss S. views the female with a sense of anxiety; she feels erratic about the female and has a tendency to be evasive and avoidant when she deals with the female. She attempts to defend against her sensual impulses toward the female by projecting them on to others. Actually, she remains at the narcissistic level and attempts to cope with her homosexual urges by fleeing to heterosexual involvement in the way of defense. She is one who has intense dependency and oral needs, who is weak and passive, yet who has feelings which are too hot to handle and impulses which threatened to be out of control. This is a girl who wants and needs controls and who is presently experiencing panic over an imminent loss of control. She identifies with people on an immature, self-centered level, but has little real sensitivity to and concern about people.

It is recommended that she be placed in a living situation which imposes strict controls such as a school away from home, or if this is not feasible, that she be hospitalized. In any event she should be involved in psychotherapy preferably of a group therapy nature which will be intensive. It is felt that this girl is experiencing an identity crisis and is fence-sitting at this time; thus, which way she moves will depend upon the treatment and living situation which she experiences within the next year or two.

Vocational Data:

Miss S. has never been employed, full time or during the summers. She has expressed an interest in pursuing a career as a social worker and would like to go to college.

Miss S. received a medical evaluation in December, 1971 and was found to be within normal physical limits with no physical restrictions or activities to be avoided. Client was noted to be on the Methadone program due to drug abuse. Based on a psychiatric and psychological evaluation this client is seen as currently demonstrating numerous characteristics of a behavioral disorder. Client has been involved in drug abuse, dropout behavior, and currently has experienced anxiety and depression due to her condition. This condition constitutes a substantial handicap to employment. With the provision of appropriate vocational rehabilitation services a favorable outcome is anticipated for this rehabilitation plan.

Vocational Objective:
Social Worker

Since that date of the initial interview this client has received counseling and guidance. Based on the diagnostic information obtained in this rehabilitation program, this client has been receiving attention from the Adolescent Clinic at City Hospital and the Guidance Clinic. These institutions have provided the diagnostic information which indicates at the curent time this individual is ready for the provision of appropriate rehabilitation services towards the above indicated vocational objective. In order to achieve this goal, she must receive formal vocational acadamic training within a local facility: tuition, necessary fees, and books. From the psychotherapist in this case, she will receive maintenance, clothes, and transportation in order to participate in the rehabilitation program. At the appropriate time in this individual's rehabilitation plan she will be placed within competitive employment and follow-up provided in order to insure an adequate vocational adjustment. The estimated duration of this plan at the current time is four years.

Over-All Plan and Financing:

Tuition—one semester	$235.00
Activity Fee—one semester	12.00
Health Fee—one semester	20.00
Books—one semester	50.00
Psychotherapy—15 sessions @ $30.00	450.00
Maintenance—4 months @ $80.00	320.00
Clothes	75.00
Transportation	45.00
Methadone—5 months @ $47.00	235.00
TOTAL	$1,442.00

B. T. S.

White—Male—nineteen

Single

High School Graduate

Drug abuse characterized by an inability to adjust vocationally and socially.

Referral Source:

Mr. S. is a nineteen-year-old-white male. Two years ago, this client was in a vocational rehabilitation school unit. During his senior year he dropped out of school and left town. He has recently returned to Richmond and was referred to this vocational rehabilitation counselor by his former school unit counselor as a client in need of services due to residuals of drug addiction.

Social History:

Mr. S. comes from a disrupted family background. This client's mother died when he was very young and he was raised and cared for by various women within the family (two sisters and an aunt). The client remembers being extremely effeminate and afraid of his peers. His father has been a disabled alcoholic for a long period of time. Mr. S. had interrupted relationships with his father and received no financial support or guidance while growing up. The client stated that he separated completely from his father when he was fifteen years old. Ever since he has been on his own, searching for his identity and attempting to cope with his emotional problems.

Mr. S. has been a drug user since his high school years. This client was a heavy user of amphetamines and eventually became dependent upon these drugs. He has also used LSD and speed. His leaving high school during his senior year was due primarily to drug abuse. After Mr. S. dropped out of school, he went to Canada, gradually worked his way across the states and finally became a "speed freak" in San Francisco's Haight Ashbury. He lived with a couple and their child. During his stay in Haight Ashbury, Mr. S. was seen by a psychiatrist in a Free Clinic where he was found to be an extremely depressed youth with homosexual drives and a drug dependency (see psychological). He was placed in a drug treatment center and withdrew from drug use.

Mr. S. is a seemingly bright young man who is attempting to work out his problems and his loneliness without family guidance and support. He has been living with friends and acquaintances for the past two years. He is seen by the vocational rehabilitation counselor as cooperative, alert, and quite willing to bend to survive.

Educational History:

Mr. S. completed eleven and one-half years of school before dropping out and going to San Francisco. While there he did manage to finish his remaining course work and graduated from a local San Francisco high school. Also while in California, Mr. S. qualified for civil service by passing the Civil Service Examination. He is an intelligent individual who expresses a desire to go to college or to learn a skill or trade.

Vocational History:

Mr. S.'s vocational experiences are limited due to his home environment, drug abuse, and age. He never has worked while living in this city. While in San Francisco he did qualify and passed the Civil Service Examination. He then secured a job with the postal department as a clerk in the concentration center. He earned three dollars per hour. He held this job for two weeks before he was forced to quit due to drugs. This client managed to find odd jobs and eventually worked his way back to this city. He has since been unemployed receiving support from his friends and relatives.

Psychological Data:

Psychiatric Abstract From the Haight Ashbury Free Clinic

Mr. S. presents symptoms of anxiety and depression. He is a highly dependent youth and has been placed in a situation with which he is unable to cope with—following a failure of a mother substitute relationship. He has been clinging to this relationship for some time as a defense against his very strong homosexual drives. However, he has recently entered into a homosexual relationship with another young man, and as a consequence feels that he has achieved some resolution of his identity conflicts.

This client has been a drug user for many years and has recently become dependent upon amphetamines. It is quite probable that his present emotional state is in part due to wasting effects of continued use of amphetamines, LSD and other psychedelic drugs.

In summary, Mr. S. has an inability to function in the appropriate masculine roles and has resolved his psychosexual conflict through a homosexual adjustment.

Since data was not obtained in regard to Mr. S.'s school cumulative record, the Revised Beta and the Kuder Preference Test were administered by the vocational rehabilitation counselor. The Revised Bata revealed a score of 120 placing Mr. S. in the upper limits of average intelligence. The Kuder Preference Test indicated this client's interests are in the fields of literature and art.

These findings were discussed with Mr. S. He stated he has done considerable writing of poetry and prose and apparently has talents in those areas. Mr. S. intends to further develop these talents in college. But, at the present time he strongly wants to become self supporting preferably through sales or clerical work. These are his stated goals at the present.

Medical History:

Mr. S.'s medical history reveals he has had no systematic difficulties or apparent illness except the residuals of drug abuse. Mr. S. was sent

to a local physician for his general medical examination. On the basis
of the following report no further recommendations were made.

General Basic Medical Examination Record:

Frequent headaches—no	Difficult vision—yes
Hearing—no	Fainting—no
Extreme fatigue—yes	Asthma—no
Nervous system—normal	Unusual gain or loss of weight—no
Persistent cough—no	Cough producing blood—no
Pain in chest—no	Short breath—no
Unusual irritability—yes	Fever—no
Swolen ankles—no	Difficult in thinking—no
Loss of appetite—no	Frequent indigestion—no
Difficulty in memory—no	Rheumatism—no
TB—no	Convulsions—no
Hernia—no	Varicose veins—no
Operation—no	Accident—no
Hemorrhoid—no	Burning in urine—no
Diarrhea or constipation—no	Height—73", Weight—129 lbs.
Eyes—20/20—left 20/20 right	Hearing—o.k.
Nose thorax—negative	Mouth or teeth—normal
Lymphatic—normal	Chest & Lungs—normal
Heart and circulation—normal	BP—100/50
Abdomen—normal	Genito-urinary system—normal
Ano-rectal—normal	Skin—normal

Mr. S.'s primary disability has been diagnosed as an emotional disorder characterized by an inability to stabilize in work. A secondary
disability has been diagnosed as residuals to drug abuse. Mr. S. expects
to later complete his education in college but at this time he needs to
gain his independence and self-esteem. Because of his exceptional
talents intellectually and his personal insights into his problems along
with his withdrawal from drugs usage, there is reasonable expectation
that he can be gainfully employed.

Plan:

A vocational plan was written with sales clerk as the vocational objective. This vocational choice was based on the client's intellectual
ability, experiences, and interests. It was felt by the counselor and the
client that time was needed for the client to plan his future. A stock
clerk position was found with a local department store. The client will
earn $50/week.

Services Rendered:

Guidance and Counseling
General Medical Examination
Transportation
Rent for a month
Food bills for a month
Clothing
Job Placement
Follow-up
Cost to Vocational Rehabilitation—$250.00
Client was closed; status twenty-six rehabilitation

Case Reopened:

Six months later, Mr. S. came and told his rehabilitation counselor he quit his job after six weeks. The position as a stock clerk was not challenging enough for Mr. S. He stated he needed to be more deeply involved in some occupation more in line with self-image.

Mr. S. appeared to be hostile, depressed and lonely to the vocational rehabilitation counselor. He blurted out his feelings in a somewhat philosophical manner. He spoke of moving many times in the past six months. He wanted to talk about the state of the economy and he did not believe there was a job "out there for him." He has been disappointed in not getting a job as a mail clerk.

His Kuder Preference Record Vocational (KPRV) was again interpreted for him. Some effort was made to explore which move would be more in the direction of his long range goals.

"Library Assistant" and "Proofreader" seemed appropriate jobs for consideration. Local opportunities might include copy editing with a newspaper. Literary and musical interest of a quiet professional caliber were also suggested by the KPRV. Mr. S.'s intelligence supports this. An appointment was made for Mr. S. to take the General Aptitude Test Battery (GATB), which will possibly confirm his musical mastery.

It was felt that Mr. S. may have real potential as a composer and arranger if he is willing to go through formal training. At this time he frowns upon formal education and wants to get a job. He does not feel academic discipline is that important since he picks up things very quickly on his own, including some composing of music.

GATB scores indicate Mr. S. is capable in most areas:

G—133	Q—154
U—145	K—140
N—130	F—106
S—107	M—91
P—121	

Mr. S. was informed of the results. The conversation tended to center around music as his long range area of interest. He has considered music school. The vocational rehabilitation counselor stressed the importance of some concrete long range planning and the use of his talents. An appointment was made with the chairman of the music department of City University.

Mr. S. would first like to work in the Post Office to prove to himself that he can hold a job for at least one-half year. An appointment was made with the Post Office about a job as a clerk.

In his interview with the chairman of the music department, Mr. S. played some of his original compositions. The chairman felt Mr. S. has good potential in the area of music and persuaded him to apply for admission as a music student.

Mr. S. then talked to the personnel director at the Post Office concerning employment. He trimmed his hair and presented a neat appearance for the interview. He mentioned his prior use of drugs to the personnel director. The vocational rehabilitation counselor felt this probably killed any chances of him getting a job.

The client was then urged to search for jobs in the city. He found a job in a medical lab and was hired by Doctor Hane. Mr. S. discussed the possibility of on-the-job training as a lab assistant under Doctor Hane's direction. It is a thirteen month training program.

Mr. S.'s GATB reveals that for the vocational profile of the Medical Lab Assistant, he has more than sufficient scores to qualify him for this work (Requirements G-110, S-95; P-110; Clinet has G-133; S-107; and P-121).

The Kuder Performance Test did show a correlation of seventy-nine percent in scientific computation and the clerical field. He is well motivated to pursue this goal having had discussed this with Doctor Hane of the Department of Anatomy—under whom he will be working. This program offers ample opportunities for future employment since a local hospital expects to hire all of these trainees. The client will learn to disect and prepare specimens for slides and to do all the jobs related there to and to operate completely with full responsibilities as a medical lab assistant. Tuition will be payable to the Department of Anatomy for this training at a rate of $86/month. Maintainance to be sought through the Department of Public Welfare and the Training Services Project at a rehabilitation center.

Total Cost of Services $2,318

Doctor Hane will be supervising training and totally responsible for all of Mr. S.'s weekly hours, progress and reporting to the counselor. Job duties:

1. Learn the preparation of tissue and various techniques.
2. How to assist in surgical operation of animals.
3. Learning the ordering and caring of equipment.

4. Learning the care and treatment of animals for research.
5. Learn to use all equipment.
6. Learn the proper method of mixing and using stain chemicals and dyes.

Mr. S. received a Training Service Project stipend with the stipulation that the money will not be paid if the student has:

1. Three absences in a week
2. Placed on leave for more than one week
3. Progress is unsatisfactory
4. If client leaves training program

Client entered the training program in April. After the first month, Mr. S. was doing a moderately good job. Doctor Hane felt his main problem was that of being easily offended by any types of critical opinion related to work. Mr. S. knows the techniques on paper but occasionally has a little trouble transposing this knowledge to practices. He attempts to do some things without really thinking carefully about them before doing the task. Doctor Hane has stressed the importance of his appearance and communications with his fellow workers.

The vocational rehabilitation counselor feels the client is having difficulty in regulating himself to work and personal regimentation but is making progress and is "sticking with it."

Several months later, Mr. S. was again evaluated. Doctor Hane indicated Mr. S. is learning the proper skills well and does a good job when told what to do. Doctor Hane senses a feeling of importance to the functioning of the Lab by Mr. S. Progress is being made both in technical skills and fellow relationships. The vocational rehabilitation counselor counselled his client about his appearance. He accepted this and changed it sufficiently.

In the last progress report received, Doctor Hane indicated Mr. S. is increasing in skill proficiency. Client is still having trouble in the area of seeing what is to be done. He misses things that should be done without being told. After the rehabilitation counselor felt Mr. S. was improving in this motivation, acceptance of responsibility and initiative. He has come a long way from "wandering in the streets."

During the fourth month of on-the-job training, Mr. S. began experiencing peculiar sensations which he described very vividly as the sensation of "drifting away or being unassociated with reality." He is also aware of occasional hallucinatory experiences especially of visual and especially when looking at a blank wall or into a clear sky.

Mr. S. was sent to Doctor Owens, a neurologist. In addition to the above sensations the client has had on occasion some alfactory hallucinations with varying and differing odors each time. He denies headaches, depotopia tenitius and peripheral paratheseas. The neurological examination is entirely within normal limits except for a very slight difficulty walking a tandem.

The EEG is abnormal showing some spontaneous paraxysmal dysrhythmic slowing occurring at frequent intervals lasting one to three seconds. These changes are consistent with this symptonatology and as his history might suggest. It is difficult to know the etiology of this abnormal EEG. It is likely that this is a residual of some recurrent toxia or anoxic cerebral manifestations occurring in the past.

Interpretation:

Paroxysmal dysrhythmic slowing. This change suggests a diffuse corticoil dysfunction of a chronic nature and the possibility of a lowered seizure threshold to generalize nonconvulsive and/or convulsive seizures without aura. These recommendations and changes should be improved with Valium.

Summary:

After six months in the training program Mr. S. terminated himself by leaving and going on the "road" again. It was felt by the Rehabilitation Counselor that the client had begun to take drugs again.

Vocational Rehabilitation could not accept him for services against unless he went to a drug treatment half-way house for therapy. He refused to do this. This case was then closed in Status 28—reason—failure to cooperate.

Case Reopened:

After a month, Mr. S. contacted his vocational rehabilitation counselor and asked for drug therapy and a chance to continue in his training. After a month in a drug treatment half-way house, client left. The vocational rehabilitation counselor was unable to locate Mr. S. This case was closed in Status 08.

NOTE: The vocational rehabilitation counselor last heard that Mr. S. is in Belgium traveling from place to place.

C. W. B.

Black—Male—eighteen

Married

Ninth Grade Education

Drug abuse characterized by an inability to adjust vocationally and socially.

Character disorder (inadequate personality)

Referral Source:

Mr. B. was referred to the Department of Vocational Rehabilitation by the prenatal clinic at City Hospital. He and his wife are currently undergoing family counseling prior to the birth of their child. He had previously been a client of DVR but was closed from a referred status for failing to respond to attempts of counseling or evaluation. He has been in the city's methadone treatment program for the last three years for his heroin addiction.

Social Data:

Mr. B. is a eighteen-year old male. He is married and is expecting his first child. He and his nineteen-year-old wife are presently living with his uncle in center city. They have been drawing general relief for the last year.

Mr. B. became addicted to heroin at the age of fourteen. His drug abuse began with the use of marijuana at the age of thirteen. He graduated to heroin and after three years his maximum usage was three bags a day. When he was thirteen, he lost his mother upon whom he was extremely dependent, and was virtually on his own. His father separated from his mother when he was very young. He remembers nothing about his father. It was at this time he began experimenting with drugs.

Mr. B. presents a pleasant, neat appearance. His dress reflects his constricted economic circumstances. His social life is quite limited, partly due to economic circumstances and his rather narrow range of interest.

Medical Data:

Mr. B. stated that his health is good. While he was on drugs, he suffered from malnutrition. But since he has been on the methadone program he has regained his health.

The local physician found Mr. B. to be well developed and well nourished in no apparent distress. He is oriented in all spheres. On the basis of the General Medical Examination recorded, Mr. B. seems to not have any overt physical or emotional problems. His drug seeking behavior is apparently under control by methadone.

General Medical Examination:

GENERAL APPEARANCE—This is a eighteen-year-old black male who is well developed and well nourished with no acute distress.
PULSE   78
RESPIRATION   18
BLOOD PRESSURE   115/75

SKIN AND HAIR   normal
HEAD   normal in size and shape.   EYES—brown
TEETH—good
NECK—normal
SPINE   No deformity
CHEST   Lungs are clear
HEART   normal
ABDOMEN   negative
EXTREMITIES   no gross physical abnormalities
NEUROLOGICAL   no gross physical abnormalities
REFLEXES   present
WEIGHT   142   HEIGHT   5'7"
IMPRESSIONS   This individual is in normal health

Educational Data:

Mr. B. dropped out of high school after the ninth grade. He stated his grades while in school were average and below C's and D's. His major reason for leaving school was financial—being on his own, he felt he needed to make some money. While in school he did not participate in any extra curricular activity. Overall, he found school to be of little interest or value to him.

Psychiatric Evaluation:

The psychiatric evaluation found Mr. B. to be evasive about his psychiatric history and drug history. He presents overt psychiatric symtoms of anxiety and tenseness in normal situations. Episodes of depression were noted but were not considered extremely significant. This particular individual is characterized as having an inadequate personality. It is my impression that Mr. B. is a young man, not greatly endowed intellectually. On top of this, he is passive, inadequate, dependent, and lacking drive and energy. Certainly a training program within his limits of intellect and emotional stability is in order. However, Mr. B. should not be placed in a situation which would cause frustration. He fears failure a great deal and will take it rather badly.

I would suspect he has developed sufficient obsessive defenses that will enable him to make a reasonably good employee once he can settle down into a semi-skilled "rut."

He has a tremendous amount invested, from an emotional point of view, in his present marriage. He will work hard to achieve stability in this situation.

Psychological Data:

Mr. B. was given a battery of tests consisting of the WAIS, Graves Design Judgment Test, Minnesota Clerical Test, The Crawford Small

Parts Dexterity Test, Wide Range Achievement Test, the Thurston Interest Schedule, the Incomplete Sentence Blank, Draw a Person and the Cornell Index—Form N2.

The results are indicated below:

WAIS; Norms eighteen-year-old group

Verbal Subtest	*Scaled Scores*
Information—7	Arithmetic—6
Similarities—9	Digit Span—9
Comprehension—6	Vocabulary—5
Performance:	*Scaled Scores*
Digit Symbol—12	Picture Design—6
Picture Comp.—8	Object Assembly—10
Block Design—11	

Verbal IQ—83
Performance IQ—95
Full Scale—87

Graves Design Judgment Test
raw score 56—85th percentile

Minnesota Clerical Test
raw score 149—93rd percentile

Crawford Small Parts Dexterity Test

Pins and Collar	subtest	40%
Screws	subtest	73%

Wide Range Achievement Test

Reading	3.9 grade	2%
Spelling	3.7 grade	2%
Arithmetic	4.9 grade	4%

Thurston Interest Schedule
Highest interest was the physical science, art, and business areas. Areas of least interest was computational.

Mr. B. is a person in the mid-range of dull normal verbal intellectual ability and lower in the middle average on the performance scale. His full scale score places him in the upper range of dull normal intelligence. He possesses good skills in the areas of abstract reasoning and short term memory. Hampered by poor vocabulary and limited information fund, Mr. B. lacks the ability to deal with tasks requiring social knowledge.

The results of the tests indicated that he possesses adequate manual skills to function in construction areas. He would be hampered in training that required reading skills such as heavy equipment operations.

Personality:

Responses on the Incomplete Sentence Blank suggests an immature young individual. He has feelings of hostility directed toward his father. He prizes work highly and is very concerned about his ability to function in competitive physical tasks. Also of great concern to him is his present unemployment situation.

The Cornell Index revealed Mr. B. has little trouble in relating to those around him. He is troubled about unemployment which affects his feelings of adequacy and self-worth.

It is recommended that Mr. B. avoid any training programs that require a classroom situation. He could function in a on-the-job program in the construction area.

Vocational History:

Mr. B. is presently unemployed. His longest period of employment was a longshoreman. This job lasted for two years. He left because of an apparent lack of demand for his services. He then went to work for a trucking company as a packer. He left this job because of poor pay. The last job he held was as a metal cutter for a bathtub company. This job lasted for a month. He was fired because of absenteeism. Mr. B. stated that his absenteeism was due to his involvement with drugs.

Mr. B. functions at the dull normal intelligence level and has no salable job skills. He has been addicted to heroin and is currently under treatment for his addiction. His previous employment has been sporadic and without any skill value. His inability to obtain stable employment and support his family has caused depression and anxiety. With his inadequate personality and lack of training, he has been unable to maintain permanent employment. His frustration tolerance and image is low. He also has difficulty in relating to authority figures. These conditions constitute an employment handicap.

Vocational Objective:

Carpenter's Helper

Mr. B. has had some previous experience in carpentry handiwork and with some success. He wishes to be trained as a carpenter's helper and eventually will advance to apprentice or master carpenter.

This goal is within his capabilities, provided he is adequately prepared for the work task. In order to gain the necessary training and skills the client will have to be helped to prepare for interviews, situations and questioning by prospective Union Apprenticeship programs.

Plans:

The client will be provided counseling and guidance and given help in preparing for apprenticeship program interviews and for training.

R. E. M.
Male—eighteen
Single
Tenth Grade Education

Inadequate personality with paranoid tendencies due to drug intoxication.

Referral Source:

Mr. M. was referred to the Veteran Hospital (VA) by his parents, who were very concerned about their son's drug addiction. Mr. M. began using drugs while in the Army and continued to use drugs since his discharge, two months ago. He has previously lost a job as a salesman with a major tire company, which may or may not be related to drugs. Mr. M. says he realizes the fatal prognosis and wants to get off drugs so he can go to work and make a fresh start.

Social Data:

Mr. M. is an eighteen-year-old man who was admitted to a VA Hospital for drug misuse. His parents are a very pleasant and neatly attired couple. His father is in his early forties, his mother is in her late thirties. He was their first child. There are six other children in the family. The parents describe Mr. M.'s early childhood as a very emotional one. He had temper tantrums frequently and often passed out from crying so hard that caused him to quit breathing. During his adolescent and teenage years he was alway quiet and had only a few friends. He also never has been too comfortable with girls. His parents made a point of saying he did not run around with the "hell raisers" and seemed to think that this was one of the biggest points in his favor. Although he uses drugs, Mr. and Mrs. M. feel their son is not a bad boy.

Mr. M.'s parents related some of their son's guilt feelings over problems with their younger son, Jim. It seems Jim ran away from home just two days before Mr. M. returned home from the service. Jim ran away with a thirty-five year old woman who Mr. and Mrs. M. feel was manipulating and using him.

He now feels Jim ran away because of him, although he had been quite close to his younger brother. Jim is still away from the home although his parents have heard that he is well. There are six siblings in the family, sisters aged eighteen, fourteen, eight, and five, and brothers aged sixteen and eleven. Mr. M. comes from a family that is described as comfortable with the necessities of life but never an over abundance of money. His father works regularly and is very strongly committed to the value of work; "the necessity for hard work to get any where in life." His mother is a warm supportive person who is greatly distressed over her son's use of drugs and weeps easily on discussing this.

Both parents claim they knew nothing of his taking drugs until recently when they first noticed a gross change in the patient's behavior. They described him as normal, outgoing, and happy when he first came home and then overnight be became very depressed and very frightened. Mr. M.'s rapid decompensation was followed by:

1. paranoid feelings in regards to people in the back yard laughing at him
2. attempts made by neighbors to harm his family physically and their reputation;
3. his reluctance to get off the bus when he was going down town to the employment office which caused him to stay on the bus the entire route and just go right back home and stay in the house, totally afraid to leave the house.

At this point, Mr. M. and his parents felt the need for hospitalization and very anxiously presented himself to the VA office.

He dropped out of school in the tenth grade because he was in constant trouble with the teachers. He enlisted in the Army, thinking that the Army life would be so nice. When he was disappointed and frustrated in the Army, he began taking drugs in order to relieve his depression while in Korea. He was taking Speed, Grass, and LSD. He had thirty trips on LSD in the last two years. Mr. M., a Vietnam veteran, was discharged from the Army with a general discharge under honorable conditions. According to Mr. M's information he continued to take drugs until one week prior to being admitted to the VA Hospital.

His girl friend left him because he was on drugs but now because he sought treatment, she has returned to him.

Educational History:

Mr. M. completed ten years of school and was described as an average student. He did not participate in extracurricular activities in school. He did enjoy playing basketball around the house but never played it in school. Once he got into high school he could not adjust to the high school routine. His parents were not really sure what it was, if it was that he could not grasp the material or if the classes were too competitive with the other students. During his stay in the VA Hospital, Mr. M. took and passed his General Educational Development (GED) test.

Psychological Data:

Mr. M. referred for psychological evaluation in order to assess possible organic impairment caused by his drug usage. He was adminis-

tered a battery of tests consisting of the Wechsler Adult Intelligence
Test, Bender-Gestalt, Projective Drawings and the Rorschach.

Test Behavior:

Mr. M. was cooperative, coherant, and relevant throughout the interview and testing. He manifested some interest in and motivation to
success on the tasks. The major clinical impression of this young man
was that of a beaten individual. Although Mr. M. was quite, soft-
spoken and self-denigrating generally, there were occasional sparks of
animation.

Test Findings:

The measure related to intellectual functioning suggest that this
veteran has not suffered organic impairment due to the drug use. His
Full Scale on the WAIS IQ was 105 indicating that he is currently
functioning in the normal range. (Verbal IQ—106, Performance IQ—
103) While Mr. M. seems to have the potential for bright normal
functioning there are indications that emotional and environmental
factors have interferred with his developing adequately. He performs
well on tasks that require nonverbal skills, demonstration moderately
above average ability to concentrate and attend freely to noninter-
personal tasks. His performance decreases on the more academic, verbal, and interpersonal tasks.

Mr. M.'s performance on the projective measures indicate some of
the likely sources of his emotional and intellectual difficulties. These
are quite consistant with the veteran's description of his family relationships and his schooling.

He has apparently employed denial as a major defense against
strong feelings of inadequacy. These inadequate feelings seem to stem
from the relationship Mr. M. had with his father. His father is seen as
a strong masculine figure who apparently thought little of his son and
at least unconsciously made that quite clear. Unable to deal with these
feelings and resolve this relationship, Mr. M., as he entered adolescence,
apparently took the "easy way out." "If I am nothing, I'll flunk out of
school, etc.," at the same time he was a "man" in this flunking sub-
group.

Mr. M. appears to be basically bright and a sensitive young man.
He seems aware of the raw deal he dealt himself in order to cope with
his emotional stress. This has apparently heightened his feelings of inadequacy and lack of self worth and through the denial there is a
fairly strong feeling of depression. In efforts to combat these unacceptable feelings of inadequacy Mr. M. at times comes across as hostile and
aggressive. This dynamic picture may help to explain his choice of
"Uppers" rather than "Downers" or any other drugs.

At the present time Mr. M.'s use or denial is sufficiently intact to interfere with his adequately grappling with, and resolving these inter and intrapersonal difficulties himself. It is the clinical psychologist's opinion that, if Mr. M. is, or can be, motivated enough to enter into individual psychotherapy of intensive counseling, he has the capacity for insight and growth. Additionally, when such counseling is undertaken, Mr. M. seems quite capable of furthering his education vocationally, and perhaps, even academically.

Summary:

Mr. M.'s current performance indicates he is in the normal range of intellectual functioning. There is no evidence in the protocol to suggest organic impairment or psychosis. At the present time he may be considered an Inadequate Personality with paranoid tendencies due to drug intoxication. The records suggests that attitudes within his family have fostered this self perception. Therapy could prove beneficial and is recommended.

Medical History:

Mr. M. has a history of drug usage which led to his military discharge and subsequent admission to the VA Hospital. He has been hearing voices and is panicked that some one is going to hurt him, although he does not know who this someone is.

Mr. M.'s mental and physical status reveal an eighteen-year-old male, thin, looking utterly panicked, eyes red from tears, claiming he does not trust anybody and is afraid to be in the building because "the whole world is crazy."

Mr. M. states he has been in good general health except for these feelings. Smoking, occasionally drinking, and use of LSD, speed, and marijuana are Mr. M.'s habits. He has had none of the childhood or adult illnesses and is sensitive to poison oak.

Because he is afraid, Mr. M. claims that "they" think he is a queer, and an addict, and so on. . . . . The physician felt the client was inadequate, immature, and withdrawn, with a flat affect.

Physical Examination:

Patient is in no distress, well oriented.
Eyes...................... negative
Throat....................negative
Neck.....................no adenopathy
Lungs....................clear to A and P
Heart....................negative
Abdomen.................soft, no masses, no area of tenderness
Reflexes..................patellar........o.k.
Diagnosis.................acute psychosis, parnoid type

Vocational History:
Testing and Counseling:

Prior to enlisting in the Army Mr. M. worked as an inspector for nine months at D & H, a screw machine company in his home town. After his discharge from the army, he worked for a major tire company as a salesman. Mr. M. lost this job due to his drug misuse.

A battery of vocational and interest tests consisting of the Lee Thorpe Occupational Interest Inventory, Minnesota Vocational Interest Inventory, and the Edwards Personal Preference Schedule were administered by a counseling psychologist. According to the Lee Thorpe Occupational Interest Inventory, Mr. M. showed interest in the mechanical field, and he would be satisfied in being an electronic pressman, or a stock clerk. He also stated that he would like to be trained as a steam fitter.

According to the Edwards Personal Preference Schedule, he sees himself as being an aggressive, exhibiting, showing off person. However, according to our observation, and other test findings, he is an immature, meek, fragile, and not too adequate person. In reality, he is only eighteen. He could be given some allowance to be immature. We are only glad that he now realizes that he can get along so much better without the effect of drugs.

Mr. James Smith, Mr. M.'s former employer at D & H, was approached about Mr. M.'s re-employment. Information was made concerning Mr. M.'s re-employment with D & H Company, upon Mr. M.'s release from the hospital.

Hospital Summary:

Mr. M. on admission was markedly frightened and suspicious. He stated that the whole world looked crazy to him. On the admission ward, he presented himself as a hostile and negative person. He requested his discharge against medical advice. After being coaxed by the staff, he opened his mind and admitted his paranoid feelings and suicidal ideas. While in the hospital Mr. M. continued to suffer from ideas of reference and persecution for quite awhile. He is uncooperative and angry, claiming that he was not sick. A urine test proved he was not taking his medication. He was confronted about this and he agreed to take his medication provided that it would not make him drowsy. Mellaril, 50 mg. q.i.d., was presented. Once this medication was increased, Mr. M.'s condition began to improve.

Mr. M. has shown quite a bit of improvement in his condition since being admitted. His affect now seems more appropriate and he is showing more spontaneity. He seems free from psychosis but could have flash backs in the future from his past experiments with LSD. Mr. M. has been on several passes home and has apparently refrained from taking drugs while there. The hospital staff feels that Mr. M. is ready to go back and resume working as an inspector at D & H Company. This will place him back in a familiar place where he feels he is wanted. And, he knows too where to go and what to do when he is ready for the GI bill training as a steam fitter. He also agreed with us that he will seek supportive therapy and counseling at a mental hygiene clinic. Upon discharge Mr. M. was given a twenty-one day supply of Mellaril.

R. G. L.

Black—Female—nineteen

Single

High School Graduate (Two Years College)

Drug abuse characterized by an inability to adjust vocationally and socially. Character disorder with aggressive and infantile manifestations.

Referral Source:

Miss L.'s initial referral to vocational rehabilitation was by Doctor Wood of the drug addiction clinic of City Hospital where she was a patient from an overdose attempt. The referral was made for purposes of counseling and support. Miss L. has been unable to adjust due to drug abuse. Drug misuse has handicapped Miss L. both educationally and vocationally. At the time of the suicide attempt it was felt that further treatment was needed and presently it would be unfeasible for Miss L. to receive vocational rehabilitation services. Miss L. was later referred by Mr. Trice of a local drug treatment program.

Social History:

Miss L. is a nineteen-year-old, single, black, female from Bronx, New York. She has a three year history of heroin abuse along with a potpourri of other drugs including cocaine, barbiturates, LSD and methadone. She graduated from Thomas Jefferson High School in New York where she was in the top quarter of her class. After graduation, she came to this city and attended City University for two years before dropping out and going back to New York.

Both of Miss L.'s parents are living and other significant family members include her older sister, Carol, who lives in Washington and her younger sister, Joan, a graduate of a local drug treatment program and currently a staff member.

Miss L. was recently detoxified from heroin addiction in New York via Methadone. She then came to this city to visit her sister. On the third day of her visit, she left her sister's home in an apparent daze. She was later found by her sister walking the street in a confused and disorganized state. Miss L. entered her sister's car and within five minutes had a major motor seizure. She was brought to the Emergency Room with a history of having taken ten to twelve grams of Isoniazid in a suicide attempt. In the Emergency Room, she had four more major motor seizures, poorly controlled with ten milligrams i.v. Valium doses.

Miss L. was first introduced to drugs while a senior in high school. She stated that her reasons for using drugs was to become part of the "in" crowd at school. Her first experience was with soft drugs (marijuna). She gradually progressed to LSD and finally heroin.

Medical History:

Miss L. stated that she has been in generally good health since she detoxified from heroin in New York. There is no history of hepatitis or abscess due to her drug use. Physical examination at the time of Miss L.'s suicide attempt revealed a well-developed, well-nourished, black female who was agitated, tachypneic, but awake and responding to commands. Her blood pressure was 140/90; pulse 98, temperature 101.3; respiration 28. The pupils were equal and reactive to light. The examination of the heart showed a normal sinus rhythm without murmurs or gallops at a rate of 95 beats per minute. The Neurological examination was given. Miss L. responded to commands and appeared to realize what was going on about her. Her sensory and motor systems were intact. No pathological reflexes were present. She had hyperactive deep tendon reflexes bilaterally. No muscle weakness was evident.

Thirty-six hours after ingestion, the patient was awake and oriented, breathing normally off the nasal oxygen with normal vital signs. At the time of discharge, the patient was alert and oriented.

DISCHARGE DIAGNOSIS:
1. Isoniazid toxicity
2. Seizures secondary to #1
3. Metabolic acidosis secondary to #1, resolved

DISPOSITION:
1. Appointment in medical follow-up clinic at which time a lateral chest will be done.
2. Appointment in the psychiatry clinic.

Physical examination was given after client recovered from her overdose.

General Medical Examination Record:

R. G. L.　　　Age nineteen　　　Female　　　Single

Height........5'5"　　　Weight........105

Eyes:	Normal　　　Conals
Ears:	Hearing good
Nose:	Normal
Mouth:	Normal
Throat:	Normal
Lungs:	Chest films show no evidence of aspiration pneumonia
Abdomen:	Normal
Sclerae:	Not icteric
Circulatory System:	Normal
Nervous System:	Normal
Skin:	Clear and normal
Orthopedic Impairment:	None
Laboratory Data:	
	Blood gases on the Bennett respirator showed a PO_2 of 108, pCO_2—25, ph 7.20 and a bicarbonate of 9.
	Blood sugar—199
	White blood count was 16, 900
	Sodium—150
	Potassium—4.2
	Chloride—102
	CO_2—12
	Chest films revealed a right hilar density with no evidence of pneuminia.
Extremities:	No cyanoses, clubbing, or edema
	Good periphral pulses

Educational History:

Miss L. graduated in the top quarter of her class at school. While there she was especially interested in the arts, i.e. music and painting. Although actively involved in the academics and subjects, she did not participate in extracurricular activities. She stated that she was a "loner" and had few friends. There was no indication that school authorities knew of her drug addiction.

After graduation from high school, Miss L. came to this city and attended City University for two years. This was due in part to her sister living here. Her curriculum area was Liberal Arts with emphasis in music. During her two college years, she became more involved with drugs especially heroin. Her grades began to drop and Miss L. finally withdrew after her second year and went back to New York.

Vocational Data:

Miss L.'s work experience has been limited to the summer months between school years. Her principal employment for her summers was as a waitress for a nationally known restaurant chain. This job was temporary in nature. The client has no interest in this area as far as permanent employment is concerned.

Psychological Data:

Due to her suicide attempt, Miss L. was referred for psychiatric evaluation. The report stated this client has no prior history of overt psychiatric systems. Over the past two weeks, Miss L. has had suicidal ruminations, insomnia, sadness or crying. She describes her life as one of loneliness and sadness. She indicated she was unable to form close relationships with others. It was also felt by the psychiatrist that Miss L. had occasional blurring of ability to organize thinking. With this mild uncontrolled thinking, her affect is flattened. She denied depressive systems at present.

Miss L.'s history suggests early signs of schizophrenia. The possibility exists that the central nervous system stimulating inclination of the Isoniazid may be exposing an otherwise subclinical thought disorders.

When Miss L. was asked to reconstruct the night of the suicidal attempt, she was unable to remember any of the night's experiences. She stated that when she recovered from the effects of the drugs, she did not realize why she was in the hospital.

Miss L. was seen as an above average person in general ability. The fact that she was a good student in school is indicative of her ability. It was felt that she could best benefit from an intensive drug treatment program. In such a program support and counseling could provide her with the needed tools enabling her to make an adequate adjustment. She will also be provided with constant supervision. The rehabilitation counselor concurred with these recommendations. Due to drug addiction and misuse, she has been functionally limited in that she has been unable to adjust socially and vocationally. In order to learn to live free of drugs in our society, she became an in-patient at a local drug halfway house. It was the opinion of the rehabilitation counselor that Miss L.'s disabling condition presented a definite vocational handicap in that she was unable to maintain herself in society, unable to continue in college and unable to obtain and maintain employment.

The final clinical impression was that she had a definite character disorder with aggressive and infantile manifestations.

Report From The Drug Treatment Center:

Upon first entering the program, Miss L. displayed an over-evaluation of herself in terms of an attitude of superiority. She was condescending, arrogant, uncooperative and cynical. She listened to no one and chronically alienated others around her. It was felt that this infantile behavior was a manifestation of severe feelings of inadequacy. She exhibited a rather cavalier attitude toward her own life when she first entered the program. One week prior to coming in as a program participant she attempted suicide by taking a large number of Boniazid tablets. When talking to her about this she reacts with unrealistic good humor as if it were some kind of a joke.

After not being able to be handled well in several of the local drug facilities, she was assigned to the North Street Halfway House where she finally responded. The staff members began to see the development of positive attitudes in relationship with others, a friendliness and a development of a definite warmth which was not present before. She also accepts criticism without becoming antagonistic and hostile.

Her improvement was to such a point that it was felt she could stabilize in a work situation. There has not been, on the other hand, a complete resolution of the conflicts she brought with her upon entering the program. With positive support, she has responded greatly and if this is continued in the program and on the job, more growth can be expected. Miss L.'s vocational rehabilitation counselor was notified as to her improvement and her readiness for work.

Miss L.'s primary disability has been diagnosed as drug abuse characterized by an inability to adjust vocationally and socially. A character disorder characterized by aggressive and infantile behavior has been diagnosed as the secondary disability. Due to drug addiction, she has been functionally limited in that she has been unable to adjust socially and vocationally. In order for her to live free of drugs in our society, it was necessary for her to become an in-patient at a drug treatment halfway house. It is felt that through the services and support of the drug treatment program, this client will be rendered fixed to return to gainful employment.

Plan and Summary:

A rehabilitation plan was written with detective (undercover operator) as the vocational objective. This vocational objective was felt to be reasonable and attainable in that this client is well qualified based on her varied drug experience to work in undercover work to help in identifying drug abusers. This position will be an on-the-job training situation in which she will receive training and experience as a nurses' aide as well as working as an undercover agent.

Summary of Services:

Miss L. will enter an on-the-job training situation at no cost to DVR. She will receive the necessary uniforms and transportation needed to begin this employment. She will also receive follow-up services to assure satisfactory adjustment to the job. While involved in the training and employment, she will continue as a halfway house resident where she will receive continued treatment and support. The estimated length of services is four months.

CHAPTER 12

LANGUAGE OF THE DRUG ABUSER

Compiled by

JOHN G. CULL AND RICHARD E. HARDY

THIS SECTION OFFERS A GLOSSARY of the language of the drug user. The glossary is in no way complete, but every effort has been made to select those words and terms which may be used most frequently. The reader should remember that the use of these words varies dramatically among geographic regions. A word which is popular in one area may be used very seldom in another.

These words represent the word usage of many addicts throughout the country; however, it is doubtful that any one addict would be familiar with all the included terms.

The argot which addicts use gives a clear description of their way of life. From the terms the reader will be able to discern the compensatory use of drugs by the individual with an inadequate personality and the necessity for many users for escape from reality. Many of the words in the language of the addict are words or modifications used originally by opium smokers, and a number of these words are oriental in origin.

If professionals are to be of help to members of the drug culture, they not only must understand the language of the drug abuser but also must have a feeling for the differences in his perceptions of words and his use of language. Work done by the authors (*Cull* and *Hardy,* 1973a; *Cull* and *Hardy,* 1973b; and *Hardy* and *Cull,* 1973) indicate subcultural groups use language in decidedly different fashions. Racial differences and differences in physical capacities cause individuals to use and perceive everyday language in an altered fashion. Consequently, professionals who work with drug abusers must understand the jargon of this group. This glossary is only the first step in developing this understanding.

Abe—A Five-Dollar Bill.

Acapulco Gold—A high quality of Marijuana.

Acid—LSD (Lysergic Acid Diethylamide) . Hallucinogen.

Acid Dropper—One who uses LSD.

Acid Freak—A habitual user of LSD, Cube Head.

Acid Head—LSD user.

Action—The selling of narcotics. Anything pertaining to criminal activities.

Alcohol—Booze, Juice.

Amp.—A 1-cc Methedrine Ampule, legitimate.

Amphetamines—Stimulants which are generally Dexedrine,® Benzedrine,® Methedrine,® or Biphetamine, Bambita, Bennies, Bottles, Browns, Cartwheels, Chicken Powder, Co-pilots, Dexies, Eye openers, Footballs, Greenies, Hearts, Jolly Beans, Jugs, LA Turnabouts, Lid Proppers, Orangies, Peaches, Pep Pills, Roses, Speed, Truck Drivers, Ups, Wake Ups, Whites.

Amys—Amyl Nitrate, Stimulant.

Angel Dust—PCP, an animal tranquilizer.

Artillery—Equipment for injecting drugs.

Away—In jail.

Axe—Musical Instrument.

Back up—A condition in which blood backs up into the syringe while injecting a drug into the vein.

Backtrap—To make sure a needle is in proper position when mainlining by withdrawing the plunge of the syringe before actually injecting the drugs.

Bad Trip—Bummer.

Bag—Situation; category.

Bag—An envelope of Heroin (see Nickel Bag and Dime Bag) .

Bagman—An individual who sells drugs.

Bambita—Desoxyn or Amphetamine Derivative.

Bambs—Barbiturates.

Band House—Jail.

Bang—Fix, shot; injection of narcotics.

Barbiturates—Sedatives, usually Seconal,® Nembutal,® Amutal,® Luminal,® Tuinal,® Barbs, Blue Heavens, Double Trouble, Nimbie, Peanuts, Purple Hearts, Rainbows, Red Devils, Sleeping Pills, Yellow Jackets.

Barbs—Barbiturates.

Bay State—A standard medical hypodermic syringe, usually made of glass with metal reinforcement, using a plunger and screw type needle.

Bean Trip—Intoxication from ingesting Benzedrine; a Benny Jag.

Beat—To cheat or out bargain.

Bee That Stings—A drug habit, especially one coming on; *a monkey on my back.*

Belt—The euphoria following an injection of narcotics. A shot, or a quantity of drugs to be injected.

Bennies—Benzedrine.

Benny Jag—Intoxication from ingesting Benzedrine.

Bernice—Cocaine.

Bhang—Marijuana.

Big C—Cocaine.

Big D—LSD.

Big John—The police or any law enforcement officer.

Bindle—A small package of narcotics.

Bit—A prison sentence.

Black and White—A policeman.

Black Beauty—Speed in a black capsule.

Blackjack—Paregoric which has been cooked down to be injected in a concentrated form.

Blank—Bag of non-narcotic powder sold as a regular bag (also Dummy, Turkey) .

Blanks—Gelatin capsules supposedly filled with a drug which are actually filled only with milk powder or sugar powder or sugar cubes supposedly saturated with LSD which have only food color.

Blasted—Under the influence of drugs.

Blast Party—Group gathered to smoke Marijuana.

Blotter—A piece of absorbent paper on which LSD has been absorbed.

Blow—To lose something: to smoke Marijuana.

Blow a Pill—To smoke Opium.

Blow a Stick—To smoke a Marijuana cigarette.

Blow Snow—To sniff Cocaine.

Blow Weed—To smoke Marijuana.

Blue Birds—Blues, Barbiturates.

Blue Devil—Amobarbital sodium in solid blue form.

Blue Heavens—Barbiturates.

Blue Mist—A sugar cube colored blue by an LSD preparation.

Blues—Barbiturate.

Blue Velvet—Sodium Amytal Pyribenzamine.®

Bombido—Injectible Amphetamine (Also Jugs, Bottles).

Boost—Steal.

Booster—A professional shoplifter, male or female.

Boot—Pushing and pulling the plunger of a syringe to cause a *rush*.

Booze—Alcohol.

Bottles—Injectible Amphetamines.

Boy—Heroin.

Bread—Money.

Brick—A kilogram of Marijuana compressed under pressure to retain the shape of a brick.

Browns—Long acting Amphetamine Sulfate (capsules, many colors mainly brown).

Buffotenine—A drug chemically related to DMT derived from dried glandular secretions of certain toads as well as from the *amanita* fungus.

Bum Beef—False complaint or information which usually is given deliberately to the police.

Bum Kick—Boring, unpleasant.

Bum Rap—An arrest or conviction for a crime the man actually did not commit, as distinguished from denying it.

Bum Steer—See Bum Beef.

Bum Trip or Bummer—A bad trip on LSD.

Bundle—Twenty-five five-dollar bags of Heroin.

Burned—Rendered useless or vulnerable by recognition; e.g., "A narcotic agent was *burned* and unable to continue surveillance." Also, to receive non-narcotic or highly diluted drugs.

Bust or Busted—Arrested; broke.

Buttons—See Mescaline.

Buy—A narcotic peddler; a purchase of narcotics.

Caballo—Heroin.

Cactus—See Peyote.

Cactus Buttons—See Mescaline.

Can—A car; A city jail.

Candy—Barbiturates.

Cap—A person, especially a young Black, who has to hustle to support his habit. Also, a gelatine capsule or a capsule of drugs.

Cartwheels—Amphetamine Sulphate in round, white, double-scored tablets.

Cat Nap—To get small (and very welcome) snatches of sleep during the withdrawal period.

Chalk—Methedrine.

Charas—Marijuana.

Charged Up—Under the influence of drugs.

Charley—Cocaine.

Charley Coke—A Cocaine addict (restricted to New York and New England) .

Chicago Leprosy—Multiple abscesses.

Chicken Out—Cop out.

Chicken Powder—Amphetamine powder.

Chip—Heroin.

Chipping—Taking narcotics occasionally.

Chippy—Nice-looking girl.

Chloral Hydrate—Joy Juice.

Clear up—To withdraw from drugs.

Clout—To steal, especially as a shoplifter.

Coasting—The sensation of euphoria following the use of a drug.

Used of all drugs except Cocaine. Serving an easy prison sentence.

Coast-to-Coast—Long-acting Amphetamine Sulphate in round forms found in many colors. Also L. A. turnabouts, Co-pilots, Browns.

Cocaine—Bernice, Big C, Charley, Coke, Corine, Dust, Flake, Girl Gold Dust, Happy Dust, Heaven Dust, Her, Ice, Snow, Star Dust, White Nurse.

Codeine—School Boy.

Cohoba—Powdered seeds used as snuff.

Coke—Cocaine.

Coked Up—Under the influence of Cocaine.

Cold Turkey—Sudden withdrawal without any alleviating drugs.

Come Down—The end of a trip; the depressed feeling when the drug effects are fading.

Connection—A drug supplier.

Contact—A person who has a connection or who knows a supplier of drugs.

Cooker—Bottle top or spoon used for dissolving Heroin in water over flame.

Cook-It-Up—To prepare Heroin (or other Opiates) for injection by heating it in a cooking spoon.

Cool— (adj.) In complete control.

Cool— (v.) To wait.

Cop a Fix—To obtain a ration of Narcotics.

Co-pilots—Amphetamines. Also Truck Drivers, Bennies.

Cop or connect—To buy or get; to purchase drugs.

Cop-out—To inform; to pull out or chicken out; to confess; to alibi.

Cop to—Admit to stealing.

Corine—Cocaine.

Cotton—The small wisp of cotton placed in the cooking spoon and used as a filter when the solution is drawn up into the needle.

Cotton Head—A narcotics abuser who depletes his supply of Narcotics and attempts to secure one more injection by re-cooking the cotton used from previous fixes.

Crackling Shorts—Breaking into cars.

Crank—Methedrine; stimulant.

Crash—An unpleasant ending of a trip.

Crash Pad—Apartment set up specifically for people to sleep in.

Crib—One's home or apartment. A house of prostitution. A hypochondriac with many persistent symptoms.

Croaker—Unscrupulous doctor who sells drugs or prescriptions to illicit drug users.

Crutch—Device used for holding shortened butt of Marijuana cigarette. See Roach Clip.

Crystal—Methedaine. See Speed.

Cube—LSD on sugar cubes.

Cubehead—See Acid Freak.

Cut—The dilution of a narcotic with substances like lactose (milk sugar) or quinine, strychnine, etc, in order to increase the profit of the drug trafficker.

Cut Out—To leave a certain place.

D—LSD.

Daisy—A male homosexual. Also Sissy, Queen, Sex Punk.

Dead—No action.

Deal—Sell narcotics to addicts.

Dealer—Anyone who buys or sells stolen goods. A peddler.

Dealing—Keeping on with whatever one is doing; selling dope.

Deck—Several bags of drugs.

Desoxyn—Amphetamine derivative.

DET—A chemically developed hallucinogenic drug; it has not been found occurring in nature.

Deuce—Two-dollar package of Heroin.

Dexies—Dexedrine, stimulant.

Dig—To understand; to follow.

Dime Bag—A ten-dollar purchase of Narcotics.

Dirty—Possessing drugs, liable to arrest.

DMT—A hallucinogen found in the seeds of certain plants native to parts of South America and the West Indies. The powdered seeds have been used for centuries as a snuff *Cohoba.*

Dollies—Dolophine; synthetic Heroin.

Dolly—Methadone.

Dolophine—Dollies, synthetic Heroin.

DOM or STP— (4-Menthyl-2, 5-Diemthoxyamphetamine) An hallucinogenic drug produced in the laboratory which induces euphoria and other hallucinogenic effects.

Doo Jee—Heroin.

Dope—Narcotics. Information. To drug. This term, like dope fiend, tends to be taboo among addicts, though they use both perjuratively.

Dope Hop—A prison term for drug addicts, mostly used by guards, turn-keys, and police.

Double Trouble—Amobarbital Sodium combined with Seconbarbital Sodium in red and blue capsules.

Down—Basic; depressed.

Downer Freak—A habitual user of *Downers*.

Downers—Sedatives, Alcohol, Tranquilizers and Narcotics.

Dragged—A post Marijuana state of anxiety.

Drop—Swallow a drug.

Dropped—Taken orally.

Drug—To annoy.

Dry—Without drugs.

Dummy—A bag of non-narcotic powder sold as a regular bag. Also Blank, Turkey.

Dust—Cocaine.

Dynamite—Something extra special or good.

Echos—See Flashback.

Eighth—Eighth of an ounce of Heroin.

Electric—Overpowering, this is a positive statement.

Eye Dropper—Medicine dropper used with hypodermic needle as makeshift syringe. Most addicts actually prefer it to a syringe.

Eye Opener—Amphetamines.

Fag—A pimp. Not to be confused with the general sling fag (a homosexual) clipped from faggot.

Fall—To be arrested. To receive a prison sentence. See Bust.

Fat Jay—Marijuana cigarette approaching the size of a commercial cigarette or larger. They are made large to compensate the weaker types of Marijuana.

Fed—A federal agent, usually a narcotic agent. Also, The Man, Narco.

Finger—Stool pigeon.

Finger Gee—Stool pigeon.

Finger Wave—A rectal examination for contraban narcotics.

Finif or Finski—A five dollar bill.

Fink—A stool pigeon; an untrustworthy person. Also wrong, no good rat.

Five-cent Bag—A five-dollar Heroin Fix.

Fix—Injection of Narcotics.

Flake—Cocaine.

Flash—A quick jolt of high in abdomen or across chest from Heroin shot.

Flashback—Partial reoccurence of an LSD trip.

Flea Powder—Grossly inferior Heroin.

Flipped—Becoming psychotic after an overdose of drugs.

Floating—To be high on drugs.

Fly—Sophisticated yet carefree; wise in the ways of the underworld.

Flying—See Floating.

Footballs—Amphetamine sulphate in oval-shaped tablets of various colors. Also Greenies.

Fox—Good-looking girl.

Freak—An individual who is excessive in some area; for example, *Acid Freak* or *Speed Freak*.

Freak-out—Bad experience with hallucinogenic drugs.

Fuzz—Policeman or Detective.

Gal Head—Narcotics addict.

Ganja—Marijuana.

Garbage—See Flea Powder.

Gee Stick—An Opium Pipe. Obsolescent.

George—Very good.

Get a finger wave—The process of having the rectum searched for drugs.

Gig—Job.

Girl—Cocaine.

Give Wings—To start someone else on Narcotics.

Going Up—Taking drugs, particularly *Uppers*.

Gold Dust—Cocaine.

Gold Leaf Special—A Marijuana cigarette which is thought to be very potent.

Goods—Narcotics, especially as they are bought and sold. Used by addicts or dealers in letters, phone calls, or telegrams.

Goof Balls—Barbiturates.

Goofers—See Goof Balls.

Gow—Narcotics in general, especially those used hypodermically.

Grapes—Wine.

Grass—Marijuana.

Greenies—Amphetamine Sulphate (oval shaped tablets).

Green Score—Profit made by passing counterfeit money.

Gun—Hypodermic needle for injecting Heroin.

H—Heroin.

Hack—A physician.

Hairy—Heroin.

Hang Tough—Take it easy, quiet down, stop.

Hang Up—A problem, generally a personal problem or a psychological problem.

Happy Dust—Cocaine.

Hard Stuff—Narcotics.

Harpoon—The hollow needle used with a joint. Also Spike, Silver Serpent, Pin, Machine, Tom Cat.

Harry—Heroin.

Hashish or Hash—Marijuana.

Hawk—LSD.

Hay—Marijuana.

Head—A user of drugs. Usually a user of LSD.

Hearts—Dextoamphetamine Sulphate in orange-colored heart-shaped tablets. Also Orangies, Dexies, Peaches, Bennies, Roses.

Heat—Police or Detective.

Heaven Dust—Cocaine.

Heavy—Deep or profound.

Heeled—See Dirty.

Hemp—Marijuana.

Henry—Heroin.

Her—Cocaine.

Heroin—Boy, Caballo, Doo Jee, *H,* Hairy, Harry, Henry, Horse, Joy Powder, Junk, Scag, Scat, Skit, Smack, Stuff, Tecata, White Lady, White Nurse.

High—Under the influence of drugs.

Hip—Aware.

Hippies—Those who like to associate with jazzmen, many of whom are drug users.

Hit—To shoot a narcotic.

Hit On—To ask for.

Hog—PCP.

Holding—See Dirty.

Holding—Having drugs in one's possession.

Hooked—Addicted.

Hooker—Hustler, a Prostitute.

Hop—Opium for smoking. Narcotics for injection or inhalation.

Hophead—Hype; a drug addict.

Hopped Up—Under the influence of Narcotics.

Horse—Heroin.

Hot Shot—Cyanide or other poison concealed in Narcotics to kill a troublesome addict.

Hump—To work.

Hustling—Activities involved in obtaining money to buy drugs.

Hype—Drug addict; Hophead.

Ibogaine—Derived from the roots, bark, stem, and leaves of an African shrub.

Ice—Cocaine.

Ice Cream Habit—See *Chipping.*

Idiot Juice—Nutmeg and water mixed for intoxication, largely used in prisons.

Indian Hay—Marijuana.

Informer—Stool; an addict assisting in arresting peddlers.

Iron Horse—A city jail. Most other underworld terms (Can, Joint, Band House, etc.) are also used by addicts.

J—A joint of Marijuana.

Jag—Under the influence of Amphetamines.

Jailhouse High—A high obtained from eating nutmeg.

Jeff—To be obsequious; especially Negroes in relation to Whites.

Jive— (adg.) -Worthless.

Jive— (n.) Marijuana.

Joint—A Marijuana cigarette. The prison.

Jolly Beans—Amphetamines.

Joy Juice—Chloral Hydrate.

Joy Pop—Use of Heroin in small amounts occasionally.

Joy Powder—Heroin.

Jugs—Injectible Amphetamines.

Juice—Alcohol.

Juice Head—An Alcoholic.

Junk—Narcotics, usually Heroin.

Junker—A Narcotic Addict.

Junkie—Narcotic Addict.

Key—One kilo of Marijuana.

Kick—Stop using Narcotics through complete withdrawal.

Kick Back—The addicts almost inevitable return to Narcotics after having kicked the habit.

Kick Cold—Treatment in which the addict is taken off drugs suddenly.

Kilo—A large amount of Narcotics form a pusher's point of view; technically 2.2 pounds. See Key.

Knockers—The testicles. A woman's breast.

Knock Out Drops—Chloral-Hydrate.

La Turnabouts—See Coast-to-Coast.

Lamb—The passive receptor in a homosexual relationship.

Lame—Square.

Laughing Grass—Marijuana.

Lay Dead—To do nothing.

Lemonade—See Flea Powder.

Lettuce—Money.

Lid—A small quantity of Marijuana, usually about one ounce.

Lid Proppers—Amphetamines.
Lipton Tea—See Mickey Finn.
Lit—Under the influence of drugs.
Lit up—Under the influence of drugs.
Load—See *Deck.*
Loco Weed—Marijuana.
Long-tailed Rat—Stool Pigeon.
Louse—A Stool Pigeon. (Also Finger, Finger Gee, Long-tailed Rat, Mouse, Rat) .
LSD—Acid, sugar cubes, trips. Lysergic Acid Diethylamide. Big *D*. Hawk.
Luminal—A Barbiturate.

M—Morphine.
Machine—See Harpoon.
MDA—Synthetic stimulant and hallucinogen.
Made—Recognized for what you are.
Main Line— (n.) The vein, usually in the crook of the elbow, into which the needle addict injects Narcotics.
Main Line— (v.) To inject Narcotics directly into a vein.
Maintain—Keeping your head during a difficult situation.
Maintaining—Injecting a Narcotic directly into a vein.
Manicure—Marijuana with everything removed except the leaves.
Marijane—Marijuana.
Marijuana—Bhang, Charas, Ganja, Grass, Hash, Hashish, Hay, Hemp, Indian Hay, Jive, Laughing Grass, Loco Weed, Marijane, Pot, Railroad Weed, Reefer, Rope, Tea, Texas Tea, Weed.
McCoy—Medicinal drugs in contrast to bootleg drugs.
Medical Hype—A person who has become accidentally addicted during medical treatment for illness or disease; one who obtains bonafide drugs through doctors or hospitals.
Mellowing—The period of a crash when a person in on speed.
MESC—Mescaline; hallucinogenic drug derived from the bottoms of the Peyote cactus plant native to Central America and Southwestern United States. (Also Peyote) .
Meth—Methedrine or Methadone.

Methadone—Dolly, Dolophine Amidone.

Mickey—Chloral Hydrate.

Mickey Finn or Mickey—Chloral Hydrate in a drink to knock out a victim. Also Euphemistically Lipton Tea. A powerful physic such as croton oil, slipped into a whiskey to make the victim sick or to drive him away from a hangout.

Mike—A microgram.

Miss Emma—Morphine.

Mojo—Narcotics of any kind in a contraband trade; but usually Morphine, Heroin, or Cocaine.

Monkey—A drug habit involving physical dependence.

Monkey on my-back—Early abstinence symptoms. A drug habit.

Morphine—Hard Stuff, *M*, Miss Emma, Morpho, White Nurse, White Stuff, Unkie.

Morpho—Morphine.

Mother—An individual's drug peddler.

Mouse—A Stool Pigeon.

Mr. Twenty-six—A needle (refers to the gauge of the needle).

Nailed—To be arrested.

Narc or Narcos—The law; narcotic agent.

Needle Fiend—An addict who gets pleasure from playing with the needle by inserting an empty needle for the psychological effect.

Needle Freak—One who enjoys using the needle. See Needle Fiend.

Needle Habit—A habit which is satisfied by hypodermic injections.

Needle Park—To New York addicts, upper Broadway and Sherman Square.

Needle Yen—A desire for Narcotics taken hypodermically. A masochistic desire to mainline.

Nembies—Nemoutal.

Nemmies—Nembutal.®

Nickel—A five-dollar bag of Narcotics or Marijuana; also a five-year sentence.

Nickel Deck—Five-dollar package of Heroin.

Nimbie—Nembutal.

Nimbies—Nembutal (Pentobarbital).

Nimby—Nembutal (Pentobarbital).

Nod—To be sleepy from a dose of drugs.

Nut City—A mythical place in which anyone feigning insanity is said to live.

O.D.—An overdose of Narcotics.

Off—Off of drugs, not to be taking drugs at the present time.

Off Someone—To kill someone or to beat someone up.

On Ice—In jail. To lie low or go out of sight temporarily. Wanted by the law.

On the Nod—Sleep from Narcotics.

OP—Opium.

Opiates—Narcotics. Generally either Opium, Morphine or Heroin.

Opium—OP.

Orange Owsley—See *Owsley Acid.*

Orangies—Dexedrine (Dextroamphetamine, orange colored, heart-shaped tablets).

Out-of-it—Confused, disoriented, unknowing; also, an outside person who is not part of the drug culture.

Out There—Confused.

Overjolt—Overdose of Heroin.

Owsley's Acid—LSD (West Coast slang after the illegal manufacturer, Augustus Owsley Stanley, III).

Owsley's Blue Dot—See *Owsley's Acid.*

O. Z.—One ounce of Marijuana.

Pack Heat—To carry a gun.

Pad—User's home; place where he shoots up.

Paid off in gold—Arrested by a Federal officer who flashes his gold badge.

Panic—Shortage of Narcotics on the market.

Paper—A legal prescription for drugs.

PCP—Angel dust. Peace Pill, Hog.

Peace Pill—PCP.

Peaches—Amphetamine Sulphate in rose-colored, heart-shaped tablets. (Also Roses, Hearts, Bennies, Orangies).

Peanuts—Barbiturates.
Peddler—A seller of Narcotics.
Pep Pills—Amphetamines. Also, Wake-ups, Eye Openers.
Pet—The police.
Peter—Chloral hydrate.
Petes—Chloral hydrate.
Peyote—Mescaline.
P.G.—Paregoric.
Phat—Well put together.
Piece—One ounce of Heroin; a gun.
Pill Head—Addict on pills.
Pin—See Harpoon.
Pink Owsleys—See *Owsley's Acid.*
Pinks—Seconal (Seconbarbital Sodium).
Pipe—An Opium smoker.
Plant—Stash-cache of Narcotics.
Pluck—Wine.
P.O.—A parole or probation officer.
P.O.—Paregoric.
Pot—Marijuana.
Pratt or Prat—A hip pocket.
Psilocybin or Psilocyn—Hallucinogenic drugs derived from certain
    mushrooms generally grown in Mexico.
Purple Hearts—A Barbiturate.
Purple Owsley—See *Owsley's Acid.*
Pusher—Seller or dealer of drugs.
Put on—To deceive by design; to make fun of or to mislead some-
    one.
Put the bee on—The act of begging Narcotics.
Put the croaker on the send—A *fit* or spasm by an addict to elicit
    sympathy.

Queen—Male homosexual.
Quill—Matchbook cover used to inhale Narcotics. Powdered drug
    is placed in fold.

Rags—Clothes.
Railroad Weed—Marijuana of poor quality.

Rainbow Roll—An assortment of vari-colored barbiturates, popular among addicts on the West Coast.

Rainbows—Amobarbital Sodium combined with Secobarbital Sodium in red and blue capsules. Also, Red and Blues and Double Trouble.

Rap—Talk.

Rat—Stool Pigeon.

R.D.—A Red Devil.

Red and Blues—See Rainbows.

Red Devils—See Reds.

Reds—Seconal; Secobarbital Sodium.

Reefer—Marijuana cigarette.

Riff—Train of thought.

Right On—Affirmation of a truth; encouragement or support.

Rip Off—Steal or purchase of false Narcotics.

Roach—Butt of a Marijuana cigarette.

Roach Clip—A device used to hold the butt of a Marijuana cigarette.

Rope—Marijuana. So called because when smoked it smells of burning hemp.

Roses—Benzedrine (Amphetamine Sulphate), rose-colored, heart-shaped tablets.

Rosy—Wine.

Run—Period of addiction.

Rush—The intense orgasm-like euphoria experienced immediately after injecting a drug. Also, Flash.

Sam—Federal Narcotic Agents.

Satch—A method of concealing or smuggling drugs into jails.

Satchel—A girl.

Scag—Heroin.

Scat—Heroin.

Scene—Where something is happening.

Schmeck—Heroin.

School Boy—Codeine.

Scortch—To abuse someone verbally and very severely.

Score—To find a source of drugs.

Script—A prescription written by a physician to obtain drugs.

Script Writer—A sympathetic physician; someone who forges prescriptions.

Seccy—Seconal (Secobarbital Sodium) .

Seconal—Sleeping pill; depressant, Pinks.

Send it home—To inject Narcotics intravenously.

Serpent—See Harpoon.

Sewer—The vein into which drugs are injected.

Sex Punk—A male homosexual.

Shakedown—To be arrested or held without charges in order to persuade the addict to supply information to police.

Shank—Knife.

Shit—Heroin.

Shoot—See Maintaining.

Shooting Gallery—Place where several addicts gather to shoot dope.

Shoot Up—See Mainlining.

Short—Car.

Short Go—A small or weak shot.

Shrink—A psychiatrist or psychologist.

Shucking—Wasting time.

Shy—To prepare a pill of Opium for smoking.

Silver—See Harpoon.

Silver Serpent—See Harpoon.

Sissy—A male homosexual.

Sitter—An individual who is sophisticated in the use of drugs, who will oversee others who are on LSD to make sure they do not harm themselves.

Sixteenth Spoon—Sixteenth of an ounce of Heroin.

Skin—Cigarette paper used for a Marijuana cigarette.

Skin Popping—Injecting drugs under the skin.

Sleeping Pills—Barbiturates.

Smack—Heroin.

Smashed—High on drugs.

Sneaky Pete—Wine.

Sniff—To sniff Narcotics (usually Heroin, Cocaine, or Glue) .

Snort—To sniff powdered Narcotics.

Snow—Cocaine.

Snowbird—A cocaine user.

Sound someone—To feel someone out.

Speed—Methamphetamine; any stimulant, especially, Amphetamines.

Speedball—A cocaine-heroin combination.

Speeder—A user of Methamphetamine.

Speed Freak—An excessive user of Methamphetamine.

Speeding—Using Methamphetamine.

Spike—See Harpoon.

Splash—Methamphetamine.

Split—To leave a place, sometimes in haste.

Spot Habit—See *Ice Cream Habit.*

Square—Lame.

Stable—The community of girls who prostitute for one pimp.

Star Dust—Cocaine.

Stash—A place to hide drugs or money; generally a place well hidden but readily available.

Steam Boat—A tube such as an empty toilet tissue roll which is used to increase the amount of smoke from a Marijuana cigarette going into the lungs in order to increase the effectiveness of the cigarette.

Steam Roller—See Steam Boat.

Stick—A Marijuana cigarette.

Stir—Prison.

Stoned—High on Drugs.

STP—Hallucinogen; lasts for seventy-two hours.

Straight—An addict's feeling of well-being after taking drugs.

Strawberries—An LSD preparation.

Strung-out—Confused.

Stuff—Heroin.

Sugar—Narcotics, generally Heroin.

Sugar Cube—This is quite a vehicle for LSD, a drop of LSD is absorbed by the sugar cube before being taken.

Sunshine—An orange or yellow tablet of LSD reputedly to be of a very potent strength.

Swingman—A drug peddler.

T or T Man—A big man. A Federal agent, especially a *narco*.

Take a trip—Using LSD.

Take Off—To smoke. To rob a place, especially of Narcotics.

Taste—Small quantity of Narcotics usually give nas a reward or favor.

Tea—Marijuana.

Tea Man—A marijuana user.

Tecata—Heroin.

Ten-cent Pistol—Bag containing poison.

Texas Tea—Marijuana.

THC—Synthetic hallucinogen; produces same effect as Marijuana. Tetra Hydro Cannabinol. The active ingredients in Marijuana.

The Man—Policeman or Detective.

Ticket—A dose of LSD.

Tie Off—Stopping circulation in order for veins to rise.

Tight—Close.

Tinge—See Flash.

Tired—Old or worn out.

Tom Cat—See Harpoon.

Tooies—Tuinal capsules. See Double Trouble.

Tracks—Scars along the veins after many injections.

Trap—Prison.

Travel Agent—A person who sells LSD.

Trey—Three-dollar bag of Narcotics; generally Heroin.

Tripping—Taking a hallucinating drug.

Tripping Out—Same as Tripping.

Truck Drivers—Amphetamines.

Tuanol—Sleeping pill; depressant.

Tuinal—A barbiturate. Also called Rainbows or Double Trouble.

Turkey—Clod or square. A bag of non-narcotic powder sold as a regular bag.

Turn On—To be excited by; to get high on drugs.

TV Action—Euphoria from drugs.

Unkie—Morphine.

Uppers—Stimulant; Cocaine, Speed and Psychedelics.

Vegetable—A person who has lost all contact with reality due to drugs.

Very Outside—Extremely far out or weird.

Vet—A prison or jail physician.

Vines—Clothes.

Vipe—To smoke Marijuana.

Viper—A Marijuana smoker.

Wake-up—Morning shot.

Wake-ups—Amphetamines.

Wasted—Stoned or drunk.

Way Out—Incomprehensible. The best.

Weed—Marijuana.

Wheels—Car.

White Cross—A white tablet of Speed which is sectioned with a cross.

White Lady—Heroin.

White Nurse—A term used to cover Cocaine, Morphine or Heroin; but more often Morphine.

White Owsley's—See Owsley's Acid.

Whites—Amphetamine Sulphate in round, white double-scored tablets.

White Stuff—*M,* Hard stuff, Morphine.

Wig—Head, hair.

Wig Out—To become psychotic as a result of Narcotics.

Wine—Grapes, Pluck, Rosey, Sneaky Pete.

Wired—Addicted on a Narcotic drug.

Works—Equipment for injection of drugs.

Yellow Jackets—Nembutal, Barb, depressant. Phenobarbital Sodium in yellow capsule form.

Yellows—Nembutal.

Zonked—Under the influence of Narcotics.

REFERENCES

Cull, J. G. and Hardy, R.E.: A study of language meaning (gender shaping) among deaf and hearing subjects. *Journal of Perceptual and Motor Skills,* in press, 1973a.

Cull, J. G. and Hardy, R. E.: Dissimilarity in word meaning among blind and sighted persons. *Journal of General Psychology,* in press, 1973.

Hardy, R. E. and Cull, J. G.: Verbal dissimilarity among black and white subjects: a prime concern in counseling and communication. *The Journal of Negro Education,* in press, 1973.

CHAPTER 13

COLLEGE STUDENTS AS VOLUNTEERS

Norman Manasa

VOLUNTEERISM; and, in this case the typical college volunteer program, is like a bright red apple with a rotten core (you don't know something is terribly wrong until you bite into it). Particularly during the past ten years, volunteerism has become one of the great myths of contemporary America. It has almost ascended to those heights traditionally reserved for apple pie, motherhood and the flag.

But, as I say, there is more wrong than right with the volunteer movement as it now exists. Some of the basic notions which support the theme of volunteerism should be examined and, hopefully, set to rights before too much more time passes. Volunteerism, however, like so many other things, is only an extension of man and therefore it is necessary to first bring forward some comments related to the basic nature of man himself.

As far as volunteerism is concerned, they are mainly these: (a) man needs to give; (b) man needs to exercise those powers of life within himself; and (c) man needs a governing structure which will blunt his more destructive impulses, support him when he grows weak, and bring to him the knowledge he needs to perform in a competent manner. Unfortunately, the traditional view of what volunteerism is all about acknowledges none of these things. We prefer to believe that man should give, that giving is the *right* thing for him to do. This of course implies that man has the option not to give, a view which many question strongly including myself.

It is contended by some that *altruism* is not basic to the condition of man; that he must first develop his own security and meet his own love needs before he is capable of giving to others. The implied thought here, then, is that man possesses the ability to almost hoard his natural talents and values of self, cultivating them and watching them grow until one day, when he feels he has enough, he will burst himself upon the world in an almost spiritual ejaculation of sharing.

Other thinkers, such as *Erich Fromm,* believe that it is not an option but a necessity for personal health and well-being that people be givers all the time, without waiting for that magic day when they have *saved* enough of themselves to be able to spread a little of it around.

To me, the second view is the most accurate and compelling. Carrying this theme further, it can be seen that the *need to give* is the same as the *need to have the power to give.* Man needs to exercise those powers which reside within himself; of the life within him. He needs to give of it, to share it, to have others *eat of it.* It is the nature of a tree, for example, to give of its fruit. Not to do so would result in its impotence and eventually its death. This condition is no different for man.

Another aspect of giving which we rarely consider is the whole matter of common ordinary respect. When does giving become corrupted to the point where it simply means control of one person over another? When does caring for somebody else degenerate to the condition of all too much contemporary volunteerism in that it becomes the standard bleeding-heart smother-the-little-dears-to-death-and-eternal-dependence form of narcissism and stupidity? When this happens it is difficult to say, but there is much more of it than we can comfortably abide.

And, at the other extreme, how much plain irresponsibility hides behind the banner of *volunteerism?* What great mass of volunteers simply don't show up when they've agreed to because of any number of self-serving excuses? Or how many just disappear because they find that caring for another means work? (And they sure as hell didn't sign up to do that.)

What is needed is volunteer programs, just as in any other human enterprise, is an effective governing structure which will support the volunteer when he grows weak or lazy; bring to him the knowledge he needs so that he may perform competently, and provide for self-assessment on the part of the volunteer so that he will blunt what unconscious drive he may have to usurp the integrity of another.

One last assault against the common notion of giving as contained in the concept of volunteerism should be made before going further.

The popular understanding of giving, drawn from the *Puritan ethic* is to do so unselfishly with no thought of recompense or return. But this common belief is not in keeping with the realities of things and nature. By way of analogy, we can draw an illustration from the science of physics. We say that "every action has an equal and opposite reaction." By this law we acknowledge that nothing can be done in nature without that action having an effect on its initiator. Though we sometimes forget it, man is a part of nature and so how can it possibly be that he can do something which in no way returns to affect him?

The point is this: In the reality of things as demonstrated in the condition of man there is always some return, in some way, for something given. It is not possible to do something for nothing. The return is a real one and always there, whether it comes in the form of a paycheck, prestige, position, power or just plain *feeling good*. The simple satisfaction of doing something; anything, is one's own gain. In an instance where you give, that act is its cause of change in others and it affects a change within you. In short, one can never do anything which in some way does not return a gift to the giver.

But what does all this have to do with a college volunteer program? Simply this: Any attempt to move people toward a particular goal must be built around hard and correct perceptions of what people are rather than pie-in-the-sky theories of what we believe people should be.

This means several specific things with regard to volunteer programs. First among them is the matter of attitude on the part of the volunteers and this must be looked at from several different perspectives.

People must learn to recognize as *good* the return they obtain from whatever work it is they set their hands to. Whether this be an everyday job or work done for no monetary compensation, they must accept the return as being a good thing in itself. If the work is good, the return must therefore be good.

Equally important is this cardinal rule: The volunteer must be willing to admit to himself his own ignorance. He must, in some way, believe that the person whom he has chosen to help has something to teach him which he does not already know, and that this something, whether it be about life or himself or another person, is vital to his own existence and which he therefore must learn. Somebody from a university working in the community, for example, must acknowledge that he is there not only to give, but to receive as well; to learn as well as to teach. Essentially this means that he regards the people with whom he is working with simple respect, for they too, are the givers; they too, the teacher. If this attitude is not present and obvious; and it rarely is in any traditional volunteer approach, two things of great and damaging consequence soon occur.

People, especially kids, have great instincts. If they (i.e. residents of jails, slums, migrant camps, etc.) perceive that you are there out of pity for their utter wretchedness, that you believe them to have no real worth as people expect when you give it to them by paying them some small attention they will hate you. (It was about three years ago that the militant blacks began throwing the *White Missionaries,* as they put it, out of the ghettos. And with good reason, too. Probably never in the history of the world have so many been so degraded by people with such good intentions as the blacks were in the mid-sixties.)

The other great negative consequence of the usual volunteer attitude is implied in the meaning of this statement: "The merciful can be very dangerous when they are not guided by hard knowledge and the certainty of this limitations."

It is one of the wonders of our age that great numbers of people feel they can enter a situation completely foreign to them (e.g. a ghetto) without any real training, without much of an idea of what they are supposed to accomplish there and without any concept whatever of just how they are to go about doing whatever it is they are there to do. If someone went for a job in a factory or business bearing the weight of this ignorance he would be laughing into the unemployment lines before the embarrassment could drain from his face.

Yet thousands of volunteers do precisely this every day. Why? Nobody strives to be an incompetent so it is not a result of any willful intent. Again, it seems to me, this is a result of an unrealistic attitude, but in this instance one which is born of the economic aspect of our societal make-up.

There was a time not too long ago when *volunteerism* was the virtual sole perogative of the rich and a few monks. The reason was that money (or the renuciation of money) is a tool which buys leisure time. "Social concern is a luxury" is how a friend put it recently. When a person has his physical needs satisfied (*not* his psychological or spiritual needs, I contend), then he can worry about feeding his neighbor and not before.

But after World War II we witnessed the burgeoning growth of the *affluent society* which meant that now, not just the rich, but whole masses of middle and upper-middle class people had leisure time in abundance. Many decided to use that extra time in volunteer efforts. Yet, by a peculiar triple-standard prompted by the predominant Puritan ethic, people believed it was *right* to care for others but that this was definitely an activity peripheral, to our real mission of caring for ourselves first and further, and most baffling of all, that any acknowledged satisfaction resulting from one's efforts was a source of guilt.

As a people, we felt we should provide for the *less fortunate,* meaning the *materially* poor. But because economics plays such a large part in our determinations of what is or is not moral, we therefore assumed that if someone was materially poor then he must be spiritually poor, too. The implications were that if we had money we were therefore morally intact and superior to those who had no money.

As a result, when all the rhetoric is set aside the basic themes of most contemporary volunteerism are these.

1. (a) I have money which means I'm O.K.; or
   (b) You have no money which means there is something wrong with you; and

(c) Therefore, I am a better person than you.

2. I know I have no training, no idea of what it is I'm here to do, and even if I did, I wouldn't have the faintest notion where to begin. But I'm here, and that's more than someone like you has a right to expect.

3. Don't thank me. It makes me feel guilty over again and my guilt is what put me here in the first place.

When all this is distilled into action, it means one paramount thing: volunteers too often do a lousy job.

If the volunteer does not think he is going to receive anything in return for his work, if his belief is that only he helps and that the poor and the desperate with whom he works have nothing to give in return, then human nature dictates that the work must be regarded as being of a very low priority. So why bother to be any good at it? Why bother to expend your energies on someone who has nothing to offer, who does not have the integrity to be a giver in his own right, who is essentially worthless? Especially when there are other unrelenting, compelling priorities which one must pursue (for college kids, it's good grades and credentials; for the rest of us, it's money and position).

So the result for most traditional volunteerism is that the work done is either short-lived or incompetent or both; or worse yet, done by those few hangers-on whose fanatical devotion to *helping* gives strong indication they should be residing in institutions rather than working in them.

I do not mean to say that all work done in the name of volunteerism is worthless and damaging. Some noble efforts and great and good service has been brought about because of people who are firm believers in the very things I am denouncing. But I would contend they do not acknowledge the dynamisms which spur them on; specifically the need for a satisfactory return I think it only honest that we do acknowledge the forces at work within each of us. For I have been associated with too many traditional volunteer efforts, both by individuals and groups, to hold most of it as being less than reprehensible.

Nor do I contend that volunteerism should simply vanish. It is like anything else. If done properly, the volunteer, by caring for those lost and broken people with which this world seems to be filled, can exhibit the most noble strengths of the human spirit and touch greatness itself.

The question is not whether one should volunteer; for the alternate course is to stand on the sidelines while the world flings itself into a hell of its own making. The question, rather, is this: how does one go about volunteering? To describe this, I can speak best using the illustration of my own experience.

My background for the past three years is that of the administrator of an academically-credentialed volunteer program at the University of Miami. But it is volunteer only in the sense that neither the students nor the faculty members are required to participate.

I initiated the program (which, for no particular reason, is called SUMMON) in the fall of 1969 and have served from then till the present as its director. But, as I say, it is not the traditional college volunteer program and in fact, was not founded to be such. It is, by any definition of the educational experience, an interdisciplinary academic program which draws its strengths from the structural elements most basic to this or any university.

SUMMON puts university students into situations in the community where they can help people who need their help, and just as importantly, where the students can learn a great many necessary things about themselves.

In the spring of 1969, the ideology which was to give birth to the SUMMON Program had grown from unordered and random thoughts into a philosophy sufficiently coherent to permit action. What we wanted to do was simply this: To reform the education offered by the University of Miami by bringing offcampus reality into the educational experience of students. And by doing that, to offer regular and competent service to the people of the Miami community who needed the help we could provide and who wanted it.

The thinking followed from there in this form. If we could provide an educational experience for our students by placing them in the community, and if the purpose of a university is to educate and it measures that education by awarding academic credit to the student, then it is right and proper for a university to acknowledge this form of education as it does any other; that is by giving academic credit to those students who participate.

It may be helpful to dwell on this for a moment as there are many who seem opposed to this element of academic credit which is so basic to the SUMMON Program. Several years ago a traditional volunteer program was begun at one of the great universities in the Midwest. Its director wrote an action handbook about it to tell others of what had occurred there and how their efforts could be duplicated at other universities. In this pamphlet he wrote one thing which struck me more than anything else he had to say. The thought was this: "Students should not be given academic credit for work done in the community as they will enter the volunteer program to get the credit rather than to do the work."

To me, this is nonsense, and for several reasons. First, it is not only grossly unfair to judge so sweepingly the motives of others, but impossible. We would do better, I think, to leave all judgments of motives aside (questions such as, "But is he sincere?" etc.) and simply deal on the level of productivity. Or, as it applies to accredited university programs, the levels of both productivity and learning experience. Second, his opinion smacks of the unrealistic Puritan view that a return on something freely given is somehow *dirty*. Since man receives some return by the vary act of giving, should we not then openly acknowledge that return?

This we did at the University of Miami. Nine departments, representing the Schools of Business, Education, and the Graduate School, along with the College of Arts and Sciences offer students three credits on a *Pass-Fail* basis for a semester's participation in the SUMMON Program.

In the philosophy of SUMMON, academic credit serves as a realistic and honest recognition that people are affected by whatever they try to effect.

In terms of academics, credits is the means used to acknowledge that, indeed our students do learn by participating in the type of experience the SUMMON Program provides.

It is our contention that the type of learning experience which regulated community involvement provides for students in very much consonant with the ideology of a university. The basic justification is both very old and very new. "We learn by doing," and "the community is a life-laboratory for the humanities," are both phrases which reaffirm the axiom that actual experience is, indeed the best teacher.

Chaining young adults to a desk for four years and filling them with theory, most of which they will forget after their next examination is folly. Only by the experience of application will they come to discover the true value of that theory and come to possess the artistry of the practitioner.

Moreover, the traditional college curricula does great damage. And not only to the community for which they provide little or no real service but to their own eight-and-one-half million students whom they insist must sit and grow fat while providing nothing toward the national welfare. This is a point sufficiently important to deserve more than cursory attention.

It was not all that long ago I suppose, when the young grew to adulthood in accord with the design of nature, uninhibited by the modern educational process and the emasculation resulting from unrestrained technology. Cultures based on farming for example forced all members of the family to work at an appropriate age in taking from the earth the things necessary for the survival of the family.

It was natural then for the young to grapple with reality at what we now consider to be an early age. They learned the real message of survival. And this learning was done with a direct responsibility to and for others. "Work the earth well, make her bless us, or mother and father, brothers and sisters will know hunger."

But from this came also the knowledge of one's talents and limits and the struggle saw the young graced with that integrity of accomplishment which spelled manhood.

Colleges, however, have pretty well succeeded in separating the young from reality for an unnatural time even for this society. The period of immaturity and adolescence has been extendeed beyond any reasonable boundary. Our college system has placed students in the position of being nonachievers. To accomplish something means to take on life as an equal, and then to give (or have the potential of giving) that achievement to others. Students however, are clearly the unequal partner of the student-professor relationship.

Because the only thing of value is that which comes from the professor (after all, you will be tested on nothing else), the student is not the creator, the initiator, he who acts, or he who is responsible for his own actions. He remains the passive partner, writing down all that is given and returning it as he is told. He reacts, does not freely experiment and is responsible for nothing he himself creates. He is responsible to someone else, not himself but to some professor who by all odds does not know even his name.

For this process of unnatural dependency, essentially unchanged since the primer years, to continue until someone's twenty-first birthday and beyond is not only silly but damaging. While the young farmer could say he had bent the earth itself to his will and thereby fed his family, today's college student can only mutter about his grade and, most importantly, give it to no one.

Far from moving the young to be mature and responsible, the general effect of the universities is to create a whole generation of docile, weak, incompetent, terribly inexperienced people who have little sense of accomplishment, creativity, freedom, committment, power and therefore, pride. (There's some changing needed for universities, too.)

If the SUMMON Program operates from any single premise, it is this: students are not preparing for life. They are alive now and therefore must assume the responsibilities of life so far as their situation permits. And the caring for someone else is definitely one of these responsibilities.

We intended to build a program which would not only make university students aware of this, but one that would put them in a position where they could exercise this responsibility. We would give them a good deal of freedom in their work. And we hoped they would come to understand that the impact they made would be both powerful and life-long. In this way, the student, by being the volunteer, would become a committed, innovating person who would gain an intense awareness of his obligation to the most weighty responsibility of all, a human life.

By early 1969 we had determined what it was we wanted the SUMMON Program to become. Now the question was: how do we go about building such a program?

It could be seen from all too many examples, that sending hordes of students into the ghettos or any other place, produced anything but a rapprochement between the warring cultures. The reasons for this were also óbvious. There existed virtually no controls which would guarantee the regular performance of those who had promis- ised (if not explicitly, then implicitly) to function in a competent were broken and the supposed recipients were made to feel cheap- manner. A great deal of harm was produced as a result. Promises ened and more worthless than ever. The general result was a need- less exacerbation of the suffering of those who were to have been helped while the volunteer went his merry way undaunted, and be- cause he never even knew what he was really causing, more ignorant than ever.

Another drawback to the usual volunteer program is that most volunteers have no detailed idea of what it is they are supposed to do. And when they do know what their goal is, there is little expert guidance offered to help them toward it. "Working in the com- munity" is a vague enough phrase to hide within it the whole parade of those who endeavor to *do good* but never once question their abil- ity to perform competently.

Some believe that any volunteer is better than no one at all. I do not. If there is any rule to this business, it is this: if you do not know what you are doing, stay out . . . or learn what you are doing or trying to do. Do not spend your extra hours playing with the lives of people who can become the victims of your own wretched bungling.

Therefore, we decided what was needed for the college volun- teer program was an organizational structure which accurately re- flected the same dynamics of human behavior and needs which any other successful social organism does. This structure should have within it the mechanisms which provide for constant and coordi- nated analysis on the part of both program and volunteers. It should be able to continually infuse ideas and knowledge into the participants. This is not a negotiable point. The structure must be strong so that it can do these things yet it must be sufficiently flex- ible to adjust to changes which its built-in analytical machinery indicates should be made.

SUMMON immediately found that the employment of aca- demic credit was, in large part, the answer to keep our people not only regular but competent as well. Because SUMMON is a course offered by the university, we could guarantee to community agencies that our students would work six hours each week for the four months of a semester. (Once a student is in the course, there is no such thing as *voluntary attendance.*)

Also, because academic credit was central to the program, the university faculty had to become involved in order to insure that the granting of credit was not abused. The traditional academic responsibility was not only preserved, but the expertise of an entire faculty was made available to our students (A word of caution is in order here. University faculty are a vital part of the SUMMON Program but they are not to be confused with the Oracle of Delphi. This is a whole new world for most faculty members too. Many of the old answers do not fit and they must go through their own learning experience.)

Our people were not only to perform regularly, they were to be competent as well. With all this we had not only a coherent philosophy of what we wanted to do and why, but we also commanded the necessary mechanical elements the university had to provide, i.e. academic credit and faculty participation.

But what was to be the specific structure within which the students would function? What was to be required of them? Here is how it appears in the SUMMON handbook:

SUMMON REQUIREMENTS FOR STUDENTS

In order to participate in the SUMMON Program for a semester, the SUMMON student is required to:

(a) work six hours per week on the job.

(b) submit a one-page report each two weeks. The purpose of the report is for the student to chart his own progress. It is to be typed and double-spaced, and submitted in triplicate.

(c) attend one meeting each week. These are held in a three week cycle. The first two weeks are seminars with the student's faculty advisor: the third is a meeting with the student's agency representative; then the seminars again, and so forth.

(d) keep a journal. Students are given a notebook to keep as a record of their work in SUMMON. Its purpose is to provide the student with a vehicle to gauge his own personal growth. It is solely his private property.

(e) submit a final paper at the end of the semester. Its length is a matter of the student's own determination.

And this is why we established these requirements:

(a) We found that six hours of regularly scheduled work each week of a semester would result in our students having considerable effect on individuals in the community without putting an unreasonable burden on the student's available time.

(b) This report is a simple description of the SUMMON student's progress and any problems, criticisms, or suggestions he may wish to convey. Three copies are submitted. One is given to the student's faculty representative, one to the student's agency representative, and one to the SUMMON Director. These reports help to let everyone know what is happening from the point of view of the student.

The reports also serve as a means by which the student submits himself to his own analysis. Because writing is an analytical exercise, the reports force the students to review the status of both himself and the program at regular intervals. The hope is that this mechanism will prevent a student from blindly plunging on without any self-evaluation and guidance.

c) The seminars serve two purposes. One is to give the students access to the expertise of the university faculty. The other is to make the student aware of how the theory of a particular academic discipline applies to the community situation in which he is working.

The agency meetings permit the agency staff to offer the SUMMON student information pertinent to his work.

d) If SUMMON works, it will teach students things about themselves which, while they should remain private knowledge, should not go unrecorded. This journal remains the private property of the student; no one checks to see if he makes entries or not. This *requirement* really amounts to a strong suggestion.

e) The final paper. These, like the reports, are informal. They conform to an outline drawn up by the SUMMON Director.

n.b. The SUMMON students must adhere strictly to these requirements. If they do not produce according to these guidelines, they have, in effect, broken their contract and are dropped from the program. This makes a sort of *fail-safe* mechanism to see to it that we do no damage to the people of the community by sporadic attendance, incompetence, etc.

We lose approximately twenty percent of the students who enroll in SUMMON in the first three weeks of any given semester. Generally, all the rest finish.

It took two years of trial and error before this performance criteria for our students was established as practical and efficient. There were a good many mistakes and more than a few disappointments but we have a program which does one remarkable thing—it works.

Academic credit was the main tool by which the SUMMON Program could offer regular and competent assistance to the community and at no cost to them. A rare phenomena indeed. Philosophy preceded practice and it was worth all the care and planning in advance. If we had not been able to insure these things, we would not have done anything.

But the question still remained: what *work,* specifically, were our students to do in the community? The answer to this could only be obtained by, first, determining what college students can do —period. It did not take much effort to find that college kids, unless you regard the ability to take notes as being some special talent, are not generally equipped to do much of anything. These kids have not been through twelve or more years of our ideas of formal *education* for nothing.

The one thing all college students have in common however, was that, to a man, they could read and write. So we adopted the rather shaky, and at the time, empirically unproven hypothesis that if you could read you could teach someone else to read also.

So that became what our people would do; tutoring. In the interests of accuracy it should be pointed out that *tutoring* covers a wide area of activity for the SUMMON Program. While it is true that our students work on remedial subjects with functionally illiterate inmates of the county jail, we also prepare inmates with some high school background to take the State High School Equivalency Examination so that upon release, they might have a diploma and therefore, greater chances for employment. Our work at Spectrum House, a residental treatment center for hard-core drug addicts, strives for similiar results.

Some of our students work with severely retarded children at the state facility here in Dade County. They do very basic behavior modification programming with these kids, teaching them to clothe and feed themselves for example, together with language acquisition exercises. At present our students are working at thirteen agencies, each one different from the next.

There exists a tremendous need for just this type of tutorial service. Endless numbers of people do not possess the most basic academic skills necessary to function in a literate society. And they do not reside in just the most obvious places such as jails, ghettos, etc. But, and this is a frightening commentary, they populate in huge numbers the one institution whose sole purpose is to produce a literate citizenry—the schools.

In planning the SUMMON Program, we decided that we would send our students to work in community agencies which already existed. This meant it was not necessary for us to found and build our own physical facilities by which we might advance the betterment of the local society. Any public institution, whether it be a jail, hospital, man-power training program, or school, seems by its very definition to be in perpetual and desperate need of competent personnel.

Because we decided to work at places which were already functioning and which needed the help we could provide, we did not need to incur the costs involved in building our own facilities, such as store-fronts and community action agencies. It was not necessary therefore, for us to spend the time and energies of the program's administration playing the popular game of *hustling the bureaucracy*. We could put our efforts into running a program instead of running to the foundations and the federal government for money. (In fact the SUMMON Program was fully functioning for two years before it received virtually any monetary support.)

Once the decision is made to work in community agencies which already exist instead of building your own, the vital element remaining is to secure the working cooperation of the agency staff. These are mainly people who deal not in theories, but in realities. Their first question, and properly so, will be: "What can you do for us?" And with equal justice their continuing refrain throughout the entire relationship will be: "What have you done for us lately?" The man running the county jail or the lady who heads the psychiatric section at a mental hospital generally has enough headaches as it is. They do not need and will not permit a full scale invasion of incompetents disguised as volunteers.

But if you produce for them, if you give their charges the help they themselves are unable to give, they will not only cooperate but love you and clamor for more. (It is with some embarrassment at our inadequacies and yet some pride, that SUMMON now has an unsolicited waiting list of forty-nine agencies, in addition to the thirteen we are already serving, who seek our aid.)

In building any program, it is just as important to take stock of your limitations as well as your resources, so it is important to mention this. Because we knew our people to possess very limited skills, we did not set grandiose goals for the programs (e.g. *changing society*) nor did we set vague and high-sounding goals (such as *counseling*) for our students. We do tutoring; pure and simple. We do it because our people are capable of doing it and because the people we work with need it.

But *tutoring* is a mundane and everyday term and so it seems to be a popular conception that because the word is simple, the work it describes must also be simple. This is not the case.

To attempt to instruct people in skills they must have if they are to function in this society; but skills in which they do not usually see immediate value, is extremely difficult work. Attempting to motivate people to a goal; the value of which they rarely recognize, cuts to the great question of the attitudes, the heritage, and ultimately the future of individuals and of a people. What are we? What do we want to become? Why? But these questions can be seen on yet an even greater scale.

To look in any direction in contemporary America is to see the great festering wounds which all the grand government programs, all the tremendous sums of money, all the king's horses and all the king's men cannot seem to stitch closed. Wounds that have cut so deeply into the societal body that as a country we will bleed our own lifeblood dry if they are not healed. The greatest of these wounds is caused by the conflict between the cultures and all the problems of the rich and the poor, the *haves* and the *have-nots* which that implies.

Almost all this misery, I think, can be traced to one simple axiom of human nature: people are afraid of and therefore hostile toward that which they do not know and from which they are estranged.

We fear each other. We fear ourselves. As a result and to escape the anxieties produced by this fear, we retreat into the false womb of drugs, or head for the Rockies or the suburbs, or simply stay home and brutalize someone weaker than ourselves. I suppose everybody mixes his own combination of these things and lives with them as best he can. But for most of us, all this running and hiding leaves us with little more than a cheap shot at life. While things should be getting better, they are not. And though violence, hatred and human degradation do not comprise all of our internal history, they are far too much in evidence.

Fear is the cause of such misery and waste. But what measures can be taken to counter the effects of this fear? Since people fear each other because they are apart from and therefore ignorant of each other, then the solution is to bring them together so that they would come to know each other and hence, not be so afraid any more. In other words there must be physical proximity and contact between the representatives of different cultures which occurs on a regular basis and for a prolonged period of time.

This, we are experiencing, is provided by the tutorial relationship. The SUMMON Program creates a situation where two people, one volunteer from the university and one resident of the community, bind themselves together for six regular scheduled hours a week for the length of a semester.

But raising someone's reading level for example, though we do a good job of it, is actually the lowest priority of the program. What we are really trying to do is to put people from different and warring cultures into a common situation whereby they might come to know each other simply as people. Whereby they might come to enlighten each other's ignorances and minister to each other's needs. Whereby they might come to care for each other and not be so afraid as their fathers were. Whereby we might help heal the nation's wounds.

It is through this tutorial experience that human bonds are established and warmth, comfort and intimacy can grow between two people.

When all talk about the economy, defense, law and order and all the rest is set aside, there will remain no greater need for our society than for just this type of personal interaction. For it is on the singular question of whether we can live together as people that this great nation will stand or fall.

But the college students; where are they when there is such a great need for them? Sitting in their desks mainly, writing down answers that were half-truths thirty years ago, and learning little which will hold them in good stead against the challenges of the future. They are the young, which means they have the ability to change their inherited attitudes and values and lessen their fears, and they have more leisure time than almost any other class of people in America. And there are so many of them. This is a great waste, but perhaps, the saddest thing of all is that the universities, the one institution which prides itself as being a seeker for truth, teaches its students the greatest of falsehoods: that they know when they do not.

Since the thirties, we have found that money alone, spent on great social programs, will not cure our domestic ills. We do not need more programs so much as we need people; people who can help others, who can calm their own fears and thereby cure themselves.

And there sit eight and one half million of these people, taking notes.

SUMMON is our attempt to change a part of this. We teach students the hard truth that being a volunteer, much-maligned as the phrase sometimes is and often with justification, is being a pro, not being an amateurish hit-and-miss dilettante. And that while they are not in the program to *save* somebody else, they can certainly help themselves.

There is more to the telling however, than this particular story was meant to bear. Like most other things, the SUMMON Program has to be experienced in order to be understood.

But it works. It works because it has an appropriate inner structure and because it functions within the broader structure of a university. Structure and organization however, do not determine if a program such as SUMMON, which is built for people, will be successful. Only the people in it can do that. All we did was put students into a situation where they could be effective while not demanding more from them than they could produce. We gave them some freedom, some guidance, a concrete supporting structure and we made a go of it.

But the main reason the SUMMON Program works is because of the people who are in it. People who are from all over the country; who have different fields of study, different backgrounds, different aspirations. People just like everybody else. They make the program work.

And if you could see what they do, you would know how remarkable a thing this SUMMON Program is.

CHAPTER 14

DEVELOPING EMPLOYMENT OPPORTUNITIES FOR THE YOUTHFUL OFFENDER

RICHARD E. HARDY AND JOHN G. CULL

⬡⬡⬡⬡⬡⬡⬡⬡⬡⬡⬡⬡⬡⬡⬡⬡⬡⬡⬡⬡⬡⬡⬡⬡⬡⬡⬡⬡⬡⬡⬡⬡⬡⬡⬡⬡

□ HOW TO LOCATE JOBS FOR THE JUVENILE OFFENDERS
□ PREPARING THE CLIENT FOR EMPLOYMENT
□ JOB ANALYSIS
□ RELATING PSYCHOLOGICAL DATA TO JOB ANALYSIS INFORMATION IN VOCATIONAL PLACEMENT
□ EMPLOYER OBJECTIONS AND HOW TO DEAL WITH THEM
□ DIRECT PLACEMENT
□ INDIRECT PLACEMENT
□ FOLLOW-UP AFTER PLACEMENT
□ CONCLUSION

⬡⬡⬡⬡⬡⬡⬡⬡⬡⬡⬡⬡⬡⬡⬡⬡⬡⬡⬡⬡⬡⬡⬡⬡⬡⬡⬡⬡⬡⬡⬡⬡⬡⬡⬡⬡

R EHABILITATION SERVICES HAVE been provided to the adult male for some time. Very little work has been done in terms of vocational opportunities for the juvenile offenders. Residential halfway houses have been established for juvenile offenders in place of traditional training schools. In these settings individualized and group treatment as well as vocational group exploration is undertaken.

Shore and Massimo (1966) have reported that work is not sufficient alone for solving delinquents many difficulties. They have indicated that in addition to vocational training and job placement, intensive counseling is needed in order for the youth to find permanent or semipermanent employment. Prevocational counseling is particularly necessary before comparative employment for on-the-job training begins. The reader interested in an excellent review of the vocational and social rehabilitation of juvenile delinquents should see Goldberg (1972). After an intensive study of problems associated with rehabilitation of juvenile delinquents, Goldberg has stated that rehabilitation agencies need specialists who are trained and experienced in work with juvenile offenders. These specialists should be based in local rehabilitation officers and assigned to courts close to their locale. These counselors should be committed to working with youth and should have had previous training and internships in the field of correctional rehabilitation. The counselor, according to Goldberg, should be mobile and willing to counsel with the offender in his own mileu. He also states that outreach programs in the schools, courts and local welfare agencies should be strengthened. Goldberg calls attention to the need for greater coordination between state rehabilitation agencies and correctional agencies, such as youth service agencies, community based programs for the offender, halfway residential houses for the offender, youth guidance centers, drug abuse programs, and neighborhood youth employment agenices. He further states that psychological and psychiatric consultation for the diagnostic evaluation and planning of rehabilitation programs for the juvenile offender should be provided by specialists trained in child and adolescent psychiatry and psychology. Goldberg's results show the expansion of rehabilitation of services to the offender population needs to encompass two new groups: (a) a predelinquent population that may be identified in local junior and senior high schools by behavioral problems such as drug abuse, truancy, and antisocial conduct; and (b) the youthful offender in the age group of seventeen to twenty-five, who may be identified at local probation offices, halfway houses, and county local houses of correction. Goldberg calls for new and intensified programs for the juvenile offender which are integrated with traditional agency procedures.

HOW TO LOCATE JOBS FOR THE JUVENILE DEFENDER

There is a variety of methods utilized to locate jobs for rehabilitated juvenile offenders. With few exceptions, the counselor has the same resources available to him as any person who is trying to secure his own employment.

The counselor can at times get real help from groups who are concentrating their interest on problems of the juvenile offender. These groups include various churches and religious groups, mental health associations, civic clubs (Rotary, Jaycee, Ruritan, etc.), League of Women Voters, women's clubs, and the local office of the State Employment Commission.

The counselor generally should be aware of industrial developments within the area he serves and in adjacent areas. He may also wish to turn to the three volumes of the *Dictionary of Occupational Titles* which offer a wealth of useful information for counselors. Much emphasis is given to descriptions of physical and personality requirements for various jobs. In addition, these volumes help expand the counselor's concepts about various types of jobs which are related to the general interest of the rehabilitation client.

Another important source even for youthful offenders can be that of former employers. These employers, if they do not hire the former delinquent can often give useful information. Another source of information is previously rehabilitated clients, including other young public offenders.

Local Chambers of Commerce usually provide an index which lists types of work available in most communities. Another resource is the Small Business Administration office serving the local area.

PREPARING THE CLIENT FOR EMPLOYMENT

Planning for placement does not begin once the client has had vocational training and is ready, "skill wise," for employment, but when the counselor first reads the client's rehabilitation referral form. The rehabilitation worker must constantly learn about his client in order to effectively help him secure the type of employment he needs. Jeffrey (1969) has developed a job readiness test which helps in the evaluation of job preparedness of clients. While the total instrument is not applicable to all rehabilitation offender clients, certain questions are quite helpful with most persons looking for employment.

In many cases, the rehabilitation counselor must stress training as a partial answer to many of the problems of the public offender. Overtraining a worker for a job which will affect his personal and family adjustment for many years to come is seldom done. In each case, the counselor must take an individual approach in helping his client. In the case of those who are educationally or socially retarded, various remedial programs may be necessary before actual work training programs can begin. In each case, the counselor must exercise considerable judgment concerning what his client needs in order to be totally ready for employment.

On-the-job training for young offenders can be a very effective arrangement for job preparation either inside the institution if opportunities exist or outside if arrangements can be made. Once the youth is released from the institution, the state rehabilitation agency can make "tuition" payments to the employer-trainer in order that the rehabilitation counselor can get the employer interested in training the client and evaluating his work. It may be necessary for the counselor to help the employer arrange the appropriate payment schedule for the client since he is not a trained employee in some cases and would not receive an amount equal to a regularly salaried employee.

In many cases the employer who is training the former young public offender may wish to offer him a job once his training period is completed. In this case, the counselor has killed "two birds with one stone." He has gained training opportunities for his public offender client, observed the client while he is adjusting to the job, and then secured placement for him.

JOB ANALYSIS

Every counselor should be thoroughly familiar with the techniques of job analysis for use in selective placement. The counselor has to be able to match the prospective worker's social, mental and physical qualifications with requirements of the job. Factors such as judgment, initiative, alertness and general health and capability must always be taken into consideration as well as the individual's social and economic background.

Job analysis should answer certain questions concerning the job. *What* does the worker do in terms of physical and mental effort that go into the work situation? *How* is the work done? In other words, does this job involve the use of equipment and mathematics, or does it require travel? *Why* does the worker perform the job? This component of the job analysis answers the question concerning the overall purpose or the sum total of the task and is the reason for doing the job. The worker also should understand the relationship of his task to other tasks that make up the total job.

Generally, the counselor should attempt to place clients in jobs which they can "handle" and which do not require modification. In some cases, however, minor modifications can be made with little or no re-engineering effort. The counselor will have to be careful in suggesting re-engineering of a job, since this can be a costly undertaking in many instances.

The following outline can be used in evaluating a job which is to be performed by a handicapped worker:

A. Name Used for Position Surveyed
  1. D. O. T. title
  2. Alternate titles
  3. D. O. T. definitions
  4. Items worked on in plant surveyed
B. Usual Operator
  1. Sex
  2. General characteristics

C. Physical and Psychological Demands
  1. Activities
  2. Working conditions
  3. Skill required
  4. Intelligence
  5. Temperament
  6. Other
D. Description of Physical Activities
E. Description of Working Conditions
F. Description of Hazards
G. Steps Required to Accomplish the Goal of the Work
H. Equipment Found in the Particular Plant Surveyed
  1. Identification
  2. Set-up and maintenance
  3. Modification
I. Equipment Variations Which May Be found in Other Plants
J. Preemployment Training Required
K. Training Procedure
L. Production
  1. Full production definition
  2. Time to reach normal efficiency
M. Interrelation with Preceding and Succeeding Jobs

RELATING PSYCHOLOGICAL DATA TO JOB ANALYSIS INFORMATION IN VOCATIONAL PLACEMENT

As a first step in getting to know clients well, the counselor should make arrangements to secure appropriate psychological information about them. He should either complete job analyses or use available job evaluation data to make decisions about types of information which will be of value to his clients in the job selection and placement procedure. In many instances, however, the counselor fails to synthesize information obtained from two of his most important sources: the psychological evaluation and the job analysis.

The counselor should take five basic steps, as described by Hardy (1969) in developing a successful procedure for interrelating and using important information. He should:

1. Study the needs of the client and the types of satisfaction meaningful to him.

2. Make certain valid psychological and job analysis data have been gathered.

3. Review the requirements of the job and evaluate the individual traits needed to meet job requirements.

4. Consider the environmental pressures with which the individual must interact.

5. Discuss the job analysis and psychological evaluation with the client so that he will understand what the work will require of him and what it will offer.

Both client and counselor need to have an understanding of job requirements in order to make realistic decisions. One important move should be structuring a set of goals—a guide to help the client avoid useless foundering that gets him nowhere. What satisfactions is he seeking? What is important to him in the long run and what types of work settings will provide these satisfactions? These are questions which the counselor must help the client answer.

Maslow (1954) has suggested a heirarchy of the individual needs which the counselor must understand in order to evaluate a client's psychological status—his satisfactions and frustrations. In the usual order of prepotency, these needs are for (a) physiological satisfaction; (b) safety; (c) belongingness and love; (d) importance, respect, self-esteem and independence; (e) information; (f) understanding; (g) beauty; and (h) self-actualization.

In our society, there is no single situation which is potentially more capable of giving satisfaction at all levels of these needs as a person's work, and it is the responsibility of the counselor to help his client plan for future happiness through adjustment on the job.

The worker needs to help his client become fully aware of the social pressures of the job because these are as important to the individual as the actual job pressures. A client's ability to adapt to the social interactions of the work environment will directly affect his job performance.

The counselor always must ask himself what the requirements of the job are. This question can be answered superficially or in considerable detail. A lay job analysis can give superficial requirements, but the responsibility for an in-depth job description belongs to the expert—the counselor who will often have to give direct advice to the client.

Effective placement requires effective planning. Planning cannot be really useful unless appropriate information has been obtained, interrelated and skillfully utilized so that the client and the counselor have a clear understanding of possible problems and possible solutions.

EMPLOYER OBJECTIONS AND HOW TO DEAL WITH THEM

Quite often, when considering placement, the counselor is confronted with the dilemma of determining to whom he owes basic loyalty—the client or the employer—that is, should he be protective of the client when dealing with an employer or protective of the employer. How much of the client's problems in reference to his incarceration and other handicaps should the counselor relate to the employer? Should he obscure the client's background in discussions with the employer?

If the professional relationship were bilateral and concerned only the client and counselor, the answer to the dilemma would be immediately obvious; however, the relationship is trilateral.

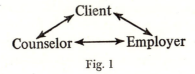

Fig. 1

As such, the counselor owes equal professional responsibility to both the client and prospective employer. Therefore, the counselor should communicate with the employer in a basic, forthright manner. The counselor is obligated professionally to be honest in his dealings with the employer.

If the counselor fails to be completely honest and forthright with the employer, he not only jeopardizes his professional relationship with the employer thereby obviating any possibility of placing clients in this area in the future, but also he takes a great chance of jeopardizing the client-employer relationship later when the employer becomes aware of the client's attributes which the counselor chose to hide or misrepresent. Consequently, we feel rather strongly that the counselor should discuss with the client what he is planning to relate to the employer. If the client refuses to allow the counselor to discuss his assets, liabilities and previous record with the employer, the counselor should modify his role in the placement process. His role should be one of providing placement information to the client, but he should not enter actively into the placement process with the client.

There are two limitations to this interchange between the counselor and employer relative to the public offender client:

1. The counselor and employer should discuss thoroughly those aspects and only those aspects of the client's background which have a direct relationship with the job.

2. The counselor should communicate with the employer on a level at which both are comfortable in the exchange of information (Hardy, 1972).

In the case of placement of young offenders, questions will often arise concerning whether or not the individual is trustworthy, reliable, violent or honest. In some cases, the employers may even be afraid of these persons. Employers may ask questions concerning how he will get the individual to cooperate in various job activities if problems arise. The employer may be concerned that the individual may not perform well for him and he may be somewhat concerned about his own safety if he were to fire the individual. All of these questions can be answered through candid open discussions with the employer. It may be necessary for the counselor to explain what probation means. It may be necessary for the counselor, with the permission of the client, to discuss the client's previous criminal record.

Quite often a counselor approaches a prospective employer regarding a specific client; and as the conversation progresses, the counselor finds himself relating information which, while highly pertinent in the rehabilitation process, has little to do with the client as an employee. In each instance which the counselor makes an employer contact for placement purposes, the counselor should have summarized previously all material in the case folder which is directly related to the client's proficiency in a particular position—both his assets and liabilities. After reviewing this summary, the counselor should refrain from relating any other information he may have derived from counseling sessions, training evaluations, or diagnostic work-ups. A mark of professionalism is the ability to communicate the essential factors relating to the client and still respect the client's fundamental right to confidentiality of case material.

A question which often arises is this one: "Why should I hire a former offender when I could hire someone who has never been in trouble?" The counselor will have to answer this question according to his own philosophy and training. Some helpful responses might include the following:

1. Ask why he should not employ individuals who have been readied for employment by a state-federal rehabilitation training program and who are, in effect, certified and highly recommended by rehabilitation employment specialists.

2. Describe the medical, social and psychiatric evaluations completed on all clients (not being specific or violating confidentiality). In other words, why not hire an individual who comes to an employer with more background information available than he usually receives on an employee.

3. Remind him that he by doing so is actually supporting what he, as a taxpayer, has already invested some money in—an employment program for juvenile offenders which is being proven to be highly successful.

Another question which frequently is raised in employment interviews concerning firing and dismissal of former offenders and the employer's reluctance to treat the rehabilitant in the same manner he would treat other employees. The counselor again will have to rely on his own resources; however an analogy may be helpful here.

Indicate that if you, as a salesman, were selling refrigerators and the employer bought one which later malfunctioned, you would stand by your product and attempt to get it in good working order. The counselor could briefly discuss follow-up procedure with the employer at this time. He might also indicate that once the handicapped employee has worked for the employer for a time, the employer will feel that he is a fully functioning, well-adjusted employee who should be treated just as all other employees are. Assure the employer of your confidence in the client.

Many aspects of the rehabilitation process depend on a good public relations program. This is especially true in the placement of clients who have been isolated from the world of work as a result of incarceration or other types of deprivation. Whether or not the client, who is known as a juvenile offender, will be offered an opportunity or even an interview will depend to a large extent on how thoroughly the counselor has conducted a public relations program. The counselor needs to spend as much time as possible contacting various civic clubs and other community organizations in order to create a climate of willingness and a desire to cooperate in the rehabilitation of public offenders. Concurrently, a survey of the business community is necessary to identify those employers who are willing to hire youthful offenders. In some instances companies have a hiring policy of giving the ex-inmate or youthful offender a preference.

DIRECT PLACEMENT

Following release or parole, if a client prefers or is allowed to reside within commuting distance of the juvenile correctional institution, the rehabilitation counselor should be directly responsible for placement. In direct placement, the counselor makes all arrangements for the client to meet with employers. The counselor is responsible for locating job opportunities and acting as an advocate for his clients. In some instances, the counselor may accompany the client to the prospective place of employment. Whether or not the counselor should be present during the actual interview will depend on a number of factors. As a general rule, the client should be allowed to conduct his own interviews.

INDIRECT PLACEMENT

When any other agency or individual locates possible job openings and makes arrangements for the employment interview, the counselor is only indirectly involved in placement. The counselor may not be able to be responsible for placement for any of a number of reasons. Not infrequently will the youth prefer or be required to live in another area of the state or county too far from the institution to be effectively served by the institutional counselor. In this instance, the counselor must seek the cooperation of his colleagues who serve that area of the state or agencies in other states in order to place these clients in employment.

There are organizations in many cities whose assistance the counselor may seek in making placements which he cannot make himself because of time and distance problems. The Austin Wilke Society in Columbia, South Carolina, was organized for the explicit purpose of aiding individuals released from prison or jails to find employment. Offender Aid and Restoration programs are located in many cities. Some of the services provided by these programs overlap with those provided by departments of Vocational Rehabilitation. General activities of Offender Aid and Restoration programs are: (1) helping the individual prepare for release and readjusting to community life; (2) operating a job placement program for ex-offenders and (3) securing support for a job placement program with the local business community. Knowledge of these and similar programs is necessary if the rehabilitation counselor who serves the public offender is going to be successful in his placement efforts.

FOLLOW-UP AFTER PLACEMENT

Follow-up refers to that phase of the rehabilitation process which occurs after job placement and which helps insure that the individual is adjusting well to the requirements of the job socially and physically. The youthful offender client often needs a longer period of follow-up than is usually provided by the rehabilitation counselor. Arrangements for follow-up visits should be made at the time of placement. Most employers dislike irregular, unannounced visits by the counselor. This may serve to create dissatisfaction especially if the employee-client is taken away from his employment duties. A good policy may be to continue talking with the client on a regular basis after working hours. The employer may be contacted by telephone and, if necessary, an appointment made to visit the employer. These contacts are evidence of the counselor's continuing interest in the client and in the employer and are also effective as a public relations tool.

A rehabilitation counselor often is tempted to consider his job completed when the client is placed on a job which appears suitable for him; however, the phase of rehabilitation which begins immediately after the person has been placed in employment is one of the most complex. Follow-up involves the counselor's ability to work as a middleman between the employer and the client. The counselor must be diplomatic and resourceful in maintaining the employer's confidence in his client's ability to do the job. At the same time, he must let the client know that he has full faith in him. The counselor, however, must somehow evaluate how his client is performing on the job and make certain that he is available to help if problems arise which the client cannot solve.

Agency regulations in vocational rehabilitation work usually require that follow-up be done after thirty days in order to make certain that placement is successful before a "case" can be closed as rehabilitated. Counselors should also consider follow-up periods of sixty to eighty days after placement. Again, this helps reassure the client of the interest of the agency and the counselor in his success and can be of value to the counselor also in developing additional employment opportunities for other public offender clients.

CONCLUSION

The counselor's responsibility in vocational placement cannot be underrated. The problems which confront the counselor dealing with the youthful public offender are real and the decisions made at this stage in the rehabilitation process not only affect the young client's immediate feelings of satisfaction and achievement; but also, of course, his long-term mental health and physical well-being. The counselor has a real responsibility to "ready" the client for employment by giving him the type of information that he needs about the job and about holding employment once it is achieved.

The counselor must be knowledgeable about job analysis and must relate all medical, psychological and social data with job analysis information in order to be successful in placement. Vocational placement is high-level public relations, especially when the counselor is working with the juvenile offender. Once placement has been achieved, the counselor must follow up the client in order to make certain that he is doing well in the job. The client should have an opportunity to evaluate his job and also the efforts of his counselor in helping him decide on and obtain the job. Effective placement requires effective planning, and counselors must constantly evaluate their knowledge of the world of work and their ability to interrelate information in order to assure the placement success of public offender clients.

REFERENCES

Bell, P. B., Mathews, Merlyn, and Fulton, W. S.: *A Future for Correctional Rehabilitation Final Report.* Federal Offenders Rehabilitation Program, Olympia, Washington, RD 2079-G, November, 1969.

Byron, W. J.: Needed: a special employment clearing house for ex-offenders. *Federal Probation, 34:3,* September, 1970.

Goldberg, Richard T.: *Vocational and Social Rehabilitation of Juvenile Delinquents,* Massachusetts Rehabilitation Commission, May 1972.

Hardy, R. E.: Relating psychological data to job analysis information in vocational counseling. *The New Outlook for the Blind, 63:7,* 1969.

Hardy, R. E.: Vocational Placement. In J. G. Cull and R. E. Hardy, *Vocational Rehabilitation: Profession and Process.* Springfield, Illinois, Charles C Thomas, 1972.

Jeffrey, David L.: *Pertinent Points on Placement.* Clearing House, Oklahoma State University, November 1969.

McGowan, J. F., and Porter, T. L.: *An Introduction to the Vocational Rehabilitation Process.* Rehabilitation Services Administration, July, 1967.

Maslow, A. H.: A theory of human motivation. *Psychol Rev 50,* 1954.

Shore, M. F. and Massimo, J. L.: Comprehensive vocationally oriented psychotherapy for adolescent delinquent boys: a follow-up. *American Journal of Orth-Psychotherapy, 36:*609-615, 1966.

CHAPTER 15

CONSIDERATIONS IN THE REHABILITATION OF THE YOUTHFUL OFFENDER

Craig R. Colvin

☐ THE COUNSELOR'S RESPONSIBILITY IN SERVING THE YOUTHFUL OFFENDER
☐ THE COUNSELOR'S RELATIONSHIP WITH THE YOUTHFUL OFFENDER

VOCATIONAL REHABILITATION has become increasingly involved with the youthful offender especially within the last decade. Program development in this area has grown dramatically with mixed results. The rationale for its existence is supported not only in the federal offenders program publication (1969) but more specifically in the Goldberg report dealing specifically with the vocational and social rehabilitation of juvenile delinquents (1972). The writers of both of these research projects state that in addition to the humanitarian aspects inherent in the rehabilitation movement the primary impetus for creating a treatment program for the offender emerged from the complimentary needs of both vocational rehabilitation and corrections. The latter research study states vocational rehabilitation has been eager for sometime to develop a new source of clientele since the agency had finally matured to the point of serving such a population with expertise.

If one examines even superficially the composition of the majority of correctional facilities, he will see that they have an abundance of clients with insufficient community resources to provide at least minimum treatment services. In terms of the total correctional system, it is quite obvious that the youthful offender and juvenile delinquent have the majority of services at their disposal and yet when one considers the merits of these services in comparison to those found in the community, the lag is most depressing. Therefore, it becomes obvious that these two agencies, vocational rehabilitation and youth corrections, join forces in an attempt to provide meaningful services which will increase the probability of the youthful offender returning to the community as a respected and trusted citizen.

Even though enthusiastic advances have been made, the majority of the articles pertaining to youthful offender programs state that rehabilitation of the inmate within the institution has never quite caught up to the age old concept of restraint and to some degree retribution. Without question to be effective with this population it is mandatory professionals realign philosophies regarding institutionalization. The present day ideologies existing in our country are undergoing massive and sometimes disruptive changes. This writer is confident, and agrees with Goldberg (1972), that vocational rehabilitation can play a vital role in the assertion of rehabilitation techniques and methodologies enabling the youthful offender after a predetermined treatment program to reenter the community as a productive member.

As stated earlier (Colvin, 1972), the mere act of putting grandiose ideas down on paper will not produce programs benefiting the youthful offender. But, it is a noble start. Hopefully this chapter will be the vehicle by which some vocational rehabilitation counselors as well as others held accountable for this population will become involved (i.e. effect meaningful behavior change). Again, if this chapter does nothing more than create an awareness within people that youthful offenders deserve professional guidance, it has served its purpose.

People knowledgeable of the legal aspects of rehabilitation realize that before any state rehabilitation agency can provide services three basic criteria of eligibility must be met. Each of the following questions (criteria) must be answered "yes" before the youthful offender can be considered for rehabilitation services; (1) Does the individual have a disability?; (2) Does the individual possess a handicap to employment?; (3) Is there a reasonable expectation that vocational rehabilitation services may help the individual toward engagement in a gainful occupation? One realizes that even though these three criteria represent a particular agency's guideline for establishing some type of professional relationship, other agencies and/or individuals will probably have other requirements which must be met prior to their commiting staff and/or money toward the rehabilitation of the youthful offender.

These eligibility requirements were formulated and written into law in 1920 via the Smith-Fess Act. As such these criteria must be met no matter what target population or individual is being considered for services. The mere fact that a youthful offender is or has been incarcerated does not automatically signify he is eligible for rehabilitation services; he must have his eligibility established on the basis of an individual evaluation as is the case of *any* applicant for services (*Rehabilitation of the Public Offender*, 1967).

Since 1965, the law does not state the client's disability must be a handicap to employment; however, this relationship continues to be implied and has been the *modus operandi*. Even though the youthful offender is usually characterized as not being over the age of twenty-one, the ramifications surrounding the work ethic must still be considered even though this group of inmates usually have not established an employment record which would amount to anything.

THE COUNSELOR'S RESPONSIBILITY IN SERVING THE YOUTHFUL OFFENDER

This writer feels that incarceration definitely is a handicap to employment in and of itself. Imprisonment *per se* is a social stigma and has such an overbearing influence on the individual after release that it is next to impossible for him to locate a suitable job or make an adjustment within a school setting. Citizens in the community do not differentiate between the types of offenses committed let alone the type of people convicted for these crimes or their ages; citizens visualize the majority of inmates and most youthful offenders as hardened criminals committed to the institution for violating severely societal norms. As professional rehabilitation workers we must differentiate between each inmate and individually evaluate his need for and desire to receive appropriate rehabilitation services.

As evidence of vocational rehabilitation's involvement with the youth camp there can be established a mutual relationship for the ultimate objective of helping these young clients. But in order to do so the rehabilitation worker must make a justifiable alignment or assessment of personal and professional ideologies. Therefore, the acquisition of new values or at least a new perspective on old ones must be achieved prior to working with the correctional institution and specifically the inmate population (Colvin, 1972).

We all have our "hangups" both personal as well as professional. Many of us in corrections and rehabilitation invision idealistic approaches to youthful offender treatment. Before involving many people in a theoretical or academic exercise, a realistic attitude is necessary. This means the counselor has to maintain a level of maturity capable of functioning within a professional framework.

The quality of maturity is a necessary component anyone working with youthful offenders must possess. Without it the naive counselor soon will fall to the manipulative devices of some offenders, will be "snowed under" with inmate requests for counseling sessions and in a short period will become so overly involved with some delinquents that the only resource is to resign.

If a counselor cannot face realistically those problems confronting him, he surely will have a difficult time in the youthful offender facilities. Every day will be filled with a new "crisis" situation that seems to require the counselor's undivided attention. If he is insecure in his personal life this will soon become evident in the counselor's professional activities. Decisions must be made with professional authority; yet, if the decision is wrong or inappropriate the counselor must have the strength to admit such a mistake.

If, as a professional, you are anticipating a great deal of "success" in rehabilitating the youthful offender, your expectations will be somewhat limited. No matter what degree of preparation one might have prior to engaging in correctional rehabilitation, the criteria utilized to evaluate success must be re-evaluated. Most publications concerned with this topic are first to mention the failure syndrome surrounding this atypical population (the inmate) : he has been a failure in society, he has been a failure to himself, he has even been a failure in his crime, and has been a failure to those who have tried to help him in the past. No rehabilitation counselor is going to come along and change things overnight. This is not to say that rehabilitation or any other related disciplines should not attempt to bring about change. We must design, realistically, a plan for constructive rehabilitation which is relevant to the youthful offender's own needs rather than the needs imposed upon him by some counselor representing a "bureaucratic organization."

False values, the inability to make decisions, insecurity, a poor attitude toward one's work and other forms of inappropriate behavior will become magnified many times if one enters the correctional rehabilitation field. After all, these types of behavior and personality problems are manifested within the majority of youth the counselor has the responsibility of serving! Therefore, prior to accepting an appointment within a youthful offender facility it is advantageous for the counselor to examine critically his own behavior and attitudes toward the job. This soul searching will go a long way if it is approached with conscientiousness. One's assignment in the penal institution for the youthful offender can be either a rewarding professional experience or it can become truly a prison of work.

THE COUNSELOR'S RELATIONSHIP WITH THE YOUTHFUL OFFENDER

Following the counselor's development of an affiliation with those people held responsible for affecting the youth's behavior change within the institution, we should examine the counselor's own involvement with the youthful offender. This section will be directed toward several factors that influence the counselor-youthful offender relationship and how the counselor can improve or strengthen his competency in working with this population.

Utilization of Diagnostic Information

In respect to the history of incarceration and especially society's involvement with the youthful offender, correctional personnel only recently have begun accumulating adequate diagnostic material on each individual entering the system. These diagnostic reports or workups usually include a comprehensive medical examination with appropriate laboratory tests; a rather elaborate psychological test battery composed of the Wechsler Intelligence Scale for Children or Adults, the Minnesota Multiphasic Personality Inventory, Kuder Preference Record, Bender-Gestalt, Perdue Pegboard, etc.; and a host of other personality and achievement tests. With some juveniles a psychiatric examination may be necessary. In addition to these reports a detailed social history is gathered containing educational, religious, and economic information. This affords the professional working with this youth group to assess all of the factors surrounding his involvement and eventual provision of services.

A thorough and objective analysis of this existing material should be made prior to the professional's interview with the potential client. After a counselor has perused such diagnostic material, he should determine whether or not additional information is required. If such material is deemed necessary, the counselor in conjunction with the correctional unit can activate a program to secure such necessary information.

Counseling With the Youthful Offender

Generally counseling as practiced by rehabilitation counselors does not vary to any significant degree from one rehabilitation setting to another. Nevertheless there is a definite aura existing between a correctional unit counselor and his inmate client which normally does not exist between a field counselor and his client in the community. An "on guard" or defensive attitude prevails between counselor and the youthful offender which does not lend itself to the establishment of a favorable counseling relationship. The counselor feels somewhat compelled to remain "uptight" so as not to become a pawn of the delinquent's manipulative devices. Often the neophyte counselor will progress in the relationship assuming that because of the client's youthful age he (the client) will not be taking advantage of the counselor. Until an individual gets involved with his population, this philosophy probably prevails; yet after the initial period of job orientation goes by one soon realizes that many of the youthful offenders have a sophisticated manipulative and deviant behavioral pattern well developed. For the correctional rehabilitation counselor to be effective in performing his responsibilities, he must discuss his role with the youthful offender during their initial interview. The counselor must set somewhat rigid limits on the relationship he establishes with this young man, yet convince him that you are there to help him rehabilitate himself. As one readily can imagine such an arrangement is no simple matter that can be sloughed over nonchalantly; to achieve this precarious balance requires a great deal of insight and perceptiveness on the counselor's part.

Youthful Offender Motivation Versus Youthful Offender Manipulation

Motivation as defined by Webster means a "stimulus to action or something that causes a person to act." If there is one reoccurring characteristic or quality found within the youthful offender population, it is motivation; but we must ask ourselves, "motivation for what?" There is both an unconscious as well as conscious desire operating within the youthful offender that can be defined as motivation. One might even call it a driving impulse which suggests a power arising from personal temperament and desire. Often the newly employed counselor feels that he has found an individual who truly wants his services as well as the desire to improve his lot. Another factor which he has either failed to consider or has repressed is the fact that this individual has been locked up in jail, sentenced, and then sent to either a youthful offender camp or a correctional facility specializing in the containment of juvenile delinquents, etc. Since this is most often the case, these clients have one thing on their mind and that is freedom. To them freedom is returning to their environment outside of the penal setting where they might resume whatever activities were in progress prior to arrest, conviction and incarceration.

Probably freedom occupies his mind more than any other single facet connected with his institutionalization; his main objective is to get out of the youthful offender facility as soon as possible. Even so, each individual responds differently to the ever present desire for freedom: there is the young inmate who will resort to escape to reach his freedom; another will quietly sit back and wait out his time in idleness (this is his definition of idleness since the system forces him in some way or another to fill his time either in productive work, training or in some other capacity deemed appropriate by the institution) ; a third type will try to con his way out; and then there is the individual who will work conscientiously toward earning his freedom by productive work and obeying the institution's regulations.

Rehabilitation will find the greatest degree of success with this last individual, and yet it will be difficult for the counselor to separate one from another during the initial interviews. As an example, the motivation of one youth may be directed toward manipulation of the professional staff. From our side we often see this individual's external behavior as being conducive for positive rehabilitation efforts. Because of the youthful offender's isolation, he will strive to manipulate or convince some professionals that he is "motivated" toward whatever objective they are wanting him to achieve.

Upon release from the institution, this young person usually rejects the likely benefits of rehabilitation programs. As an illustration of this writer's experience in working with the juvenile delinquent and youthful offender, he has seen individuals who really looked forward to their training in an area such as the institution's bakery shop. As their counselor, it was felt that adjustment and progression in this area was more than satisfactory and that upon release there would be no difficulty in placing them in the labor market especially within the bakery industry. Prior to their departure from the institution, this counselor made the usual arrangements regarding work and a place for them to stay within some residential facility. After no more than one week on the job some of these young men left without leaving word as to their whereabouts while others came to me asking for training in another area. This counselor asked them why and their answer invariably was that the training they received in the camp reminded them of their institutional days. Others felt that the pay was not good enough and they were looking "for the big money."

Additional Considerations

When the juvenile delinquent or youthful offender makes a mistake, we have a tendency to ridicule or punish him unduly; if this same mistake were to be made by one of our clients or even a member of our own family, it is anticipated that he would not be reprimanded as severely. Mistakes are a vital part of the learning process. We have to examine and, if necessary, to re-examine continually the reasons underlying their failure. We must concentrate and channel our professional efforts toward affecting a realistic treatment program.

Realistically we must give the young person more responsibility for his actions. As is found in most correctional institutions today, inmates are told when to get up, when to wash and shave, when to eat, when to go to the bathroom, when to go to work, when to participate in recreation, etc. What happens to this individual when it comes time for him to reenter the community and face the every day grind? Self-control has been inhibited or even squelched during his institutionalization and after release we expect him, if by magic, to regain all of those intricate components which are identifiable as "normal" behavior patterns exhibited by the majority of the people found in our society today.

Treatment, rehabilitation, habilitation, or any word which expresses a return to normalcy, must include responsibility for one's own behavior. This behavioral change process has no predetermined solution which can be applied to all people; individual approaches to individual problems are required if we expect to see positive results. Such an approach necessitates greater coordination and teamwork of all disciplines that have dedicated themselves to helping the juvenile delinquent and the youthful offender.

REFERENCES

Colvin, C.R.: The correctional institution and vocational rehabilitation. In J. G. Cull and Richard E. Hardy (Eds.) *Vocational Rehabilitation: Profession and Process.* Springfield, Thomas, 1972.

Colvin, C. R.: Eligibility determination of the public offender in R. E. Hardy and J. G. Cull (Eds.) *Introduction to Correctional Education,* Springfield, Thomas, 1973.

Fulton, W. S. (Ed.): *A Future for Correctional Rehabilitation.* Final Report, Federal Offenders Rehabilitation Program, State of Washington, Division of Vocational Rehabilitation, November, 1969.

Goldberg, R. T.: *Vocational and Social Rehabilitation of Juvenile Delinquents.* Massachusetts Rehabilitation Commission, Boston, May, 1972.

Rehabilitation of the Public Offender. Fifth Institute of Rehabilitation Services, U. S. Department of Health, Education and Welfare, RSA Series #68-36, May 22-25, 1967.

INDEX

Cobb, J.A., 55, 63
Cocaine, 130, 143, 180, 201
Cohen, Melvin, v., 153, 159, 163-165
Cold turkey program, 170
Colvin, Craig R., v., 262, 263, 265, 271
Community centers, 105
Community social agencies, 35
Conformity behavior, 175
Cooper, D., 39, 61
Correctional
  administration, 35
  facility, 263
Counseling
  prevocational, 249
  rehabilitation, 101, 204, 251, 258, 268
Court workers, 66
Crime Index offenses, 7, 33
Criminal
  behavior, 12
  justice system, 37, 96
  law, 4
Criminalistic parents, 45, 47
Culbertson, Robert G., v., 72
Cull, John G., vi., 99, 152, 169, 171, 175,
  178, 179, 207, 248, 261
Cultural norms, 14
Culturally disadvantaged, 13

D

Delinquency, 12, 26
  rates, 28
Delinquent
  adjudged, 23
  agency, 23
  alleged, 23
  behavior, 25, 44, 51, 74
  detected, 23
  legal, 23
  peer group, 93
DET (diethyltryptamine), 120
Detention facility, 76
Detoxification, 167, 170
Deviant child behavior, 56
Dextro-amphetamine, 128
Dictionary of Occupational Titles
  (DOT), 250
Disrupted homes, 45
DMT (dimethoxyptamine), **120, 162**
Dole, A.A., 53, 61

Douvan, E., 44, 61
Dressler, David, 28, 31
Drug
  abuse, 141, 180, 181
  abuser, 153
  addiction, 39, 100
  culture, 175
  oriented society, 95
  rehabilitation, 138
  related offenses, 8
  therapy, 191
Drugs
  antipsychotic, 130
  mood altering, 110
  narcotic, 132, 176
  psychedelic, 117, 186
  psychoactive, 166
  tranquilizer, 142, 156

E

Economically deprived families, 28
Economically disadvantaged class, 12
Educational system, 88
Ego disorganization, 114
Emotional disorder, 26, 187
Emotional disturbance, 47
Employment opportunities, 248
Epstein, L., 159
Ex-drugee, 175
Ex-inmate, 258

F

Facility
  correctional, 263
  detention, 76
Family, broken,
  broken, 12
  characteristics, 44
  counseling, 70
  disharmony, 100
  dynamics, 80
  evaluation, 59
  guidance, 185
  leadership, 42
Fejet, D., 166
Fitzgibbons, D.J., 160, 163
Flashbacks, 116
Foster
  family, 59